Slavery in the Age of Memory

Slavery in the Age of Memory

Engaging the Past

Ana Lucia Araujo

BLOOMSBURY ACADEMIC
LONDON • NEW YORK • OXFORD • NEW DELHI • SYDNEY

BLOOMSBURY ACADEMIC
Bloomsbury Publishing Plc
50 Bedford Square, London, WC1B 3DP, UK
1385 Broadway, New York, NY 10018, USA

BLOOMSBURY, BLOOMSBURY ACADEMIC and the Diana logo
are trademarks of Bloomsbury Publishing Plc

First published in Great Britain 2021
Reprinted 2021 (three times)

Copyright © Ana Lucia Araujo, 2021

Ana Lucia Araujo has asserted her right under the Copyright, Designs
and Patents Act, 1988, to be identified as Author of this work.

For legal purposes the Acknowledgments on p. xi constitute an
extension of this copyright page.

Cover design by Tjaša Krivec
Cover image: Female Silhuette: Slave Belonging to Mrs. Oyley
(© Glenn Tilley Morse Collection, Bequest of Glenn Tilley Morse, 1950 /
The Metropolitan Museum of Art).
Background image: Coolidge Collection of Thomas Jefferson
Manuscripts: Farm Book, 1774–1824, page 30, by Thomas Jefferson
(© Collection of the Massachusetts Historical Society)

All rights reserved. No part of this publication may be reproduced or transmitted
in any form or by any means, electronic or mechanical, including photocopying,
recording, or any information storage or retrieval system, without
prior permission in writing from the publishers.

Bloomsbury Publishing Plc does not have any control over, or responsibility for,
any third-party websites referred to or in this book. All internet addresses given
in this book were correct at the time of going to press. The author and publisher
regret any inconvenience caused if addresses have changed or sites have
ceased to exist, but can accept no responsibility for any such changes.

A catalogue record for this book is available from the British Library.

Library of Congress Cataloging-in-Publication Data
Names: Araujo, Ana Lucia, author.
Title: Slavery in the age of memory : engaging the past / Ana Lucia Araujo.
Description: [New York] : [Bloomsbury Academic], 2019.
| Includes bibliographical references and index.
Identifiers: LCCN 2020025160 (print) | LCCN 2020025161 (ebook) |
ISBN 9781350048492 (paperback) | ISBN 9781350048485 (hardback) |
ISBN 9781350048478 (ebook) | ISBN 9781350048508 (epub)
Subjects: LCSH: Slavery. | Slave trade. | Memory–Social aspects.
Classification: LCC HT871 .A73 2019 (print) | LCC HT871 (ebook) |
DDC 306.3/62–dc23
LC record available at https://lccn.loc.gov/2020025160
LC ebook record available at https://lccn.loc.gov/2020025161

ISBN: HB: 978-1-3500-4848-5
PB: 978-1-3500-4849-2
ePDF: 978-1-3500-4847-8
eBook: 978-1-3500-4850-8

Typeset by Integra Software Services Pvt. Ltd.
Printed and bound in Great Britain

To find out more about our authors and books visit www.bloomsbury.com
and sign up for our newsletters.

For Alain Bélanger

CONTENTS

FIGURES

ACKNOWLEDGMENTS

This book was written with the support of many colleagues, friends, and institutions. I am indebted to the administration of the historically black Howard University, as well as to my colleagues and brilliant students. The Howard University family provides me with resources, freedom, and inspiration to conduct my research and its beautiful community is what gives meaning to my work on slavery and its afterlives. I am also grateful to various scholars who over the last five years invited me to give talks about the research that gave birth to this book. In 2015, I presented parts of this book at Leiden University; I thank Wayne Modest and Damian Pargas for inviting me. I also presented segments of the book in a conference panel at the Université du Havre, and in a keynote lecture at the Université de Montpellier. I thank Eric Saunier, Lawrence Aje, and Nicholas Gachon for these invitations. I also spoke about this book project during a plenary panel at the International Conference *Transforming Public History from Charleston to the Atlantic World* held at the College of Charleston in 2017; I thank Simon Lewis, John White, and Rachel Donaldson for inviting me.

Alex Balch invited me to give a keynote lecture and lead one session of the Renkei Pax Workshop at the University of Liverpool in 2017; the time I spent in Liverpool greatly enriched my work. Maria Lúcia Bastos Kern invited me to give a keynote lecture at the *Conference of the Brazilian Committee of Art History*, Bahia Art Museum in Salvador (Brazil), and another lecture at the Symposium *O Triângulo do Atlântico e as artes visuais*, at Pontifícia Universidade Católica do Rio Grande do Sul, in Porto Alegre (Brazil). Both lectures helped me in shaping the last chapter of this book. In 2017, invited by Abou Bamba, I also presented a combination of various chapters in a lecture at Gettysburg College. Historian and friend Olivette Otele invited me to give a talk in the *International Conference People of African Descent in Reluctant Sites of Memory*, held in Bristol in 2018. Susanne Seymour invited me to give the Annual Public Lecture for the Institute of Slavery at the University of Nottingham in the UK. The week I spent in Nottingham visiting slavery heritage sites and meeting with scholars, artists, and activists enriched my work. I am particularly grateful for having the opportunity to share my work with Amy Potter and Steve Hanna, who not only provided me with insights regarding the "wall of names" but also shared data about the profile of visitors to the Whitney Plantation Museum. Thanks to Ibrahima Thiaw, Deborah Mack, Laurie Obbink, and

Danilyn Rutherford, I had the opportunity to present my work during the week-long Wenner-Grenn International Conference *Transatlantic Slavery and the Making of the Modern World*, in Sintra, Portugal, in October 2018. My paper as well as the presentations of other scholars helped me rethink certain chapters of this book. Likewise, I thank Ariella Azoulay for inviting me to speak at the Pembroke Center at Brown University and am also grateful to Mariana Dantas and Kim Yeong-Hyun for bringing me to Ohio University to give the Wealth and Poverty Public Lecture in 2018. Thanks to Maria Betlem Castella Pujols and Karo Monet I also presented my work at the Seminar *Memòries històriques, Memòries incòmodes* Grup d'Estudis de les Institucions i de les Cultures polítiques (Segles XVI–XXI), Universitat Pompeu Fabra, Barcelona, Spain. The feedback provided by the participants of the seminar gave me insight into reworking several elements of the book's second chapter.

I am indebted to Armelle Enders for making possible a month-long visiting professorship at University of Paris VIII in March 2019. This very intense month allowed me to present parts of this book in different seminars. Armelle Enders and Malika Rahal provided beneficial comments during their Seminar *Histoire globale du temps présent: Expériences extra européennes du second XXe siècle*. I also thank Emmanuelle Sibeud for inviting me to her seminar *Histoire sociale des populations noires en France*, and for the comments provided by Sarah Fila-Bakbadio, Audrey Célestine, and Syliane Larcher. I also thank Alejandro Gomez for giving me the opportunity to speak in his seminar at Université de Paris I, Sorbonne. Inês Beleza Barreiros and Ângela Xavier invited me to present my work at Universidade de Lisboa, in Lisbon, Portugal. I appreciate Anne-Claire Faucquez, Androula Michael, and Renée Gosson for allowing me to share my work in a conference at the Université de Picardie-Jules-Vernes in Amiens, France. Also, while in France, I was able to pay additional visits to the Nantes History Museum and the Museum of Aquitaine. I am grateful to Matthieu Dussauge for putting me in contact with the colleagues of the Museum of Aquitaine. Laurent Vedrine, Paul Matharan, and Katia Kukawa welcomed me at the museum and shared with me observations about the collections as well as numerous materials that helped me better shape the fourth chapter of this book. I am also indebted to Krystel Gualde for receiving me at the Nantes History Museum and for providing me with important information regarding the formation of its collections and the museum's approach for exposing slavery. I thank these curators for allowing me to use photographs taken at the Nantes History Museum and the Museum of Aquitaine.

I am particularly grateful to many colleagues and friends who helped me along the way answering questions, and equipping me with sources and advice: Daniel Domingues, Madge Dresser, Kirt van Daacke, Lisa Earl Castillo, Annette Gordon-Reed, James DeWolf Perry, Scot French, Christopher Fennell, Kate MacMahon-Ruddick and Lucia Stanton. Anthropologist Carole Lemée generously provided me with information about Marthe Adélaïde Modeste Testas, as well as with a stunning photograph of the monument honoring her, unveiled after my last trip to Bordeaux. She also gave me access to a picture showing Bordeaux's new street name plaques, elements that helped at the very last minute to balance my analysis of the Bordeaux case. Historian Lopez Matthews at the Moorland Spingarn Center helped me in numerous ways, including scheduling last-minute visits to consult the archives.

Mary N. Elliott answered numerous questions and guided me several times through the *Slavery and Freedom* exhibition at the National Museum of African American History and Culture. Júlio César Medeiros also gave me important information regarding the panel of names displayed at the New Blacks Institute of Research and Memory in Rio de Janeiro. Many thanks also to Mary Elliott and Douglas Remley for their assistance to obtain permissions to use photographs of the National Museum of African American History and Culture. I am also grateful to artists William Adjèté-Wilson and Rosana Paulino for making available photographs of their works and allowing me to publish them. I also thank artists Charles Fréger and François Piquet for giving me permission to publish the photographs of their works. I also thank John McKee (Thomas Jefferson Monticello), Dawn Bonner (Mount Vernon), Joy Banner (Whitney Plantation Museum), and Jean-François Maniçom and Richard Benjamin (International Slavery Museum in Liverpool) for providing me permission to use pictures taken at these institutions. I am also grateful to Dawn Bonner at Mount Vernon and John McKee at Monticello for their assistance regarding the use of photographs taken at both sites.

This book also benefited from my interactions with Katrin Sieg with whom I co-convened the conference *Decolonizing the Museum*, funded by Georgetown University, held at Georgetown University and Howard University campuses. The conference organization, the preparation of my paper, and the panel discussions contributed to clarify several points in two chapters of this book. I am also thankful to Ibrahima Seck and John Cummings, who tirelessly responded to my questions regarding the establishment of Whitney Plantation Museum in Louisiana, United States. Nikki Taylor, Chair of the Department of History of Howard University, also supported me with her positive energy and enthusiasm, and especially by allowing me to take time to research and write this book. Andrew Maginn, PhD candidate in the Department of History, assisted me in finding a few sources as well.

I presented the fifth chapter of this book in my own seminar *Slavery, Memory, and African Diasporas* at Howard University, for which I received insightful comments from Nikki Taylor, Andrew Maginn, Emily Kugler, Jane Hooper, and Thomas A. Foster. I also shared the first chapter with the *Memory Studies Seminar* led by Michael Rothberg at University of California Los Angeles, and the third chapter with the faculty seminar of the Center for the Humanities and the Public Sphere of the University of Florida. I thank Professors David Myers, Michael Rothberg, and Barbara

Mennel for respectively inviting me to speak at the University of California Los Angeles and at the University of Florida.

I am indebted to the four anonymous scholars who reviewed the initial book proposal. I am especially grateful to the two dedicated anonymous reviewers who provided me with very detailed comments, suggestions, and corrections that helped dramatically improve the final version of this manuscript. One of these reviewers, Charles Forsdick, who later revealed his identity to me, gave me precious additional references; I am indebted to his great generosity. My special thanks go to my editor Maddie Holder who encouraged me several times to persist in this project when I was ready to give up. I also thank Dan Hutchins and Abigail Lane, editorial assistants at Bloomsbury. I am grateful to Emma Goode, with whom I started working on this project. I thank Kristy Johnson for copyediting the first draft of the manuscript as well. I am thankful for the cover designers, who accepted all my suggestions and produced a poignant book cover.

This book could not have been completed without the support of my lovely husband Alain Bélanger, who encouraged me with his words of knowledge, love, and wisdom during the entire process of researching and writing this book, and who sacrificed summer vacations and holidays to allow me to work on this project. This book is dedicated to him. Finally, let me acknowledge that Aby, our feline buddy, is also my great supporter; he kicked me out of bed every single morning to write this book, and can't wait to see me start the next one.

Introduction: Slavery and Memory

The idea of this book emerged in the days that followed the massacre that took the lives of Reverend Clementa Pinckney, Cynthia Hurd, Reverend Sharonda Coleman-Singleton, Tywanza Sanders, Ethel Lance, Susie Jackson, Depayne Middleton-Doctor, Reverend Daniel Simmons, and Myra Thompson by white supremacist Dylann Roof, at the Emanuel African American Methodist Episcopal Church, in Charleston, South Carolina, United States. The site of the massacre had already been the stage for acts of terror. Among the founders of the church was Denmark Vesey, sentenced to death for plotting a slave insurrection. After his condemnation in 1822, the church building was burned and was only reconstructed after the end of the Civil War. Since the 1990s, a memorial paying homage to Vesey is featured at the church. Before committing these murders, Roof visited and posed for pictures at several slavery sites in South Carolina, including former plantations that today welcome thousands of tourists. In some of these pictures, he proudly appears holding a Confederate flag, a pro-slavery symbol appropriated by white supremacists.[1] The aftershocks of this series of connected events that in many ways give life to William Faulkner's famous quote "the past is never dead, is not even past" continued to evolve in the subsequent months.[2] In various cities of the United States, black residents, along with activists and ordinary citizens, occupied the public space and demanded the removal of the Confederate battle flag from public buildings. Likewise, all over the United States, demonstrators made calls for taking down Confederate memorials and monuments honoring pro-slavery individuals.

These public battles over the slave past may have surprised scholars, politicians, journalists, and ordinary citizens. Yet, despite its national contours, the monuments' war was, to a lesser or greater extent, neither a new nor an isolated trend. As early as the nineteenth century, African

Americans protested the creation of monuments honoring pro-slavery individuals.[3] Also, with the end of the Cold War and the fall of the Communist regimes in Eastern Europe, citizens of several countries such as Ukraine, Poland, Hungary, and Russia called for the removal of monuments paying homage to Communist leaders.[4] Comparably, since the 1990s, black citizens have demanded the removal of statues and the renaming of streets honoring slave merchants in the UK and France. In the United States, outcries for the removal of Confederate monuments and the Confederate flag also reemerged in the same period along with demands to build monuments to honor black social actors who fought against slavery and championed claims for citizenship during Reconstruction.[5] In March 2015, South African students ignited a successful campaign to take down a statue of Cecil Rhodes (1853–1902) from the campus of the University of Cape Town. This movement gained attention all over the world and led more universities in South Africa and the UK to join protests demanding the fall of other statues representing Rhodes and other monuments symbolizing colonialism and Apartheid.[6]

As these movements surfaced, more than ever, the interest in all dimensions associated with the slave past continued unfolding with mandates for the creation of public monuments, memorials, and museums honoring enslaved and black social actors. The past of Atlantic slavery, propelled by the rise of social media, reached the public sphere and the public space in unprecedented ways. In contrast with the private realm, in this book public sphere is conceived as a political space between the individual citizen and the state, where social agents engage in debates on a variety of public issues. Likewise, the public space relates to the tangible dimension of the public sphere, the physical location where these social actors create social connections and participate in public debates.[7] On an almost daily basis, newspapers, magazines, and websites report the discovery of new slave burial grounds, the releasing of motion pictures and documentary films, the unveiling of exhibitions and websites, the organization of conferences, the development of heritage sites and museums, as well as the publication of books examining the issue of slavery and race. Therefore, the calls to remove pro-slavery public markers were intertwined with the demands of memorializing black social actors in the urban landscape of societies that benefited from slavery and the Atlantic slave trade. Yet white social actors claiming a southern Confederate heritage continued arguing that removing statues from the public landscape was an enterprise led "by radical leftists who seek to erase our history."[8] Scholars and activists opposed and denounced these claims.[9] As continuing confusion about the concepts of history, memory, and commemoration prevailed in these debates, I decided to write a book to contribute to this discussion.

This book investigates the ways slavery and the Atlantic slave trade have been remembered and memorialized by individuals, social groups, and societies between the middle of the nineteenth century until the present. I show that current debates about slavery are more than simple attempts to come to terms with the past but are rather associated with persistent racism and racial inequalities that prevail in former slave societies or countries where slavery existed. Exploring several case studies from the Americas, Europe, and Africa, I review the concepts of history, collective memory, cultural memory, public memory, official memory, and public history. I show how these various modes of engagement with the past relate to slavery and the Atlantic slave trade in both analogous and differing ways and how sometimes they are also intertwined. How do social actors and groups in countries such as the United States, Brazil, England, France, and the Republic of Benin confront the slave past of their societies? Does the collective memory of a Brazilian-born slave merchant like Francisco Félix de Souza have any elements in common with the memory of the founding father of the United States Thomas Jefferson? How do slave cemeteries in Brazil and the United States and the walls of names of Whitney Plantation Museum speak to other initiatives honoring enslaved people such as those found in the Royall House in Massachusetts (United States) and the Georgian House Museum in Bristol (UK)? Is there any connection between the demands to rename streets of Liverpool and the protests to remove the Confederate flag from the Capitol building in South Carolina in the United States? What shared problems and goals have led to the creation of the International Slavery Museum in Liverpool and the newly opened National Museum of African American History and Culture Washington DC? How have black and white social actors and scholars influenced the ways slavery is represented in George Washington's Mount Vernon in the United States? Why have artists from Brazil, France, the Republic of Benin, and the United States, who identify as either blacks or whites, used their works to confront the debates about slavery and its legacies? Addressing the notions of history, cultural memory, collective memory, public memory, official memory, and their dialogues with public history and art, *Slavery in the Age of Memory* explains how ordinary citizens, social groups, governments, and institutions grapple with the past of slavery and the Atlantic slave trade. The book illuminates how and why, over the last five decades, the debates about slavery have increasingly become so relevant in the societies where slavery existed and participated in the Atlantic slave trade.

But before moving further, it is important to clarify the use of certain terms considered throughout this book. Many scholars dedicated entire works to study the notions of history and memory.[10] In this book, history and memory are conceived as forms of human discourse (either oral or written) about people, things, situations, and events that actually occurred or allegedly happened in the past. In other words, these two modalities of discourse that engage with the historical past have many elements in common and are shaped by those who produce them. Yet, despite the artificial dimension of this task, establishing distinctions is imperative. Historical discourse is an imperfect account based on primary sources (such as a written document, a visual image, an object, or an oral account) produced in a specific moment of what is conventionally defined as past. Historian Marc Bloch, for example, pointed out that the past is also a convention, that is, "by definition, a given that nothing will change anymore," even though the knowledge about the past is always in progress and is "constantly changing and improving."[11] Anthropologist Michel-Rolph Trouillot underscored that "history means both the facts of the matter and a narrative of those facts, both 'happened' and 'that which is said to have happened.'"[12] Historians not only aim to establish facts; they examine, select, classify, organize, and interpret these facts in the light of existing evidence.[13] Ultimately, normative history produced by academic historians is an organized account that attempts to explain the past. Yet, historians rarely witness the events they narrate and very often have no direct access to the social actors who witnessed the experiences they recount. Despite high aims of objectivity and in many cases, serious attempts to tell the truth, history written by historians is also biased. As David Lowenthal observes, historians are also aware, "they cannot avoid manipulating the evidence."[14] Consequently, like memory, history also "conflates, exaggerates, abridges; what is crucial or unique is made to stand out, uniformities and minutiae fade away."[15] Yet Paul Ricoeur probably conveys the most insightful dimension of the relation between history and memory. Refusing the opposition between these two modes of discourse, he sees memory as the "womb of history, in as much as memory remains the guardian of the entire problem of the representative relation of the present to the past."[16]

Although memory and history remain in constant interaction, living experience is usually assigned as the realm of memory, not history. Collective memory is alive and relies on intergenerational transmission of remembered experiences shared by a group.[17] Still, transmission occurs at various levels. Members of different generations of a given group may remember an event they directly witnessed, whereas other members of the same group may also remember the same event despite having experienced it through mediated forms, such as radio, television, and the internet.[18]

Collective memory is closely related to identity because it is linked to the group. However, collective memory is not the mere addition of multiple memories of members of a given group. It is rather a modality of memory that is deeply shaped and even determined by the group that can be as vast as a nation or as small as a family unit. As argued by Maurice Halbwachs, because individuals share common experiences in each society, collective memory exists and is transmitted within specific social frameworks such as the institutions of family and religion. Therefore, individual recollections allow collective memory to reorganize a representation of the past that relates to the prevailing views of a given society. But whereas specific groups assemble this memory manifested through the recollections of individuals, specific persons also remember the past by seeking to position themselves into the group's point of view.[19] Ultimately, collective memory is plural, fragmented, and dynamic. Through its various frameworks, collective memory is not only shaped by social institutions but also modeled by class and gender. Like other forms of memory, collective memory does not preserve the past, it rather reconstructs the past.[20]

Although overlapping the notion of collective memory, cultural memory emerges beyond the transmission occurred among individuals and generations that shared common experiences. Cultural memory, as conceived by Jan Assmann, incorporates a certain materiality. It operates through a variety of tools, such as rites, commemoration ceremonies, texts, material traces (like monuments and objects), and other mnemonic devices that activate meanings connected to what happened, but that at the same time go "beyond their practical purpose."[21] In other words, cultural memory is materialized and ritualized, hence it is also referred to as a synonym of material heritage because of its link to physical remains "that have significance for a particular group or society."[22]

Whereas collective memory of slavery can be confined to the private circles of groups such as families, public memory is achieved through an engagement with the public sphere. In different historical periods, whether through actual or imagined stories, societies and groups choose to highlight selected elements of their pasts. When making these choices, social groups put forward specific features that help them gain social visibility and recognition and therefore acquire political power. In other words, while in dialogue with other modalities of memory such as collective memory and cultural memory, public memory is conveyed by groups carrying specific political purposes. Memory, then, becomes public in contexts in which, to some extent, organized groups asserting a certain identity experienced the rupture of their connections with their community, or imagined community of origin.[23]

Bearers of public memory rely on the past to legitimize their claims, but they engage the past through verbal discourses and actions carried out in the present. Public memory, like collective memory, is a mode of memory that can only exist through the voices and actions of established living groups, composed by individuals who assert their presence in the public arena through relations of power. But in contrast with collective memory that presumes intergenerational transmission, public memory (sometimes also referred to as part of a larger branch identified as historical memory) is a political instrument to build, assert, and reinforce collective identities. Otherwise stated, individuals develop identity narratives or discourses about who they are, what are their origins, what gathers them together, and what makes them different from others. Obviously, these discourses are grounded on the connections of these individuals with given communities, even though these associations become explicit under specific circumstances and contexts. Constructed through the interactions among different groups with specific political agendas, public memory is about power relations. Each group in play fights to make its views of the past dominant in the public space. Very often, the group that wins this symbolic battle is successful in making these memories official. Ultimately, these memories acquire an official status when legitimate political authorities, such as international institutions, governments, and universities, embrace and recognize these memories by assigning them a permanent status and favoring them with the monopoly of public instruments.[24]

When discussing all these modes of memory as they concern specific cases and national contexts, I rely on the work of philosophers, anthropologists, historians, and sociologists who explored the notions of race, racialization, white supremacy, and racism to argue that race and white supremacy are predominant frameworks through which the different modalities of memory of slavery in the Americas, Europe, and Africa manifest themselves.[25] I contend that race (as a socially constructed political idea according to which human groups are subjectively classified through perceived physical features) has shaped the multiple representations of the slave past. I mean that the construction of racial hierarchies in a modern world "created as a *racially hierarchical* polity, globally dominated by Europeans" largely impacted the ways slavery is remembered and memorialized in various Atlantic societies.[26] Racialization, as theorized by Charles Mills and Jemima Pierre, is a "contract between those categorized as white over the nonwhites" and is a key factor "in the long historical arc of Europe's relationship with Africa and Africans."[27] Likewise, as argued by Achille Mbembe, race and identity are closely interconnected: "the racial signifier is still in many ways the inescapable language for the stories people tell about themselves, about the relationships with the Other, about memory, and about power."[28] Through different paths, Mills and Mbembe agree that the rise of modernity between the end of the fifteenth century and the long eighteenth century gave birth to the "racial contract." In other words, they concur that modernity "coincided with the appearance of the principle of race."[29] This new order is characterized by the emergence of the ideology of white supremacy and racism. In the context of the rise of the Atlantic slave trade and the European colonization of the Americas, these authors conceive white supremacy as an ideology, a "power structure of formal or informal rule, socioeconomic privilege, and norms for the differential distribution, of material wealth and opportunities, benefits, and burdens, rights and duties."[30] In this system, racism operates as an instrument of the ideology of white supremacy. In other words, racism is a belief naturalizing individuals racialized as nonwhite to be inferior, while simultaneously placing white persons in positions of superiority. But more than an abstract belief, racism engenders actions and practices that systematically discriminate against nonwhite individuals in various societal spheres. Still, as Eduardo Bonilla-Silva maintains, racism contributes to fuel white supremacy as an ideology, reinforcing a structure in which the dominant racial groups not only receive awards but also reproduce "their systemic advantages." In this dynamic, racism is more than a simple idea "but the social edifice erected over racial inequality."[31]

The Atlantic slave trade imposed on West African and West Central African men, women, and children the most voluminous transoceanic forced migration in history. Starting at the end of the fifteenth century in Europe and the Americas, this process of racialization meant that being black and being human with the legal status of a "slave" gradually became synonyms. Over time, in most societies that largely relied on slavery or in societies involved in the Atlantic slave trade, race became the most influential element to determine whether individuals or groups represent people who benefited from or who were victimized by slavery. As a socially constructed category, one's race encompasses a combination of elements, such as physical features, ancestry, religion, language, social position, and wealth. With the rise of the Atlantic slave trade, populations of African descent in the Americas were associated with individuals who were victimized by this inhuman commerce and kept in bondage. Still how a person of African descent is identified in different societies can vary. Typically, ancestry is arbitrarily determined by the origins of one's ancestors. Yet these personal roots are always compounded and overlapping. In West Africa and West Central Africa, racialization mainly operates through lineage but is also combined with other elements such as bodily features. In the United States, skin color is certainly central, but African ancestry has been the key element to determine if a person is black, brown, or white. In Latin America and the Caribbean, however, in addition to skin color, wealth and social position are relevant factors to determine if one individual is categorized as white or racialized as black, brown, or indigenous.[32] Because former slave societies such as Brazil maintained slaves and their descendants in disadvantaged social and economic positions, underprivileged individuals have been historically racialized as black. Likewise, constructed racial models in operation in the Americas also established that people of European descent carry physical characteristics such as light skin as well as light and straight hair. Identified as whites, these men and women have historically occupied higher social ranks in societies where the institution of slavery existed and have been typically identified with the groups who supported slavery and financially benefited from it.

Of course, these distinctions are not always as clear as they look on the surface. In societies where slavery was pervasive such as Brazil, although on a small scale, there were black individuals who traded in slaves and other black residents of urban and rural areas who owned slaves as well, though very rarely in great numbers.[33] African societies that evidently provided captives to the Atlantic slave trade have had and still have their own wealthy elites. Elite groups include descendants of men and women of royalty who led wars and raids against neighboring states and villages to acquire prisoners to be sold in the Atlantic slave trade. Moreover, not all whites and people of European descent owned slaves. Intergenerational poverty exists among white populations in Europe and the Americas, making it also hard to associate light skin and European ancestry with previous generation's slave ownership.[34] Similarly, in many former slave societies, individuals identified as whites carry African ancestry that they either ignore or conceal to dissociate themselves from the stigma associated with slavery.

Although race is a social construct and not a biological concept, racial lines shape the way individuals and groups position themselves regarding the involvement of their ancestors and countries in slavery and the Atlantic slave trade. Individuals categorized as white and racialized as black continuously reconfigure these racial identities that in the long run orient their possible claims. In countries such as the United States, men and women identified as whites who did not directly inherit the wealth generated by slavery still enjoyed the benefits of not being victims of racial discrimination. Ultimately, the ways these groups represent themselves along these fabricated racial designations orient how they assert themselves in the public arena.

Individual and collective memories of individuals and groups remained alive for a very long time, especially in the private realm. But especially after emancipation during the nineteenth and twentieth centuries, these memories started occupying the public sphere, eventually shaping the public and official memory of slavery and the Atlantic slave trade. Unlike most other regions of the Atlantic world, during the second half of the eighteenth century, former slaves in the United States started publishing slave narratives, which soon transformed into a genuine literary genre.[35] In 1935, during the Great Depression, as part of the New Deal US President Franklin Delano Roosevelt launched the Federal Writers' Project, an initiative aimed at funding written works and supporting writers. From 1936 to 1938, men and women employed in this project were assigned to interview freedpeople in seventeen southern states. Despite the biases of the interviewers, this ambitious and unprecedented initiative produced the most comprehensive collection of testimonies provided by former enslaved individuals in the Americas, thus offering clues to understand the collective memory of freedpeople in the United States.[36]

On the eve of the Second World War, slavery became the object of representations in US popular culture as well. Embodying elements of the collective memory of slavery carried out by white descendants of slave owners, novels and movies such as *Gone with the Wind* imparted a nostalgic image of the old slaveholding South.[37] Reinforcing depictions of enslaved men and women as submissive subjects, the United States exported these representations of slavery to other former slave societies such as Brazil.[38] Yet, with the rise of the Civil Rights Movement in the 1950s, African American activists, writers, artists, and other social actors challenged white renderings of passive slaves. Probably one of the most successful examples of this transformation is Alex Haley's novel *Roots: The Saga of an American Family* (1976) and its 1977 television adaptation.[39] Both the book and the television series promoted new African American representations of enslaved men and women that emphasized resistance and resilience.

The decolonization of Africa and the Caribbean also transformed the memorialization of slavery. If most monuments conveyed submissive representations by often portraying crouched and bent bodies of enslaved men, women, and children until the first half of the twentieth century, starting in the 1960s, an emerging public memory of slavery favored the commemoration of bondspeople and freedpeople who organized insurrections.[40] Especially in the Caribbean, several monuments rendered individuals who resisted bondage and fought against slavery. Representing slaves in body positions that demonstrate resistance (with raised arms and breaking chains), many new statues featured identifiable individuals such as Gaspar Yanga in Mexico, Benkos Bioho in Colombia, Carlota in Cuba, Bussa in Barbados, and Zumbi of Palmares in Brazil.[41] Despite these initiatives that paid homage to enslaved historical actors who acquired prominence because of their roles in fighting slavery, the presence of ordinary enslaved men and women tended to be erased from heritage sites of former plantations or urban settings where slavery existed. Either in Brazil, Colombia, or the United States, the crucial role of the enslaved workforce and their numerical importance in slave societies were rarely recognized. But in the last three decades, the slave-owning past of these societies became more visible. The end of the Cold War favored the visibility of historically excluded groups asserting their identities. This general framework also propelled international exchanges boosting global connections among black organizations and populations of African descent. On the one hand, black social actors and activists increasingly started occupying the public space to claim the history of men and women who resisted slavery. On the other hand, historians also began paying more attention to individual trajectories of enslaved men and women who coped with the hardships of slavery by emancipating themselves or by negotiating better work and living conditions. Relying on a myriad of firsthand narratives and testimonies of enslaved persons especially in the United States, these scholars began giving a central place to the lived experiences of bondspeople.[42] This phenomenon did not occur in isolation. Before the end of the Second World War, initiatives memorializing the Holocaust emerged through the publication of victims' testimonies that embraced individual stories, which since then have been depicted in motion pictures, novels, documentary films, museum exhibitions, and memorials featuring men and women who resisted the Nazi regime.[43]

During the 1990s, heritage sites of old plantations of tobacco, wheat, and cotton opened to visitation in the United States also started giving more visibility to the institution of slavery, a dimension once totally evacuated from these spaces designed to underscore the luxurious lives of slaveholding elites.[44] As put by Stephen Small and Jennifer L. Eischstedt, during the tours of southern plantations, docents often made references to slavery by using the passive voice, one of the various devices conceived to symbolically annihilate the physical presence and the work provided by enslaved persons.[45] Still, despite older timid attempts and more recent robust efforts to call attention to slavery in former plantation heritage sites, bondspeople continued to be portrayed as nameless individuals.[46] Even visitors to richer plantation sites such as Thomas Jefferson's Monticello, which over the last two decades made considerable efforts to interpret slavery, still object how these sites whitewashed their history.[47] As scholars studying slave trade heritage tourism in US southern plantations have emphasized, to a greater or lesser extent, even the sites that brought slavery to light remain perpetuating the dehumanization and the invisibility of enslaved men and women.[48]

Like collective memory, public memory of slavery and the Atlantic slave trade is carried out by men and women whose histories are in one way or another associated with these past atrocities. During slavery and immediately after the abolition of slavery, enslaved persons and, later, freedpeople gathered themselves to commemorate specific dates, especially emancipation.[49] As the formerly enslaved passed away in different societies of the Americas, men and women identifying themselves as descendants of bondspeople preserved a collective memory of the experiences lived by their ancestors. In this context, slavery and the Atlantic slave trade operate as a template through which the members of a group situate themselves regarding other groups in their societies. Occupying different positions as descendants of enslaved victims, middlemen, slave merchants, or slave owners, the claims these individuals and groups presently convey in the public sphere can greatly differ.

This book draws from my earlier work and new case studies. Most examples come from the United States, France, and England, even though I briefly explore some case studies in Brazil and the Republic of Benin, countries which I extensively examined in previously published works. As each chapter centers on one specific modality of memory, my selected examples of heritage sites, plantations, museums, monuments, and artworks are based on to what extent they embody such modes of memory, on how they relate to each other, and also on their national and international visibility. Obviously, several other books could be written by utilizing other examples.

The multisited and unconventional archive that I relied on to write this book is composed of public discourses found in memoirs, oral interviews, pamphlets, and newspaper articles, as well as monuments, memorials, heritage buildings and sites, museum exhibitions, and artworks. The book is divided into six chapters. In Chapter 1, "Weaving Collective Memory," I examine the formation of a collective memory of descendants of slave traders, slave owners, and enslaved people. I look at the examples of slave merchants such as Francisco Félix de Souza from the old Kingdom of Dahomey (the present-day Republic of Benin) as well as slaveholders such as Thomas Jefferson and his descendants. Through the study of these cases, I show how race, family, religion, and, to some extent, gender were central frameworks that shaped the development of a collective memory of slavery and the slave trade. Chapter 2, "Shrines of Cultural Memory," discusses the notion of cultural memory in relation to slavery. Like collective memory, cultural memory of slavery is also racialized and deeply shaped by white supremacy structures. I look at how naming practices have been incorporated in memorials honoring enslaved people by specifically examining how initiatives commemorating slavery incorporated "walls of names" to recognize the humanity of enslaved men, women, and children. By exploring a few case studies in the United States, the chapter investigates how effectively this specific kind of memorial has been employed to recognize and pay homage to the victims of slavery. In Chapter 3, "Battles of Public Memory," I argue that public memory is a political and racialized mode of engagement with the slave past. Analyzing examples from England and the United States, I explain how activists, associations, individual citizens, and sometimes academics occupy the public sphere to demand public powers to give visibility to slavery in the public space. These demands certainly address the need of recognizing the deep involvement of Britain and the United States in the slave trade and slavery. Yet, in due course, these social actors exposed the pervasiveness of white supremacy, deeply embedded in the urban landscapes of these societies, by also fighting the persistence of racism and racial inequalities. In Chapter 4, "Setting Slavery in the Museum," I show that in some cases the battles of public memory generated tangible results. Through a discussion of the contexts of France, England, and the United States, I examine how the Nantes History Museum, the Museum of Aquitaine, the International Slavery Museum, and the National Museum of African American History and Culture heard the claims of black citizens and their white allies by eventually incorporating slavery and the slave trade in their exhibitions. In Chapter 5, "Memory and Public History," I delve into the dialogues between memory (in its various modalities) and public history in Mount Vernon and Monticello, the plantations of George Washington and Thomas Jefferson. Even though the history of these two sites is fully documented, memory still prevails over public history initiatives that attempted to shed light on the lives of hundreds of enslaved men, women, and children who labored these plantations. Overall, I propose that race and white supremacy continue to model the ways memory and public history engage with the slavery's past. In Chapter 6, "Art as Memory," I discuss how visual artists in Europe, Africa, and the Americas have engaged with the problem of slavery and the Atlantic slave trade. By looking at the works of Cyprien Tokoudagba, Romuald Hazoumè, William Adjété-Wilson, Rosana Paulino, Nona Faustine, and François Piquet, I explore how their artworks incorporate the work of memory while at the same time participating in political debates regarding race, racism, and white supremacy. Eventually, in the book's conclusion, I contend that although separated in different categories, the various modalities of memory often overlap and interact with each other. However, the understanding of the several modes of memory studied throughout the book allows scholars and students to better seize the multiple ways individuals, groups, and institutions grapple with slavery's past in the present, and how this past is constantly reshaped to respond to the persisting legacies of these human atrocities.

1

Weaving Collective Memory

Over the generations, despite myriad of obstacles, enslaved men and women and their descendants have managed to preserve a collective memory of the period in which they lived in bondage. Marked by gaps, absences, and unanswered questions, in most cases collective memory of slavery is accessible through oral accounts passed on by the last generations of enslaved individuals. As collective memory relies on transmission, the families of rich slave merchants and slave owners, who today still carry the names of their ancestors, tend to have better preserved oral accounts, narratives, documents, and artifacts, permitting them access to parts of their past, which, in turn, nourishes their collective memory. This same kind of transmission could hardly occur among bondspeople and their descendants. Regardless of exceptions, most enslaved persons and freedpeople remained illiterate. Moreover, they faced myriad obstacles that deprived them of the very basic means for livelihood. Hindrances such as being prevented from accumulating property, and family separation, seriously complicated the propagation of reminiscences, knowledge, and experiences to their descendants.

This chapter discusses what collective memory is and how it relates to slavery and the Atlantic slave trade. I argue that in the context of these atrocities collective memory is racialized, gendered, and shaped by the ideology of white supremacy. Therefore, this modality of memory is neither homogeneous nor immutable.[1] This is the reason why it would be inappropriate to refer to a collective memory as being true or false, because memory, like history, to varying degrees, is always biased.[2] By exploring examples from West Africa and the Americas, this chapter shows how certain narratives predominate among specific groups in former slave societies and societies that were deeply involved in the Atlantic slave trade. I open the chapter by examining the contrasting ways the descendants of slaves and slave traders have addressed the slave past in their own families and at the local level in the Kingdom of Dahomey, today part of the Republic of Benin, a small country in West Africa. Next, I discuss how descendants of slave merchants and slave owners in the United States have engaged with the slave-trading and slave-owning pasts of their families, in contrast to the ways groups who identify themselves as descendants of slaves remember this tragic history. I analyze three examples that have become well known in the United States. I start with the case of Thomas Jefferson (1743–1826) and his enslaved black family, the Hemingses. I also explore two other examples: first, the Balls, a large slave-owning family from South Carolina; second, the DeWolfs, a family of slaveholders and slave merchants from Rhode Island. I emphasize that collective memory of slavery and the slave trade is never uniform. Instead, it varies among various groups and sometimes among different members of a same group, depending on how they position themselves in relation to these past atrocities.

Intertwined Memories of Slavers and Enslaved

Can descendants of slave merchants celebrate the slaving past of their families? At various times and in different places, the progeny of some slaveholding families and slave traders have continued to take pride in their ancestors' slaving activities. Until the rise of the Civil Rights Movement in the United States, many descendants of slave owners, especially in the South, were not at all ashamed of the fact that their ancestors owned slaves. Perhaps today, these families no longer dare to make public statements praising their slave-owning past. Yet, in West Africa today, many scions of slave owners and slave merchants still commend their families' slave-trading activities in private and public spaces.

The Republic of Benin, a West African country encompassing the region of the old Kingdom of Dahomey, offers one of the richest cases for the study of collective memory of the Atlantic slave trade. Dahomey emerged in the seventeenth century in the hinterland of the Bight of Benin (bay stretching from Cape St. Paul in Ghana to the Niger River's Nun outlet, in Nigeria) and started expanding its territory in the early eighteenth century. The kingdom was ruled by a dynasty of speakers of Fon, a Gbe language that is part of the Volta-Niger subdivision of the Niger-Congo family. Since its inception, Dahomey was a militarized state, in which warfare played a central role.[3]

Engagement with Europeans gave Dahomey access to firearms. These weapons afforded the kingdom an advantage to lead raids and wage war against its neighbors, including the Ewe in the west, the Mahi in the north, and Yoruba-speaking groups located mainly in the northeast area, up to present-day region of Abeokuta, in Nigeria. The Dahomean army took many prisoners during these raids and military campaigns.

Some captives remained enslaved in the kingdom's territory, where they performed religious duties, agricultural labor, and domestic service. Others were sacrificed during religious ceremonies. But most captives were sold into slavery. Among them was Oluale Kossola (*c.* 1841–1935) known as Cudjo Lewis, who was brought to the United States on board the slave ship *Clotilda* in 1860. Kossola narrated in detail how he was captured during one of these raids, then transported by middlemen to the coast, where along with others he was sold to slave merchants and shipped to the Americas.[4]

During the eighteenth century, Dahomey expanded. After conquering the Kingdom of Hueda in 1727, the kingdom seized the port of Ouidah, gaining direct access to the coast. Ouidah alone exported nearly 22 percent of the enslaved Africans sent to the Americas.[5] In the next decades, Dahomey became a major player in the Atlantic slave trade in the Bight of Benin. Yet the kingdom did not have a monopoly on the slave trade in the region. In this same period, the Oyo Empire, located northeast of Dahomey, became one of its fiercest rivals. After successful raids during the first half of the eighteenth century, Oyo forced Dahomey to pay huge tributes, an imposition that lasted until the 1820s. Over the eighteenth century, Ouidah became the second largest slave port in Africa, second only to Luanda in present-day Angola. But progressively Oyo came to control slave ports such as Porto-Novo in the modern-day Republic of Benin. Gradually other ports such as Lagos and Badagry, in contemporary Nigeria, acquired importance as well. Slave merchants from Europe and the Americas established themselves in Ouidah and other Bight of Benin ports. Moreover, during the nineteenth century, hundreds of freedmen and freedwomen who left Brazil after a failed slave rebellion settled in the region.[6] Back in West Africa, several of these formerly enslaved individuals became slave merchants or worked on activities related to the infamous trade.

The Republic of Benin's complex involvement in the Atlantic slave trade shapes the collective memories of the descendants of slave traders, slave owners, and enslaved persons. How do freedpeople who left the Americas to settle in Ouidah, as well as heirs of slave owners and descendants of the Dahomean royal family, collectively remember slavery? How do descendants of men and women who were kept in slavery on African soil and those of freedpeople from Brazil who settled in the region remember slavery and the Atlantic slave trade? Understanding these multiple dimensions of collective memory helps us to see that bondage and the trade in human beings have been conceived differently for multiple social actors and groups during the period of the Atlantic slave trade. These different views that have survived in the present still model the relations among the descendants of these different groups. In other words, these questions provide clarification of such nuances, which are important to comprehend today's debates around the history and legacies of these atrocities.

The slave merchant Francisco Félix de Souza (1754–1849) is one of the most controversial figures embodying the slave-trading past of Dahomey and the present-day Republic of Benin. Souza was most likely born in

Salvador (Bahia) in Brazil in 1754.[7] He first arrived in the Bight of Benin in 1792 and may have remained in the region for nearly three years, before returning to Brazil and then back to West Africa in 1800. In the early nineteenth century, the slave trade between the Bight of Benin and Brazil was at its summit. Souza first settled in Ouidah to work at the Portuguese fort of São João Batista da Ajuda, moving on later to become the fort's director.[8]

Souza's wealth and political power made him a pivotal figure in the construction of the collective memory of the Atlantic slave trade in the Republic of Benin. His influence was based on a large network including the Dahomean royal family, other slave merchants, as well as freedmen and freedwomen who left Brazil to settle in Ouidah. The importance of Souza's large and extended family along with his intrepid life as a slave trader has inspired novelists and screenwriters who often represented him as an adventurer. His legacy is still alive among his clan and in the Republic of Benin's collective memory.[9]

In Ouidah, a city whose current population is estimated at around 92,000 residents, Souza is a well-known character. Since the nineteenth century in Dahomey and until today in the Republic of Benin, the collective memory of the Atlantic slave trade is manifested through a variety of modalities. Religion is one of these frameworks. The collective memory of slavery, especially in the Souza family, is shaped by Catholicism, the religion of the clan's founder. But another influence is Vodun, a West African religion characterized by trance, possession, and the belief in the existence of a great number of deities.[10] Family in and of itself is a key framework of collective memory. Among Souza's descendants, the Atlantic slave trade is remembered through stories about their forefather. These recollections are also fashioned by the clan's current relations with the Dahomean royal family and with the descendants of his collaborators and other men and women who depended on him, among whom there were persons locally enslaved.

Souza's slave-trading activities impacted not only his immediate circle but also the lives of a wide range of individuals, including the Dahomean royal family; European and American-born slave merchants; the men, women, and children owned by him; as well as entire families of freed individuals, who over the nineteenth century settled in Ouidah and the neighboring towns. Each of these groups and their descendants remembers the slave trade, and Souza's involvement in it, in different ways.

Souza's earliest activities in Ouidah coincided with the reign of the infamous King Adandozan, who ruled Dahomey from 1797 to 1818. Although Adandozan is an important figure in the Republic of Benin's collective memory of the Atlantic slave trade, his successors to the throne erased his name from the list of Dahomean kings. The king acquired a bad reputation because after taking power he allegedly transgressed local customs by selling into slavery Dahomean-born individuals, including noblemen and noblewomen, involved in the plot that led to the assassination of his father.[11] However, he was not the first king to break this rule. Actually, preceding and later rulers also sold members of the royal family into slavery. Indeed, Adandozan governed Dahomey during a period of economic and political crisis, when Ouidah's slave trade activity, the kingdom's main source of revenues, went into decline. Following the end of the British slave trade in 1807, Britain increased the pressures to prohibit the slave trade from Africa to Brazil, one of the main destinations of enslaved Africans embarked in Ouidah. Moreover, during the same period its position as the largest West African slave port was threatened by the growing importance of Lagos.[12]

After a clash with King Adandozan, probably because of debt related to the slave trade, Souza was jailed in Abomey, the capital of Dahomey. In prison, Souza encountered Prince Gakpe, Adandozan's half-brother and future King Gezo, who organized his escape, a story depicted in Werner Herzog's motion picture *Cobra Verde*.[13] Later, Souza supported the prince in a coup d'état that removed Adandozan from power. Once made king, to pay back his support, Gezo awarded Souza with financial advantages and political power. Over the next years, Souza became one of the wealthiest slave merchants of West Africa and Gezo's most important intermediary in Ouidah's slave-trading activities. Because of his close ties with the Dahomean royal family, Souza is still today considered the founder of a dynasty of sorts and referred to as the Viceroy of Dahomey, even though this title did not exist. In his family, Souza is remembered as a great leader, a wealthy and seductive man, whose exceptional qualities made him a key player in changing the course of Dahomean history.

Souza's relations with Gezo also contributed to the development of other dimensions of the collective memory of the Atlantic slave trade in Dahomey. Oral tradition, today largely accepted by scholars, states that when Adandozan took power, he sold Gezo's putative mother, Na Agontimé, who subsequently may have been sent into slavery to Brazil.[14] As Souza was Brazilian, oral tradition also emphasizes that Gezo gave Souza the task of traveling to Brazil to find his Dahomean enslaved mother. But despite the existence of several cases of emissaries sent to the Americas to rescue African noble individuals sold into slavery, there is no evidence that Souza effectively traveled to Brazil to accomplish this task or that Na Agontimé was ever rescued. A persistent familial recollection by the members of Souza even today, this story is an important example on how Souza is associated with the collective memory of the Atlantic slave trade in Dahomey, not as a slave merchant who sold individuals into slavery but rather as a redeemer.

British travelers who sojourned in Ouidah also contributed to construct an image of Souza as a compassionate man. Contemporary accounts not only depicted him as disposed to liberate his slaves but also described him as a man concerned with human rights. Scottish traveler John Duncan reported that Souza and other slave dealers were all benevolent to their slaves. Likewise, Duncan stated that slaves did not perform much work in Dahomey. Also, Souza treated his slaves so well that they refused to be freed.[15] Likewise, British naval officer Frederick E. Forbes underscored that Souza's values differed from those of the indigenous population, because he opposed the practice of human sacrifice.[16] Travelers who met Souza also attested to his projected image as a great philanthropist, substantiating that he saved the lives of many captives he purchased for export preventing them from being sacrificed in Vodun religious ceremonies. Souza's descendants still remember him through a praise-name that, according to them, states that he bought an enslaved man to give him back to his family. However, this praise-name indeed asserts that Souza "bought the child and the child's mother," conveying a clear reference to Souza's power and wealth.[17]

Religion as a Framework of Collective Memory

The collective memory of the Atlantic slave trade as embodied by Souza and his lineage also operates within a religious framework. Both Portugal and its Brazilian colonies were Catholic societies governed by a monarchy. As a Portuguese subject until 1822, year of the Brazilian independence, Souza is perceived not only as a Catholic but also as the one who introduced Catholicism in Dahomey in the early nineteenth century. Yet the Brazilian slave trader also embraced other local religious traditions, especially Vodun. Therefore, when Souza settled in Ouidah, King Gezo ordered the installation of several Vodun shrines in the city to protect him. Still today the descendants of the priests sent to Ouidah during Gezo's reign remain close to the Souza family. These religious chiefs were captives captured in neighboring regions. Whereas some were brought to Ouidah to be sold into slavery and sent to the Americas, others remained enslaved locally.[18] Their presence exposed the conflictual relations between Souza and the Dahomean royalty, as through them the king could exert control over the slave merchant and his family.

Upon his death, Souza himself became a sort of Vodun deity. Following the local tradition, his body was buried inside his original house located in his compound in Ouidah, transforming it into a family memorial. The memorial houses a gallery of portraits of various important male members of the family. It also includes the slave trader's tomb and his original bed, which is prepared every day as if he were still alive. The religious framework of Souza's collective memory is emphasized in a large statue of a barefoot Saint Francis of Assisi. Lying at one end of the white marble tomb, the statue of the Catholic saint implies that practicing Catholicism and selling human beings were not conflicting activities. In addition to Catholicism, other religious traditions are represented in his memorial. Close to Souza's tomb is a large ceramic jar that according to his family members was brought by him from Brazil. This jar contains water, used in libation rituals aimed at healing members of the family. Embedded in a religious construct that mixes Catholicism and Vodun, the collective memory of the slave merchant and his progeny remains alive through a variety of artifacts and rituals, in which Souza's Brazilian origins play a prominent role.

When showing the site to visitors, Souza's family members explain that when their ancestor died, the King of Dahomey sent a dozen slaves to be sacrificed and buried in his tomb. But Souza's children rejected the ritual and ordered instead the men to be freed. Despite this Westernized and humane image of the family opposing both local religious practices and human sacrifice, historical evidence does not corroborate this story. Indeed, the slave dealer was honored like a traditional Dahomean chief. During his memorial service, four enslaved individuals were sacrificed, two on the beach and two others on his tomb.[19]

Souza also had his own vodun named *Dagoun*, a term probably related to the word "dragon." Souza's *Dagoun* is a serpent (*dan*), associated with *Sakpata* (deity of earth and diseases, such as smallpox) and *Heviosso* (deity of thunder). Versions about the origins of Souza's *voduns* vary. Highlighting the encounter among Portuguese, Brazilian, indigenous, and African cultures, the first version states that Souza wore a ring with a serpent's effigy, offered to him by his mother, who according to family fabled accounts was an indigenous woman from Amazonia in Brazil. As time passed, locals started believing that the serpent, similar to a *dan*, usually associated with wealth, was at the origin of the slave merchant's opulence. The second version states that Souza adopted a *vodun* to protect his family from high infant mortality, of which many of his relations were aggrieved by. The third and more current version states that when King Gezo invited Souza to settle in Ouidah, he gave him two *voduns* to protect the city. The first was placed at the city's entrance and the second at the city's exit. To protect him, he also received a third *vodun* called *Dagoun*.

However, there is a fourth version analogous to the first one, which states that Souza brought two snakes from Brazil for his own protection. When the snakes died, they were buried close to the slave merchant's compound, but some days later, a termite mound appeared in the exact place they were buried. Although Souza ordered the mounds to be destroyed, new ones continued appearing. Helpless, Souza asked assistance of King Gezo, who sent his Vodun priests to Ouidah. The priests discovered through divination that Souza's reptiles were indeed sacred Vodun snakes. This finding led to the construction of a temple to worship them, located where the first termite mound appeared and not far from the Souza's compound. Souza's Vodun deities fulfill several functions. They maintain the myth of his humble background. They promote the idea of his mixed Brazilian origins. They contribute to keep together the members of his family and their dependents. They also help to highlight his power and wealth, legitimizing the persisting political and economic importance of the Souza family in Ouidah and the Republic of Benin.

Collective Memory of the Enslaved

The collective memory of the Atlantic slave trade among the members of Souza's clan greatly differs from that of the descendants of enslaved men and women who still live in Ouidah and neighboring towns. Because Souza's memory relies on the encounter between Portugal, Brazil, and West Africa, he is at times perceived as an African chief and at other times as a white Brazilian-born individual who carried Europeanized culture. Racialization and white supremacy play a central role in the construction of the Souza family's collective memory of slavery. Still today, its members clearly establish a distinction between themselves and the descendants of slaves who returned from Brazil and became associated with the family through marriage or business ties. The descriptions of these differences include mentions of lighter "coffee and milk" skin color and alleged European "thin" physical features.[20] Yet, as argued by Jemima Pierre in her work about Ghana, this claimed "whiteness" is connected to not only physical appearance but part of the overall framework of white supremacy. Whiteness is associated with a series of qualities such as "development, modernity, intelligence, innovation, technology, cultural and aesthetic superiority, and economic domination," therefore representing the "unearned privilege for the group racially designated as White."[21] Indeed, on several occasions, including during interactions with visitors of the family's compound in Ouidah, Souza's African-born descendants depict their ancestor as a white person and as a successful businessman who saved the captives allocated for human sacrifice by selling them into slavery. Unlike the descendants of slave merchants in former slave societies such as the United States who today adhere to the framing of Atlantic slave trade as an inhuman commerce, most of Souza's relatives do not convey feelings of guilt. On the contrary, they typically express pride in being the scions of a powerful man who according to them represented Luso-Brazilian white values, including Catholicism. In conversations and interviews, Souza's descendants also justify the activities of their ancestor by stressing that in his time the Atlantic slave trade was a legal activity. However, this narrative, like many other expressions of collective memory, contradicts historical evidence. Indeed, the busiest and most lucrative period of Souza's slave-trading activities corresponded to the period when the slave trade was already prohibited on the Bight of Benin.

During the era of the Atlantic slave trade several men, women, and children captured during wars waged by Dahomey against neighboring states were kept enslaved on Dahomean soil. While some of these prisoners were sacrificed in religious ceremonies, others were kept as slaves and employed in agricultural and domestic activities. Rich locals also purchased captives with great knowledge of Yoruba religions to provide them with spiritual protection. Like other wealthy Dahomey's residents, Souza and his family owned slaves. Their descendants, such as the late historian Émile-Désiré Ologoudou (1935–2019), lived in Ouidah and neighboring cities. Ologoudou's ancestor landed in Ouidah in 1830, when the slave trade in the region would have been already prohibited. His forefather (a Yoruba speaker) was on board of a slave vessel that left from Abeokuta to the Americas. But the vessel experienced technical difficulties while bordering the West African coast and was forced to anchor in Ouidah. As reported by Ologoudou, Souza bought all six hundred enslaved Africans who were on board the slave ship, thereby sparing them from being sold and sent into slavery in the Americas.[22] Although it is hard to determine how many of these dozens of captives remained enslaved locally, Ologoudou's account supports the view, which prevails in Souza's family, portraying the ancestor slave merchant as a benevolent man who rescued the captives, preventing them from being sold overseas or being killed in religious sacrifices.

But the line separating the collective memory of descendants of slave merchants, slave owners, enslaved persons, and freedpeople is not always clear. Souza is considered the founding father of the Luso-Afro-Brazilian community that emerged in the Bight of Benin during the nineteenth century. Yet this community was composed not only of slave merchants. Many of its members were freedmen and freedwomen who left Brazil to settle along that portion of the West African coast, especially after the backlash that followed the Malê rebellion in Bahia in 1835. The term "Malê" (derived from the Yoruba word *imale*, meaning Muslim) did not refer to an ethnic group but to the African-born Muslims who composed a small fraction of the enslaved population in Bahia. Although most slaves and freed individuals practiced African-based religions such as Orisha and Vodun, Islam empowered a variety of groups especially Yoruba speakers. Together they organized the Malê rebellion scheduled to erupt on the eve of January 25, 1835; however, police authorities discovered and dismantled the conspiracy. Hundreds of suspects were arrested. According to the Brazilian criminal code at the time, only the leaders of the rebellion could get prison or death sentences. Many suspects were sentenced with hundreds of floggings and forced labor.[23]

Thus, to prevent new rebellions, the provincial assembly of Bahia passed a law on May 13, 1835, aimed at control and repression of African-born freed and enslaved individuals. The first article of the law allowed the government to deport freed African-born men and women who were suspected of participating in rebellious activity, as these men and women did not enjoy the privileges of Brazilian citizenship.[24] Hence, many freed individuals who allegedly participated in the Malê rebellion were sentenced with deportation to the Bight of Benin. Fearing the backlash resulting from the wave of oppression that imposed many restrictions on African-born individuals, the deportees were followed by family members along with their slaves and former slaves. Together they settled in cities such as Accra in present-day Ghana, Lomé in contemporary Togo, in several present-day cities of the Republic of Benin such as Petit Popo, Agoué, Ouidah, and Porto-

Novo, as well as in Badagry and Lagos in today's Nigeria. In these towns, they joined the existing group of slave dealers of Brazilian and Portuguese origin who had been established there since the eighteenth century.[25] In Ouidah, Francisco Félix de Souza received these returnees, who settled in the surroundings of his compound.[26]

After settling in Ouidah and neighboring towns, several of these freed individuals engaged in the Atlantic slave trade, the only activity that could provide them with economic prosperity. This reunion of slave merchants and freedpeople, who also brought to the Bight of Benin their own human property, gave birth to a unique community in which the collective memory of slavers and enslaved was woven. Carrying Portuguese and Brazilian last names, these men and women shared religious and cultural values, such as Catholicism and Westernized "manners" that placed them closer to the Europeans in comparison to the indigenous population. Yet the experiences of slavers and former enslaved persons as individuals and part of a group shaped in different ways how they engaged with bondage and the Atlantic slave trade. In this emerging community, there were victims and perpetrators, and persons who had been victims and became perpetrators.

In the first category, there were African-born freedpeople, who were raised with the daily fear of being abducted. They witnessed war, raids, and kidnapping that led to the destruction of their villages. Many were captured in the Bight of Benin's hinterland to be sold in the coastal areas. Most of them dealt with the trauma of family separation, the long and deadly walks to the coast, and the horrible Atlantic crossings in the interior of slave ships. Once in regions like Bahia, they were stripped off their original names and were forced not only to acquire a different language but also to adhere to Catholicism. Yet they discovered new trades and resisted. Ultimately, they learned how to navigate a new society and culture, while facing excruciating working and living conditions.

The slave merchants belonged to the second category. Most of them had never been enslaved, were born in Europe or the Americas, and therefore were designated as whites, a visible marker that distinguished them from African-born freed returnees. The experience of slave traders with the Atlantic trade involved buying and selling captives, as well as owning slaves as property. They certainly observed and interacted with enslaved Africans who waited to be sold in ports on both sides of the Atlantic Ocean. But to these men, the atrocious commerce was a positive experience, associated with economic prosperity and not with suffering. This dimension can explain how and why presently the descendants of slave merchants in West African societies such as the Republic of Benin are not ashamed but rather proud of their ancestors, who they perceive as successful individuals. Moreover, these men sold most enslaved Africans to the Americas. Therefore, unlike freedmen and freedwomen who returned to West Africa, the Euro-American ancestry of African-based slave dealers was never challenged by the descendants of men, women, and children they sold overseas.

In addition, there is another complicating factor that makes it difficult to separate victims and perpetrators. Once established in the various towns of the Bight of Benin, several newly arrived freedmen became slave merchants. Consequently, this group's collective memory carries two conflicting sides, because its members lived two opposed dimensions of the Atlantic slave trade's experience, first as enslaved Africans and freed individuals who returned to the continent, and then as traders who purchased and sold human beings. In short, in former Dahomey the experiences of being enslaved and being a slaver were not necessarily separated but rather intertwined. Because of these intersected positions, as well as the presence of descendants of merchants and enslaved persons in a same family, explicit and implicit conflicts continue emerging today. Although Luso-Afro-Brazilian slave owners and former enslaved individuals formed a community, slave merchants and their progeny have continuously stigmatized freedpeople and their descendants.

In addition to these groups, there are also the descendants of men and women who were kept enslaved locally. Many of these individuals were Yoruba speakers, recognizable through their names, even though not all individuals with Yoruba names are descendants of bondspeople. Because all these men and women are black, their differences remain invisible to newcomers who are unfamiliar with these complex connections. Yet, through their last names, native languages, religious practices, way of dress, music and dance traditions, and other physical markers such as scarifications, locals know very well about their slave origins. In the Souza's family, for example, a simple conversation around ancestry can reveal that descendants of family members who married former enslaved men and women returned from Brazil are not considered genuine bearers of the slave merchant's legacy so often associated with Luso-Brazilian origins.

Still, both the offspring of individuals who were sent into slavery to the Americas and returned to the region as freedpeople and Souza's descendants refer to conflictual and ambiguous relations with Fon speakers and members of the Dahomean royal family. In local towns, the collective memory of the descendants of men and women who were captured, sold, and sent to the Americas continues to emphasize the traumatic relations between Fon speakers and the residents of Kétou, a Yoruba town located in the present-day Republic of Benin, which was constantly raided by the Dahomean army during the era of the Atlantic slave trade. For example, when an unannounced visitor knocks at the door of a house in Kétou, the house's owner may answer: "Is this a man, or is this a Fon?" This saying shows how Kétou's Yoruba speakers collectively remember the circumstances of enslavement of their ancestors and how they continue to associate these captors with a specific ethnic group. The Fon who captured their ancestors are perceived as cruel and inhumane individuals, who therefore do not deserve to be called "men." Although Souza was the greatest ally of King Gezo when he seized the throne in the early nineteenth century, members of the slave merchant's family collectively remember how the king held their forebear and later his successors under strict control. This influence greatly increased during the period that followed the end of the slave trade, when Souza's successors played an important role in favoring Portuguese presence in Ouidah, when other European powers such as France were positioning themselves to establish their colonial presence in the region.

Like in the families of slave dealers, the Dahomean royal family cultivates a congratulatory collective memory of the Atlantic slave trade. Its ancient rulers waged war to expand the kingdom's control of other territories and to capture captives locally employed in a variety of activities, who were offered in human sacrifices during Vodun religion ceremonies or who were sold and sent into slavery to the Americas. This collective memory not only has been preserved in royal circles but has also been publicly displayed through a series of bas-reliefs decorating the walls of the Abomey's royal palaces depicting Dahomean soldiers capturing war prisoners in the battlefield. Still, the collective memory of the Atlantic slave trade among the members of the royal family also preserves sad episodes. After all, even a few of its members, such as King Gezo's mother Na Agontimé, were sold into slavery following internal disputes during periods of succession to the throne.[27]

Thomas Jefferson in Black and White

Unlike West Africa, starting with the rise of the Civil Rights Movement, the descendants of slave traders and slave owners in the United States became more cautious in explicitly displaying too much pride in the slaving past of their ancestors in the public sphere. Still, in the last two decades, a few relatives of slave merchants and slave owners started publicly acknowledging the dishonorable past of their families and recognizing that slavery generated their wealth and persisting position of privilege. Although slavery and the slave trade were pervasive realities in these families from the South and the North of the United States, their involvement in these atrocities remained an uncomfortable topic of discussion even in the domestic circles. Therefore, collective memory of slavers and their descendants in the United States was marked by meaningful silences rather than by explicit public assertions.

Like among the Souza's enslaved property, the collective memory of the families enslaved by US founding father Thomas Jefferson (1743–1826) was much better preserved than those of bondspeople owned by less prominent individuals.[28] But among the many enslaved people owned by Jefferson during his lifetime, some families were more successful in preserving and transmitting their collective memory of slavery because of their privileged position in relation to those who were not related to the founding father or who were owned by ordinary people. Take the example of the Hemingses, owned by John Wayles (1715–1773) in Virginia. After the death of his third wife, Wayles had six children with Elizabeth Hemings (1735–1807), the enslaved daughter of an African-born bondswoman and a certain captain Hemings, after whom she received her last name.

All six enslaved children fathered by Wayles became half-brothers and half-sisters of the future first lady of the United States Martha Wayles Skelton (1748–1782), his daughter with his first wife Martha Eppes Wayles (1712–1748). In 1772, Martha Wayles Skelton married Thomas Jefferson and moved to Monticello, her husband's tobacco plantation, located on a top of a mountain near Charlottesville, Virginia. After her father's death in 1773, she inherited 135 enslaved persons, including Elizabeth Hemings and her ten children, six of whom were her half siblings. During an entire decade of marriage, Martha remained busy giving birth to six children, of whom only two daughters survived. Meanwhile, Jefferson, as widely known, actively participated in the revolutionary process that led to the American Revolutionary War (1775–1783). In addition to being a delegate to the Second Continental Congress in 1775, Jefferson was also a primary author of the Declaration of Independence, ratified in 1776, the same year he was elected to the Virginia House of Delegates. In 1779, Jefferson was elected governor of Virginia. In 1783, nearly one year after Martha's death, he was appointed delegate of Virginia in the Congress of the Confederation. In 1784, he moved to Paris to become minister plenipotentiary to France with his older daughter. James Hemings (1765–1801), an enslaved man owned by him, who was the son of Elizabeth Hemings and his deceased father-in-law also followed him. In France, James continued to have advantages unknown to other Virginia enslaved men. He earned a monthly wage and freely circulated in the city. Moreover, he learned French, and after taking cooking lessons for several months, he became a chef de cuisine at Hôtel de Langeac, Jefferson's residence in Paris.

In 1787, Jefferson's youngest daughter Mary Jefferson (1778–1804), alias Polly, moved to Paris to join her father and older sister. She was accompanied by the fourteen-year-old enslaved girl Sally Hemings (1773–1835). Like James, Sally was the daughter of Elizabeth Hemings (1735–1807) and therefore Martha Jefferson's half-sister. In Paris, she also enjoyed the special treatment reserved for the enslaved children of Martha's deceased father. In the last two years of his term in Paris, Jefferson continued the tradition initiated by his father-in-law. By 1789, just before his return to the United States, he impregnated the young Sally with her first child. This relationship and pregnancy added an incestuous layer to the already-established history of sexual contacts between Virginia white masters and Hemingses enslaved women. Sally had at least six children with Jefferson, but only four survived. Between 1790 and 1801, year of Jefferson's election as president of the United States, Sally gave birth to four children. Within the next seven years, she had two other children, all of them fathered by Jefferson.

Scholars have portrayed Jefferson in his various roles as a politician, a father, and as a monogamous loving husband. But starting in the twentieth century, he was also depicted as a virile man who had relationships with several women.[29] But despite this more recent emphasis, most scholars have remained silent about whether Jefferson or his father-in-law had sexual relations with their slaves when their white wives were still alive.[30] While emphasizing the existence of affective bonds between these white slaveholders and their enslaved women, these works suggest that Wayles only had sexual relations with Elizabeth Hemings after the death of his third wife. Likewise, because these studies describe these encounters as romantic relationships and not as sexual adventures, they tend to suggest that Jefferson had sex with Sally Hemings alone by omitting if his sexual advances were also extended to other enslaved women in Monticello.[31] But whatever were the possible benefits of maintaining sexual relations with their owners, bondswomen such as Sally who gave birth to enslaved children fathered by their masters were neither their mistresses nor their wives. They were not in a position to refuse their owners' sexual demands. Contrasting with other enslaved women in Monticello who also faced the strenuous conditions of bondage, Sally could neither freely choose to have other sexual partners nor decide to make her life with a man who publicly recognized her children.

Because of these long-lasting sexual interactions, the collective memory of slavery carried by the Hemingses is not only racialized but also intertwined with and greatly shaped by the memory of their owners. Jefferson's white descendants visibly remembered him as a kind man who was generous with his enslaved property. Similarly, the intrinsic power relations of white supremacy imposed on the Hemingses impacted the few surviving accounts of their lives under slavery, which typically describe Jefferson as a good master and omit any references to coercion and sexual abuse. This image is also visible in the written narrative left by Madison Hemings (1805–1877). His account rarely uses the term "slave." He designates his grandmother Elizabeth Hemings as being the concubine (a woman whose social status is below that of a wife) of John Wayles, whereas his mother, Sally Hemings, is referred to as a body servant (a personal maid) of Jefferson's youngest daughter.

Madison Hemings provides few explicit descriptions of the living and working conditions of his enslaved relatives. Instead, he describes Jefferson's personality and daily activities.[32] Remembering his childhood, he recalls that Jefferson "was not in the habit of showing partiality or fatherly affection to us children." Madison's memories are racialized by emphasizing that his white father's coldness was reserved to his enslaved children, as he and his siblings "were the only children of his by a slave woman." This distance contrasted with Jefferson's demonstrative attitude toward his "white grandchildren," who recollected not only their grandfather's kindness but also the numerous gifts received from him.[33] At the same time, Madison underscores that he and his siblings had privileges that other enslaved persons did not have: "We were permitted to stay about the 'great house,' and only required to do such light work as going on errands. [...] We were free from the dread of having to be slaves all our lives long, and were measurably happy. We were always permitted to be with our mother [...]."[34] Woven within the fabric of white supremacy, the collective memory of slavery among the Hemingses embraces white values depicting the good master who allowed his enslaved children to have access to the white house.

Despite living in bondage, the Hemingses were more stable than other enslaved families. This stability and their kinship with the Jeffersons allowed them to preserve an identity based on their biracial origins that survived slavery. Once again, white supremacy operates as a framework of collective memory of slavery that places light skin, mixed-race, enslaved children produced from the sexual contacts between slaveholders and enslaved women at higher ranks than the offspring of enslaved couples. Similar to the Souzas, whose descendants proudly emphasize the mixed-race origins of their ancestor, the Hemingses were conscious that racial mixture was an advantage that distinguished them from other slaves of Monticello and the neighboring region. Although this privileged treatment cannot be dissociated from their blood ties with two white families (the Wayleses and the Jeffersons), their reported light skin color allowed them to get preferred treatment and feel special. Indeed, as historian Annette Gordon-Reed shows in her groundbreaking history of the Hemingses, contemporary social actors described Elizabeth's daughters and granddaughters as "extremely attractive women."[35] Likewise, according to other slaves who lived in Monticello, such as Isaac Jefferson (1775–1846), Sally Hemings "was near white... [and] very handsome: long straight hair down her back."[36] It is clear that in the framework of white supremacy and in the context of an eighteenth-century slave society such as Virginia that valued European physical features, being beautiful was also a euphemism for appearing white. Basically, if either Elizabeth Hemings or her children had very dark skin and other physical features associated with people of African descent, their alleged assimilation to Jefferson's family would be nearly impossible, and references to them as beautiful would be very hard to find.

Today the guides who tour Monticello slave quarters accurately tell visitors that unlike other slaves Jefferson paid wages to the members of his enslaved family. Likewise, they emphasize that some male Hemingses had Jefferson's permission to freely circulate in Virginia and to offer their services in exchange of wages.[37] Still, despite enjoying the privileges of their proximity with the master's family, the Hemingses of Monticello were all enslaved. They were not free individuals who could go wherever they wanted. Except for the period spent in urban residences in Paris, Philadelphia, Washington, and New York, Jefferson's enslaved children and their mother all lived in slave quarters that dramatically differed from the Monticello's mansion. Even though they were not as much exposed to physical punishment as other bondspeople on the plantation, they were controlled and were also victims to violence and abuse.[38] In his will, Jefferson freed his surviving enslaved sons Madison and Eston. The two other enslaved siblings, Harriet and Beverley, were not formally freed, but before his death Jefferson gave them permission to leave Monticello. Not much is known of what happened to them. For more than a decade, historian Pearl M. Graham made attempts to identify the descendants of the two siblings.[39] More recently, historian Catherine Kerrison explored other possible hypotheses but with no conclusive results.[40] But whatever was their fate, the two siblings legally remained enslaved, although the absence of written manumission records suggests that they were able to pass as whites. Passing as whites meant they had to change identities as they were criminals. In a similar fashion, upon Jefferson's death, his daughter Martha Jefferson Randolph (1772–1836) authorized Sally Hemings to leave Monticello as well. Still, like Harriet and Beverley, she was never legally manumitted. In her fifties, unlike her two children, she could not go away and attempt to live as a white woman. To this day, the place where she was buried is unknown. Needless to emphasize, neither Sally nor any of Jefferson's enslaved and freed offspring inherited property, marking another crucial difference between his enslaved black family and his free white family.

Most Hemingses and the members of other enslaved families owned by Jefferson were not able to read and write. Although they orally transmitted stories and experiences associated with the time they lived in bondage, written history of Jefferson's family largely overshadowed the memories of his human property. Moreover, many contemporary social actors and even further generations of historians perceived the memories of these other bondspeople as unreliable. But the collective memory of Jefferson's white family was also carefully constructed since the time he was still alive. In his correspondence with his white daughters, Jefferson actively engaged in developing a narrative emphasizing his white family's happiness.[41] This idealized representation of alleged familial bliss certainly shaped the way his enslaved children ended up perceiving themselves, most likely in much the same manner. But, in fact, the very existence of Jefferson's enslaved descendants stained this fabricated and idealistic image of an accomplished family, to the point that in the family correspondence, Jefferson's white descendants never referred to the Hemingses by their names, making them invisible.[42] During the second half of the nineteenth century, this erasure became deliberate denial. Jefferson's white descendants contested Hemingses's collective memories by repudiating the testimonies attesting that their patriarch sired six children with Sally Hemings.

Yet the construction of the harmonious image that rejected the existence of Jefferson's enslaved descendants was not only a family enterprise. Historians and archivists also contributed to prevent the collective memory of Jefferson's black family from surfacing. In 1938, Madison Hemings's granddaughter, Nellie Johnson Jones (1869–1964), wrote to lawyer Stuart G. Gibboney (1877–1944), then the president of the Thomas Jefferson Memorial Foundation, offering to donate Jefferson's artifacts, preserved by her great-grandmother Sally Hemings that remained in her possession, but he declined her offer.[43] It is very possible that by that time highlighting the provenance of these objects could drive attention to the fact that Jefferson fathered children with an enslaved woman. Also, over the twentieth century, institutions and librarians explicitly prohibited the circulation and publication of correspondence that ultimately supported the accounts of Madison Hemings and Isaac Jefferson, who both stated that Jefferson was the father of Sally's enslaved children.[44]

Jefferson's Enslaved "Family"

Jefferson himself never publicly acknowledged he had sexual relations with any enslaved women. But he had at least two relationships with married women. First, he admitted that when he was young he had "offered love to a handsome lady."[45] The lady's name was Betsey Walker, the wife of his old friend and classmate John Walker (1744–1809).[46] But according to the betrayed husband, Jefferson's sexual behavior was not an isolated adventure of his bachelor's days, as he persisted in his inappropriate conduct for several years, even after he married Martha Wayles Skelton.[47] Second, during his time in Paris, Jefferson also had an affair with the artist Maria Luisa Caterina Cecilia Cosway (1760–1838), who by the time of the affair was also a married woman.[48]

Among black Americans, a collective memory of Jefferson's abuse of enslaved women remained alive well after the end of slavery, confirming once again that in the context of slavery collective memory and public memory are racialized. In 1853, former enslaved man William Wells Brown (1814–1884) published in London the novel *Clotel; or the President's Daughter: A Narrative of Slave Life in the United States*. Considered as the first novel published by an African American, the book explores the life of Clotel and her sister Althesa, two mixed-race enslaved women, who were daughters of Thomas Jefferson and Currer, one of his bondswoman.[49] On April 20, 1940, the newspaper *The Afro-American* published a one-page article about Jefferson's black children. Denouncing the degeneracy that marked the sexual lives of slave owners in the United States during slavery, the article highlights that despite legal prohibition of miscegenation, slaveholders maintained continuous sexual relations with enslaved women with whom they had children. Moreover, the article also suggests Jefferson was a promiscuous man who maintained a "harem of 5 slave girls."[50] Indeed, the description of Jefferson's sexual relations with enslaved women as a "Congo Harem" had been used several times by his enemies in the early nineteenth century, even before his election as president of the United States.[51]

Similar stories circulated among descendants of Monticello's enslaved men and women, who did not idealize the owner of their ancestors. Although rarely highlighted in existing studies, sexual abuse is also part of the Hemingses's collective memory of slavery. This dimension was brought to light by Pearl M. Graham who rediscovered Jefferson's farm book and conducted pioneer research on Jefferson's relationship with Sally Hemings.[52] Graham maintained an extensive correspondence with Dorothy B. Porter, librarian and curator of the Moorland-Spingarn Research Center at the historically black Howard University, during her quest for information about the relationship between Jefferson and Sally Hemings. Graham's correspondence with Porter and other informants clearly shows how she sought to obtain from her interviewees stories and oral traditions that passed down among the families in order to construct a coherent narrative of what happened to the descendants of Jefferson's enslaved children. Still, as one of her correspondents Charles H. Bullock (1875–1950), a leader of the Colored Young Men's Christian Association (YMCA) movement from Charlottesville, Virginia, brilliantly observes, "slavery conditions were such that many things happened which will never be made clear."[53]

If the collective memory of the enslaved is often blurred, in 1948 and 1949, several descendants of the Hemingses told Graham that in addition to Sally, Jefferson had sex with other enslaved women. Moreover, a descendant of Mary Hemings (1753–1834), the oldest daughter of Elizabeth Hemings and half-sister of Sally Hemings, reported that Jefferson had children with three colored women, including Mary.[54] Such accounts are not surprising as several members of this branch of the family were either sold or given as gifts after Jefferson's death. Although Joseph Fossett (1780–1858), Mary's son with William Fossett, was freed in Jefferson's will, his enslaved wife Edith Hearn, Monticello's cook, was sold after Jefferson's death, along with nine of her ten children.[55] Unlike other descendants of the Hemingses, these traumatic experiences of family separation certainly ruined the idealistic view of Jefferson and his white family as benevolent slave owners.

Likewise, in an article published in the magazine *Ebony* in 1954 and in interviews given in the 1990s, descendants of Mary's two children corroborated this view by insisting that Jefferson was their ancestor. Also in another interview to Graham, three daughters of Mary Cole Kenney, descendant of a member of the Hemings family, referred to Jefferson's "promiscuity." Among others, they stated that he used to force himself on one enslaved washerwoman, when she was returning laundry to the mansion. A resident of Charlottesville also told Graham that oral accounts transmitted within his family highlighted that Jefferson "was unscrupulous in his sexual demands upon colored women."[56] Graham did not take these statements lightly. Although centering her early research on the relationship between Jefferson and Sally Hemings, in a letter to W.E.B. Du Bois almost a decade later, she clearly stated that she wanted to write an article on Jefferson's "descendants, real or supposed, by colored women other than Sally."[57]

During the nineteenth and the twentieth centuries, several of Sally's progeny passed as whites.[58] This identity shift broke their ties with bondage by also disrupting the family's collective memory of slavery. For the light-skinned Hemingses who passed as whites, a black identity was closely associated with past slave legal status. Therefore, to ensure their social mobility, references to it had to be suppressed. Among the Hemingses who embraced African ancestry, like many descendants of slaves in other societies, their past lives under slavery were often surrounded with silence. As new generations distanced themselves from slavery, collective memory of life in bondage remained largely confined to the family private circles.[59] Despite these obstacles, over the last three decades, this context started changing largely because DNA evidence confirmed Jefferson's paternity of Sally Hemings's children. These new findings led a growing number of Hemingses to publicly display their ancestry associated with slavery and claim Jefferson as their ancestor.[60]

Slave Owners and Enslaved in the North and the South

The heirs of slave owners and slave merchants in the United States also started digging up their collective memory of slavery. During the 1990s, Edward Ball and Katrina Browne, descendants of two of the most important families of slave owners and slave merchants from the South and the North of the United States, uncovered the collective memories of their ancestors, once confined to the domestic circles, and made them known to the public. Whereas Ball brought his family's collective memory to light through the publication of a book, Browne took the same path by producing a documentary film. Although their stories differed at many levels, during their young years, neither Ball nor Browne was fully conscious of the slaving past of their families. But in both cases, their families carried a collective memory of slavery and the Atlantic slave trade, which was transmitted to them through narratives in which slave ownership was occasionally mentioned. Consequently, it took them a deliberate effort to recover and publicize these chapters of their families' past.

The Ball family of South Carolina was one of the richest families of the south of the United States. Its patriarch was Elias Ball (1676–1751), an Englishman, who inherited land, assets, and nearly twenty-five enslaved persons from his aunt in South Carolina. In 1698, Ball left England to take possession of his inheritance. In South Carolina, he became the patriarch of six generations of rice planters and slave owners. In this region, where plantation slavery was widespread, the past associated with slavery was neither hidden nor forgotten. Like the Souzas in Benin, the collective memory of slavery among southern slave-owning families remains alive. Indeed, until the rise of the Civil Rights Movement, relatives of slave owners often publicly expressed pride of their past.

The slave-owning past of the Balls was never a secret. But when Edward Ball decided to write a book about his family history, he was the first member of the clan to bring the issue of slavery to the public sphere. Like in other families of slave owners and slave traders, his interviews with older relatives revealed that implicitly or explicitly they were conscious of their family's deep involvement with the inhuman institution. As late as the 1990s, older members of the family called African Americans "negroes." Not surprisingly, according to these members, their ancestors treated their slaves very well, and such benevolent treatment was reciprocated with gratitude.[61] For example, one of these relatives, Dorothy Dame Gibbs (1906–1999), stated that the "Negroes considered themselves part of the community…They considered the Balls their family."[62] Despite this paternalistic statement made by many descendants of slave owners in former slave societies, Gibbs evidently failed to explain whether her ancestors considered the "negroes" part of the family. Instead, she emphasized that her white ancestors treated their enslaved property with kindness. They neither inflicted physical punishments on them, nor sold family members separately. But as expected, collective memory of slavery is racialized and plural. Eventually, Edward Ball recovered historical records showing that this embellished view of slavery existed only in the collective memory of white members of the family.[63]

If collective memory of slavery stayed alive among the families of slave owners in the South of the United States, this heritage remained less noticeable in the North. Although slavery existed in the North until the first half of the nineteenth century, history books, textbooks, documentary films, and popular narratives traditionally described the region as the realm of abolitionists and where slavery had long been eradicated. Yet, following the steps of Edward Ball and thanks to the support of a few family members, the descendants of James DeWolf (1764–1837), one of the greatest northern slave merchants, gradually uncovered their slaving history and made it publicly acknowledged.

DeWolf was born in Bristol, Rhode Island. His father Mark Anthony DeWolf (1726–1792) was a slave trader when Rhode Island was still one of the thirteen British colonies. Following the American Revolutionary War, along with his brothers, DeWolf also engaged in the commerce of human beings, first as a ship captain and later as a slave merchant, transporting slaves from West Africa to the West Indies and Cuba. In 1790, he married Nancy Ann Bradford (1770–1838), the daughter of Rhode Island governor, William Bradford (1729–1808). Eight years later, DeWolf became a member of the Rhode Island House of Representatives, a position he intermittently occupied until his death. Like Souza in Benin, DeWolf accumulated economic and political power. Between 1821 and 1825, he was elected senator for Rhode Island. By the time of his death, he was considered the second richest man in the United States.

Unlike the Balls who owned slaves and large rice plantations since the seventeenth century, the DeWolfs's involvement in the Atlantic slave trade occurred later. Yet, like Souza in Dahomey who was very active during the period of the illegal slave trade, the family continued trading in human beings after 1787, when it had already been prohibited in Rhode Island. Moreover, the clan persisted in the infamous business after 1808, when the international slave trade to the United States was legally banned. Although not in Bristol, additional evidence reveals that the family's abominable commercial activities continued until 1820.[64] In Bristol, the DeWolfs owned and managed several ventures associated with the slave trade, including distilleries, mills, insurance companies, and a bank.[65] Even after 1842, when slavery was abolished in Rhode Island, the DeWolfs continued making profits from five coffee and sugar plantations in Cuba, where final emancipation occurred only in 1886. Today, many descendants of the clan belong to wealthy families in the United States.

Despite the family's well-documented participation in the Atlantic slave trade, its members avoided publicly emphasizing this controversial dimension of the economic activities of their ancestors. Certainly, slaving was and still is part of the DeWolfs's collective memory, but over the last two centuries references to the slave trade became blurred. Largely repressed, they came to light only through fragments, especially among older family members. But during the 1990s, nearly the same time that Ball published his book *Slaves in the Family*, this silence was broken by Katrina Browne, a descendant of James DeWolf, then in her late twenties. Browne, a Princeton University alumna, created the Public Allies, a nonprofit organization dedicated to diversifying young-adult leadership in 1992. Curiously, one year later, the first program of Browne's new venture was launched under the leadership of its executive director, Michelle Obama, the future first black first lady of the United States, whose ancestors were enslaved in South Carolina.[66] On her end, after learning about her family's history, Browne gradually became familiar with her ancestors' participation in the Atlantic slave trade.

Similar to Ball, Browne delved into the family's history and eventually decided to document it through film. In 2000, she contacted nearly two hundred of DeWolf's descendants. As reported in her documentary film, only sixty responded to her call. Among those who responded, some elegantly expressed their concerns. For example, one relative clearly articulated how the project disturbed him. He feared the impact on his public life, especially his relations with black colleagues, indicating that in a country like the United States a past associated with slavery still highly impacts present-day race relations. Moreover, he was also afraid that black activists would pressure him to pay financial reparations. To him, what his ancestors did was not his fault. Despite refusal and indifference, nine family members agreed to participate in her project. The journey into the family's slaveholding and slave-trading past was scheduled to start in Bristol, Rhode Island, where the DeWolfs's main businesses were located and where they lived for most of their lives. From Bristol, the group would continue with a trip to Ghana and Cuba, two locations where the family developed its slave-trading activities.

During the summer of 2001, ten DeWolf descendants met for the first time in Bristol. As shown in the documentary film, on July 4, the group attended together the Sunday service in Saint Michaels Episcopal Church. Like among the Souza's family, in many ways Browne's film confirms Halbwachs's thesis. The documentary reveals the intersections of religious and family frameworks in the construction of collective memory of slavery and the slave trade. As the DeWolfs attended the church for more than two centuries, still today its building displays several references to male family members involved in the slave trade, including stained glass decorating its windows. Yet, unlike Souza's family members in West Africa who think that the slave trade was an issue of the past, Browne's journey focuses on the necessity of repairing the harm caused by her ancestors. In contrast with the descendants of slave merchants in West Africa, and certainly because of her religious background, her approach emphasizes a certain level of guilt and the need of taking responsibility for the actions of her ancestors.

However, the documentary film also exposes how the collective memory of the Atlantic slave trade varies among the different members of the family depending on a series of factors, including age and gender. Keila DePoorter, for example, was raised in a very wealthy branch of the family in Bristol. She recalls that among her family members there were forbidden discussion topics: "one of our ancestors said that we should never talk about sex … religion … politics … and … the negroes."[67] Exactly like in Ball's family, on a smaller scale, this recollection illustrates at how the ideology of white supremacy operates as a framework of collective memory of slavery creating what Charles Mills refers to as "a racial fantasyland."[68] Although the two families profited from slavery and the slave trade, in the clan's invented reality the enslaved should remain invisible, reason why the members of the slave-owning family should avoid speaking about those who provided them with unpaid work. Despite the superficial silence regarding slavery, the existence of the same interdiction in a southern slave-owning family and in a northern white family is a clear indication of their association with the Atlantic slave trade and slavery. It also suggests that both families engaged with the past of slavery and slave trade in similar ways.

Like DePoorter, Browne brings to light other early references to the family's association with the slave trade. During her childhood, the DeWolfs were often described as pirates, "adventurers in the high sea," in ways that other slave merchants such as Souza in West Africa are still depicted today. In her documentary film, she also highlights a mural executed by her great-grandfather narrating the history of Bristol. The painting, representing a huge map, shows a white settler shooting an indigenous man and depicts two black men in uniform driving a carriage. Indeed, Browne's documentary film emphasizes that the DeWolfs were not only slave traders but also owned enslaved Africans. In 1803, James DeWolf gave as Christmas gifts to his wife an African girl named Adjua and an African boy called Pauledore.[69] When adults, the two enslaved Africans, Adjua D'Wolf (1794–1868) and Pauledore D'Wolf, married each other and might have had children. In contrast with what DePoorter claimed, the existence of the enslaved couple remained visible and survived in the family's collective memory not only in a nursery rhyme but also because they were put to rest in the family's cemetery in Bristol, though only Adjua's tomb is marked.[70]

Because Adjua and Pauledore continued working for the DeWolfs after the abolition of slavery and were buried in the family's cemetery, collective memory seems to reinforce the narrative that the two Africans were well treated and integral members of the family, a motif that constantly appears in public and private slave-owning family narratives.[71] All these stories reveal that although no longer being highlighted in the public sphere, slavery and the slave trade were quite embedded in the DeWolfs's collective memory. Thus, despite the initial shock, Browne quickly realized that although repressed, she already knew about her family's slaving past.

In the DeWolf family, collective memory is gendered. Male relatives who agreed to participate in Browne's journey to find their family's slave-trading roots varied in their reactions to and engagement with the DeWolfs's controversial past. In the documentary film, Tom DeWolf, who carries the name of the main slave merchant ancestor, explains that his grandfather died when his father was only two years old, therefore stressing that they did not "know anything about any of this" because they are from a different branch of the family. Hence, he argues that "there's no amnesia, there's no guilt, there's no nothing, it didn't exist."[72] Another male family member, Dain Perry, who grew up in Charleston, South Carolina, where slavery heritage was a given, explains that some of his relatives feel guilt and "very weighted down by" the family's history. But he adds that he is fortunate to not feel that way. Yet, this assessment changed when the family started its journey to the slave trade heritage sites in Ghana and Cuba. During a meeting with African Americans and Ghanaians at Cape Coast Town Hall, Perry publicly told the audience that he was raised in a racist environment in the South and also acknowledged that he was "terribly racist."[73] In further parts of the documentary, he also expressed his embarrassment by the fact that even though they were Christians, three generations of the family participated in the Atlantic slave trade. Likewise, Ledlie Laughlin, another older male family member who was aware of the family's controversial legacy, explains that it is very difficult when he tries to imagine being in his ancestors' boots and surmises that their "stomach for violence must have been extraordinary."[74]

Female members of the DeWolf's family better conveyed their embarrassment associated with the clan's slaving past. In *Traces of the Trade*, Keila DePoorter, the oldest female in the group, explains that she was christened as Edith Howe Fulton. The Howes have been associated with the

DeWolfs since the eighteenth century, when Abigail DeWolf (1755–1833), a sister of the DeWolf brothers, married a man named Perley Howe Jr. The link between the two families was reinforced during the nineteenth century when Edith DeWolf (1877–1966), DePoorter's grandmother, married her distant cousin, Halsey DeWolf (1870–1964).[75] In 1975, with the intent of getting rid of the family's heavy legacy, DePoorter decided to change her name.[76] Her story shows that for several DeWolfs, especially the women, bearing the name of a family that was deeply involved in the Atlantic slave trade for three generations was a burden, that even though carried unconsciously, was very hard to endure.

James DeWolf Perry V was also aware of the family's slaving history. He knew that in 1791, his homonymous ancestor, a sea captain, was indicted for murder. DeWolf ordered to throw overboard an enslaved woman he believed had smallpox to allegedly prevent her from infecting the other captives being transported in the ship. After being charged, he escaped to the West Indies and five years later the judge dropped his arrest warrant.[77] Like DePoorter, DeWolf Perry V also raises the issue of naming among the members of the family. As the fifth in line to carry the same name of the slave trader ancestor, he reports that when his son was born in the 1960s, he asked himself if he would transmit the family's legacy by naming him James DeWolf Perry VI. But unlike his female cousin, he did not attempt to distance himself from the family's legacy and instead named his son according to the tradition. Like his father, James DeWolf Perry VI demonstrates his understanding of the family's past not in terms of guilt or regret but as part of a larger historical context. By emphasizing the great profits made by his ancestors in the trade, he dispassionately assesses that they may not be very different from their forebears. He considers the possibility that if he were in their shoes he, and his family, might "well have been involved in the slave trade."[78] During their journey, other members of the DeWolf family eventually arrived at similar conclusions. As they continued delving into the family's slave past, they also realized their ancestors were not alone in the slave trade business. As in other societies involved in the inhuman commerce, even though merchants made incredible profits, they needed the support from the local community whose prosperity greatly depended on the slave trade.

Conflicting and Changing Collective Memories

Slavery ended in the Americas more than one hundred and fifty years ago. Slaveholders, slave merchants, and enslaved people acquired experiences and obtained knowledge while living in the shadow of the inhuman systems prevalent during the period. This vast amount of information was transmitted to their lineage through oral and written accounts. Although remembering is an individual faculty, memory has a collective dimension. An enslaved man captured in the hinterland of the Kingdom of Dahomey probably shared with other enslaved men and women in the same region similar recollections of being seized, brought in coffins to the coast, and transported in a slave ship to the Americas. Sometimes, these personal reminiscences manifested through images, smells, and sounds, which were then heard, recorded, and passed down to further generations through written and oral accounts. Individuals were not isolated. They had experiences in common with other members of their groups and reconstructed the slave past together. To this end, collective memory is a shared set of information, stories, experiences, and knowledge acquired by several individuals and communicated to their descendants. Although recollection is a key component of individual memory, transmission is a vital element to the existence of collective memory of slavery and the slave trade.

Enslaved victims and slavers as well as their descendants may have shared experiences and information. But as groups, their collective and individual memories were racialized; they differed and were often opposed. As Maurice Halbwachs underscored, social frameworks such as language, family, and religion shape collective memory, which is not a simple combination of the recollections of several individuals. Instead, remembrances are instruments that allow collective memory to rearrange an image of the past that fits the dominant thoughts of a given society in a given period. While a group collects remembrances, which manifest through the individual recollections, individuals also remember the past by attempting to place themselves into the point of view of the group.[79] In this complex game, collective memory is also shaped by larger contexts, such as those of an entire nation, a state, a city. Individual and collective memories of slavery and the slave trade are racialized, gendered, and interwoven in the fabric of white supremacy. Collective memories of slavery are not static entities. Carried by living individuals, they change over time and never remained intact during the various centuries of slavery's existence in the Americas.

Collective memory of slavery and the Atlantic slave trade is neither continuous nor homogenous. Despite the existence of conjoined elements, the examination of oral and written accounts by descendants of enslaved people and slave merchants in countries such as the Republic of Benin demonstrates that this mode of memory is not only shaped in contrasting ways among different groups but may indeed vary among the members of the same group. Despite the diverse contexts, the collective memory of relatives of slave merchants, slave owners, and bondspeople in the Republic of Benin shares similar elements with the collective memory of descendants of enslavers and enslaved in the North and the South of United States. In these two spaces separated by the Atlantic Ocean, representations of the past depicting slave traders and slave owners as benevolent individuals continue to prevail in contrast to images portraying these individuals in a negative light. In these two areas, collective memory of slavery is racialized. On the one hand, references to racial mixture usually emphasize "white" physical traits, such as light skin and straight hair, and European ancestry as positive qualities that allow individuals to dissociate themselves from slavery. On the other hand, African ancestry and features such as dark skin are perceived as undesirable qualities linking peoples to slavery and the Atlantic slave trade. In all these areas, collective memory of slavery is molded by class, age, and gender, and impacted not only by the actions of particular social actors but also by changes in national and international contexts. The examples of the family lines of slave owners, slave merchants, enslaved people from the Republic of Benin and the United States reveal the multilayered dimension of collective memory of the Atlantic slave trade and slavery. Although their views may be conflicting, they are not unchangeable. The views of the descendants of those directly associated with the Atlantic slave trade are impacted not only by the past social position of their ancestors and by their current social positions but also by religion and family structures. Despite living in the same society, the circumstances around those directly involved in the Atlantic slave trade, either as individuals who sold slaves or as people who were sold into slavery, determine how they collectively represent the slave past for themselves and to others. Of course, the past cannot change, but the way these social actors conceive the slave past today is not eternally fixed. Representations of the past prove to be mutable much of the time, as they are shaped by internal and external frameworks, including a variety of initiatives resulting from the work of cultural memory, public memory, official memory, and public history, concepts that are further explored in the next chapters.

2

Shrines of Cultural Memory

In the last three decades, an increasing number of organized groups and social actors, who identify themselves as descendants of enslaved people, have engaged in activities memorializing the victims of slavery and the Atlantic slave trade. Although these ventures take different forms, this chapter focuses on cultural memory of slavery, a modality of memory in dialogue with collective memory, encompassing commemoration and rituals that ultimately have the power to allow people to come to terms with the past of slavery in the present. To explore these processes, I examine two different kinds of initiatives that expose how cultural memory of slavery is also racialized. I start by looking at the commemoration activities and ceremonies around burial grounds of enslaved Africans and their descendants in Brazil and the United States. I highlight the rare cases of marked tombs of enslaved individuals in France, England, and the United States. I also look at another set of more complex initiatives designated as "wall of names." This mnemonic device, utilized in memorials commemorating the victims of Atlantic slavery and the slave trade, especially in the United States, is greatly inspired by the memorial expressions created for the victims of wars, the Holocaust, and other genocides. In many ways, the creation of "walls of names" reinforces dialogues between survivors of human atrocities and their descendants, therefore embodying Michael Rothberg's idea of multidirectional memory in which the memorialization of the Holocaust and other genocides reciprocally shapes the memorialization of Atlantic slavery.[1] I argue that although paradoxically drawing from ancient plantation inventories, documents that dehumanized enslaved individuals, walls of names of slavery and the Atlantic slave trade are designed to establish a link of empathy between visitors to these memorials and the deceased victims of slavery. By naming the victims of these human atrocities, the creation of "walls of names" can be conceived as a form of symbolic reparations, here understood as "redress of physical, material, or moral damage inflicted on an individual [or] a group of individuals."[2] At last, even though not always accomplished successfully, by individualizing the victims of the Atlantic slave trade and slavery the creation of walls of names in sites that are historically marked by white supremacy is an attempt to rehumanize enslaved men, women, and children.

Unmarked Graves

Except for the Caribbean and South American contexts, where monuments and memorials paid homage to enslaved men and women who fought for freedom, the work of bondspeople has been rarely recognized in heritage sites of former plantations or urban settings where slavery existed. During the period of slavery, plantation and urban areas where enslaved, freed, and free black populations predominated were spaces of white supremacy that continued to function as such after emancipation through the gradual erasure of their presence. But during the twentieth century, two moments were crucial to disrupt this invisibility. First, the end of the Second World War greatly contributed to the decolonization of Africa and the Caribbean and the rise of the Civil Rights Movement. Second, the end of the Cold War propelled a new visibility of historically excluded groups who started asserting their identities, encouraging international exchanges and increasing global connections among black organizations and populations of African descent. Black social actors gradually occupied the public space to claim the history of enslaved men and women who resisted slavery. Historians also began paying more attention to individual trajectories of enslaved people who coped with the hardships of slavery by emancipating themselves or by negotiating better work and living conditions. Relying on a myriad of firsthand narratives and testimonies, these scholars gave a more central place to the lived experiences of enslaved people.[3] Of course, this phenomenon did not occur in isolation. Before the end of the Second World War, initiatives memorializing the Holocaust emerged. Therefore, individual stories were increasingly embraced through the publication of victims' testimonies, which since then have also been depicted in novels, films, exhibitions, and memorials featuring social actors who resisted the Nazi regime.[4]

During the 1990s, heritage sites of old plantations in the United States started giving more visibility to the institution of slavery, a dimension once evacuated from these spaces, designed instead to underscore the luxurious lives of slaveholding elites.[5] Still, despite older timid attempts and more recent robust efforts to feature slavery in most former plantation heritage sites, white supremacy prevails, and when they are portrayed enslaved persons usually appear as nameless individuals.[6] As explored in Chapter 5, visitors to richer plantation sites such as Monticello (the home of US President Thomas Jefferson), which over the last two decades has made considerable efforts to interpret slavery, underscore how these sites whitewash its painful history.[7] In other words, even the venues that brought slavery to light continued perpetuating the invisibility and the dehumanization of enslaved men and women by very often depicting them in the shadow of their white owners, and almost never providing any commentary about their daily lives, their tastes, and the world they created. In most cases, bondspeople were buried in unmarked common graves, condemned to be forgotten even in death, when at least since antiquity in Africa, Europe, and the Americas, the concern with burying the dead is perceived as a right imposed on humanity.[8]

In societies around the globe, places where the dead are put to rest, such as churchyards, cemeteries, and tombstones, constitute exemplary sites of memory designed to permanently commemorate the deceased. Earlier, before the arrival of Europeans in the Americas, members of indigenous societies interred their late members by often using sumptuous ceramic funerary urns. West African and West Central African societies that provided the enslaved men, women, and children who were brought to the Americas also developed elaborate mortuary ceremonies and burial practices to honor their dead.[9] In Brazil, as in other parts of Latin America, freedpeople as well as enslaved men and women joined Catholic brotherhoods to have access to a dignified burial service.[10] Yet, in most cases slave owners and slave merchants carelessly discarded enslaved bodies in common burial grounds and unmarked graveyards. In the United States, slaveholders consented to provide corpses of enslaved individuals for dissection in medical schools of the most prestigious universities in the country.[11] To this day, newspaper articles constantly report newly found unmarked slave graves in cities involved in the Atlantic slave trade such as Lagos (Portugal), São Paulo (Brazil), and Annapolis (United States).

Probably the most well-known burial ground containing remains of enslaved Africans was found in the United States. In 1991, during an excavation to construct a new federal building at 290 Broadway in New York City, construction workers uncovered hundreds of bones of men, women, and children, either African-born or of African descent.[12] The discovery caught many people by surprise. Introduced by the Dutch, very few people were even aware that slavery existed in New York. The Dutch West Indies Company brought the first enslaved Africans to Manhattan in the early seventeenth century. Whereas slavery continued to exist during the British rule in the second half of the seventeenth century, the slave trade through the port of New York persisted during the eighteenth century.

The unearthing of the mass grave brought to light the ignored existence of slavery and the long-lasting marginalization of black populations in New York City. As soon as the discovery emerged, African American concerned citizens claimed the place as hallowed ground. The names of the individuals buried in the site were unknown, but the discovery of the remains helped to foster research that would shed light on the lives of free and enslaved people of African descent in New York City. Archaeologists, historians, and anthropologists of the historically black Howard University in Washington DC immediately started researching the remains and artifacts uncovered during the excavation.[13] In their extensive report, these scholars concluded that the site was a former burial ground. The mass grave contained the remains of approximately 15,000 individuals, enslaved and free, who were born either locally or in Africa and who had been buried in the site during the seventeenth and eighteenth centuries. Located in a port city that imported about 8,500 enslaved Africans, the New York African Burial Ground, as it became known in the following years, is the earliest known and among the largest of its kind in the United States.[14]

Whereas government authorities, activists, and general members of the black community fought to preserve and promote the site through the construction of a memorial and a visitor's center, the African Burial Ground gradually became a shrine of sorts that over almost three decades has been the stage of ceremonies to honor enslaved Africans and their descendants. If observed from various angles, the process that led the establishment of the memorial encompassed various modalities of memory, public, cultural, and official. The development of commemoration rites as a modality of cultural memory of slavery occurred in tandem to the battles of public memory that made possible the creation of a memorial at the African Burial Ground and its status as a national monument officially recognized.

The discovery of the burial ground exposed the ways public memory of slavery is shaped by the disputes of various social groups organized along racial lines that fight to occupy public space. In other words, the unearthing and interpretation of the African Burial Ground contributed to bringing to light race and identity issues that were not directly related to the historical past of the site but to the persisting racial structures that maintained the city's past of slavery, generally invisible in the public arena. The discovery of the mass grave also occurred in a particularly political moment. In 1989, David Norman Dinkins had been elected mayor of New York City. Despite the long history of black presence in the city, he was its first (and up to this day the only) African American mayor. His election in the period marking the end of the Cold War was an indicator of the growing political strength of black social actors. In office since January 1990, Dinkins's intervention was crucial to the development of the African Burial Ground. He stated to the African American newspaper, the *New York Voice*, how fortunate he was because the site was unearthed during his tenure: "by exploring this burial ground, commemorating it, and reinterring the remains with the respect and dignity they deserve, we can go a long way toward righting an old wrong."[15]

Since the unearthing of the mass grave, black social actors identifying themselves as descendants of those buried in the site put pressure on public authorities to memorialize the burial ground. Here the descendant community was obviously a rhetorical and political designation embraced by individuals who in the New York City's context saw themselves as the symbolic heirs of the men and women interred in the burial ground.

Like in other societies where slavery existed, by claiming this constructed descendant identity, these citizens established an artificial continuous connection between the past and the present.[16] Controversy opposing federal government authorities, politicians, scholars, and activists marked the meetings discussing the next steps to preserve the site and whether a memorial should be built.

As these discussions progressed, the African Burial Ground became a shrine where ordinary black citizens and organized groups performed rituals remembering deceased African ancestors and their descendants. In September 2003, the Schomburg Center for Research in Black Culture organized a series of ceremonies that started at Howard University, where the bone remains were examined, and culminated on October 4, 2003, with the reinternment of 419 bone remains in New York's financial district (290 Broadway), the same site where they were discovered. Thousands of attendants, including various African American and international dignitaries such as Maya Angelou and the then mayor of New York City, Michael Bloomberg, attended the reburial. The commemoration of nameless enslaved and freed men, women, and children interred in the mass grave during the seventeenth and eighteenth centuries was a privileged stage to address the necessity of publicly recognizing the contribution of Africans and peoples of African descent to the making of the United States. Howard Dodson, the then director of Schomburg Center, explained that "basically everything that is including life on earth came from mother Africa and in this country, this western Babylon, we built it on our backs and on our suffering."[17] Jonathan Blount, one of the founders of *Essence* magazine, used the image of "the bones that rose up through the concrete of time" to illustrate the idea of the past that reemerges in the present, emphasizing the existing debt toward the African Americans whose ancestors were enslaved in the United States.[18]

Since 2003, every October 4, commemorative ceremonies are held in the African Burial Ground to pay homage to the men, women, and children who were buried in the site. Also, in 2003, the US Congress eventually appropriated funds for the construction of a memorial on top of the site where the human remains were found. Eventually, in June 2004, two Haitian American architects, Rodney Leon and Nicole Hollant-Denis (AARIS architects), won the competition to design the memorial. Already embodying dimensions of cultural memory and public memory of slavery, on February 27, 2006, when President George W. Bush proclaimed the African Burial Ground a National Monument it also became an official site of memory of slavery.[19]

The memorial was eventually dedicated on October 5, 2007.[20] Built with granite, the structure is divided into two sections, the Circle of the Diaspora and the Ancestral Chamber. Through a ramp, the visitor is led to the interior of a circular wall on which various Akan symbols are depicted. In many ways, the symbols replace the unknown names of the Africans and their descendants interred in the burial ground. In the interior of the court, a map of the Atlantic world evoking the Middle Passage is depicted on the ground. The Ancestral Chamber, built with Verde Fontaine granite from the African continent, was placed next to the ancestral reinternment ground. The chamber, which acts as tomb, symbolizes the interior of a slave ship and was conceived as a place for contemplation and prayer. As in other monuments, memorials, and heritage sites of the Atlantic slave trade, the idea of return is evoked by a Sankofa symbol carved on the chamber's external wall and dedicated as follows: "For all those who were lost; For all those who were stolen; For all those who were left behind; For all those who were not forgotten." In the various official descriptions of the memorial, the symbol is translated as "learn from the past," but a more accurate translation is "go back to fetch it," referring to a proverb that states, "It is not a taboo to return and fetch it when you forget," evoking the links between spiritual and material world.[21] Indeed, the choice of the emblem was not an accidental one. During the excavation, archaeologists recognized a heart-shaped symbol on the cover of one of the coffins that was identified as a Sankofa, an Akan pictogram used in burial practices in present-day Ghana.[22] Still, one scholar identified as white and who is not a specialist of West African cultures contested this interpretation. According to him, contemporary Europeans had not found evidence that the symbol was part of eighteenth-century Akan burial practices.[23] Yet as far as cultural memory goes, the Sankofa became an ancestral symbol, the core around which rituals were performed. The symbol made connections between the self-assigned descendant community and an actual and imagined Africa that was the homeland of the nameless men, women, and children buried in the African Burial Ground.

In 2010, as part of the development and promotion of the site, a visitor center housing a permanent exhibition was created in the federal building adjacent to the memorial, with the goal of celebrating the African presence in New York City and disseminating the history of the most important archaeological project ever undertaken in the United States.[24] African American tourists, scholars, and members of the African diaspora are the most frequent visitors to the memorial. During the year, and especially in October, various ceremonies to honor the African ancestors are held in the memorial. But despite its location close to Wall Street in Lower Manhattan at the heart of New York City, the promotion of the African Burial Ground was transformed by the events of September 11, 2001. The two towers of the World Trade Center, destroyed by the terrorist attacks that killed thousands of individuals, were located just over half a mile from the burial ground. This tragedy created another mass grave near the site and imprinted the collective memory of New York City's population with a more recent traumatic event. When asking where the African Burial Ground is located, visitors are often directed toward Ground Zero, where the National September 11 Memorial and Museum, dedicated on September 11, 2011, is located today. Despite these hindrances, the unearthing of the site brought to light the existence of slavery as a central institution in New York until its abolition in 1827. The African Burial Ground became a crucial marker of the presence of people of the African descent in the city and contributed to fostering the development of several other ventures focusing on the existence of slavery in New York City.[25]

In 1996, much like the occurrence in New York City, an archaeological excavation on a private residence at 36 Pedro Ernesto Street (former Cemitério Street) in Rio de Janeiro's Gamboa neighborhood uncovered a mass grave containing bone fragments of dozens of enslaved Africans.[26] The site was identified as the Cemetery of New Blacks (Cemitério dos Pretos Novos), a burial ground where newly arrived Africans who died before being sold at the shops of the Valongo slave market were buried. Although many of these recently disembarked Africans had already been baptized, their dead bodies were literally thrown in the common grave. On top of each other, naked, wrapped in mats, and buried without the performance of any Catholic rituals, their corpses were subsequently burned to avoid the propagation of bad smell.[27] Between 1824 and 1830, after continuous complaints from the residents and because of the official ban of the slave trade from Africa to Brazil, the cemetery was closed.[28]

Following this exceptional discovery, the cemetery and the area surrounding the old port area remained abandoned for a long period. Unlike the African Burial Ground in New York City, the site was not a federal building but rather a private property overseen by the City Hall. The Guimarães family, who owned the property where the cemetery was uncovered, decided to embrace the cause of protecting the site. Although they were greatly supported by Rio de Janeiro's members of a variety of black organizations, they barely received any public or official assistance.[29] Indeed, over the past two decades, the site has survived constant threats of having to close its doors.

By 1999, the site of the former cemetery was informally opened to public visitation. In 2005, as lack of public financial support persisted, the Guimarães family created the New Blacks Institute of Research and Memory (Instituto de Pesquisa e Memória Pretos Novos) at the same location to oversee the site, which in 2009 was transformed into a nongovernmental organization. This initiative coincided with the first term of President Luiz Inacio Lula da Silva and the emergence of numerous official projects promoting Afro-Brazilian history across the country. Yet, another unexpected finding drastically affected the site's position. In March 2011, as part of the project Rio de Janeiro: Wonderful Port (Rio de Janeiro: Porto Maravilha), drainage works started in the Rio de Janeiro port region. The works were intended to recuperate and revitalize the city's old port in view of the 2014 FIFA World Cup and 2016 Olympic Games. During the works, the ruins of Valongo Wharf were eventually rediscovered. The excavation also recovered numerous African artifacts, including ceramic pipes, cowries employed in religious practices, and buttons made of animal bones.[30] After a long process of nomination and evaluation, in 2017 UNESCO finally inscribed the Valongo Wharf in its World Heritage List.[31]

Both the Valongo Wharf and the Cemetery of New Blacks were incorporated into Rio de Janeiro's urban landscape. As the entire region was revitalized in preparation for the Olympic Games, tourism activity significantly increased. Likewise, slavery and the Atlantic slave trade were gradually included in the country's official national narrative that now recognizes Brazil's crucial role in it. In 2012, the site of the Cemetery of New Blacks was transformed into a memorial. Curated by Marco Antônio Teobaldo, the main exhibition was reorganized, with the inclusion of explanatory panels of text and images reconstituting the history of the site, including large photographs of Africans and Afro-Brazilians. A total of 6,119 slaves were buried in the Cemetery of New Blacks. Most of them were African-born individuals recently arrived in Rio de Janeiro. Yet Santa Rita Parish's death records included the names of 247 Brazilian-born slaves owned by poor whites who between 1824 and 1830 were also interred in the cemetery. To pay homage to all these nameless men, women, and children, the exhibition circumvents this gap by featuring a huge "panel of names" (Figure 2.1) displaying some of the few recorded Brazilian-born slaves who were also buried in the Cemetery of the New Blacks.[32]

Moreover, glass pyramids were set on the memorial's floor, allowing the visitors to see the ground from where the archaeological findings discovered in the site were removed. A sacred site, the memorial's unveiling ceremony included Candomblé priests who paid homage to the African ancestors who died without ever receiving a decent burial ground. In recent years, the community of Gamboa and different black organizations appropriated the Valongo area, organizing black heritage tours, public religious ceremonies, and spectacles of capoeira (an Afro-Brazilian martial art, combining dance and music). As archaeological research in the site of the Cemetery of the New Blacks continued in 2017, archaeologists recovered for the first time an entire skeleton of an enslaved African woman of nearly twenty years old who died approximately two centuries ago. To honor the nameless African, the archaeologists named her Josefina Bakhita (*c.* 1869–1947) after the first Catholic Church's official African saint from Sudan.[33] Here again, naming is an important gesture to recognize the importance of men and women who were enslaved in Brazil.

Despite the proliferation of unmarked graveyards where enslaved men, women, and children were put to rest, there have been a growing number of initiatives to uncover and recognize the sites of former slave cemeteries and tombs in the United States. Although the names of the enslaved who labored in plantations of US founding fathers, such as Mount Vernon (see Chapter 5 and Figure 5.1), Monticello, and Montpelier, are accurately recorded, their individual graves were unidentified. But despite the absence of individual graves, today guests to these plantation sites are invited to visit

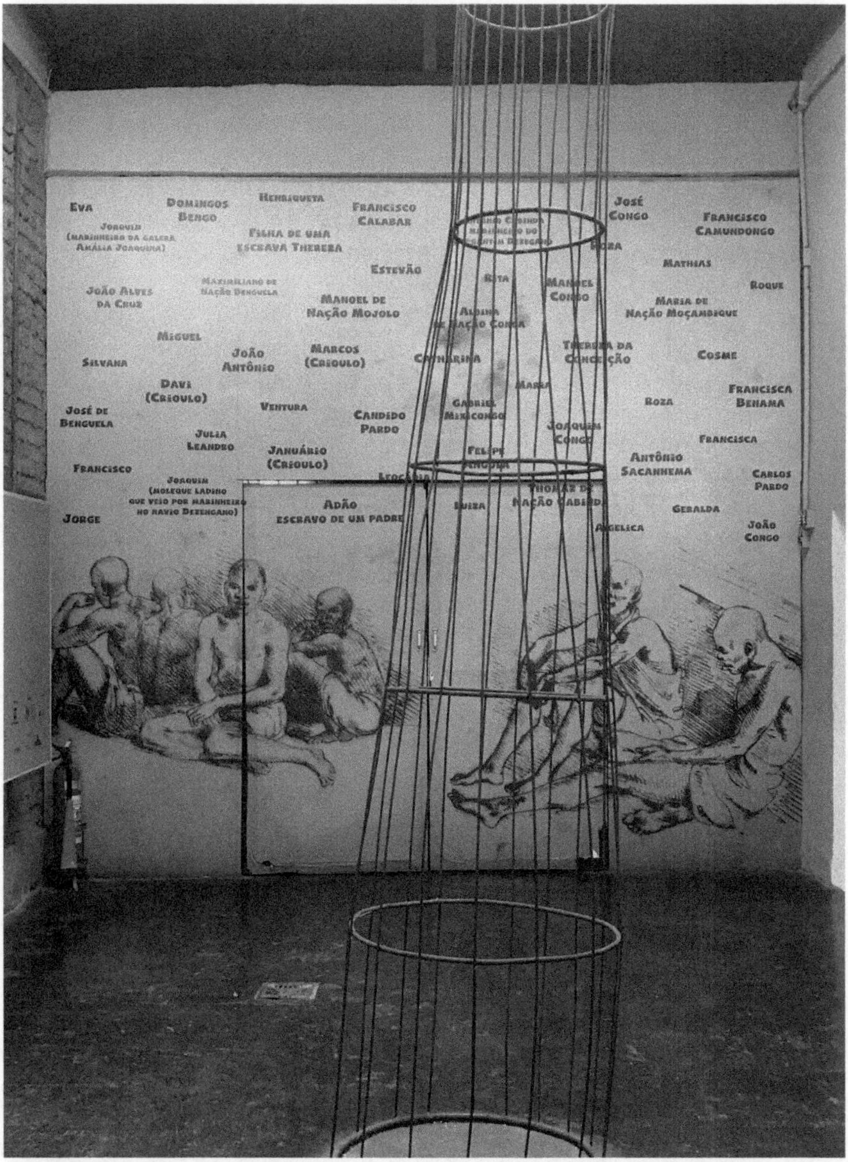

FIGURE 2.1 *Panel of Names. Cemetery of New Blacks. Rio de Janeiro, Brazil. Photograph by Ana Lucia Araujo, 2018. Courtesy: Cemetery of New Blacks.*

these burial grounds. Usually one old collective gravestone, a garden or a plaque indicates the location of these ancient cemeteries. From time to time, descendants of the enslaved persons who were members of these plantation communities gather at these sites where they perform religious ceremonies to pay homage to their ancestors.

Naming the Dead

The emergence of written systems among different societies introduced the practice of adding names and inscriptions to tombstones. These epitaphs were a means of keeping the dead as a permanent part of the world of the living, reflecting the desire to give them humanity and immortality.[34] In Ancient Greece, for example, listing names of war victims in poems, monuments, and tombstones was intended to pay homage to those who died in battle.[35]

After the Second World War, a growing number of heritage sites, memorials, and museums, especially those associated with the Holocaust, Apartheid, and Vietnam War included walls of names listing the victims of these atrocities. Indeed, as early as 1945, the pre-state of Israel initiated Holocaust commemoration through projects aimed at creating permanent memorials.[36] Starting in the 1950s, Jewish men and women mobilized efforts to unveil plaques displaying the names of victims of the Holocaust in "synagogues, cemeteries, public buildings, and Jewish National Fund groves."[37] In 1957, the government of Israel unveiled the Yad Vashem in Jerusalem, labeled as the first official memorial especially constructed to commemorate the martyrs (and not the victims) of the Holocaust and Second World War. Taken from a verse of the Book of Isaiah, in its literal translation from Hebrew to English, the designation "Yad Vashem" meaning "a monument and a name" evokes the practice of naming as the best way to perpetuate the memory of the Holocaust victims. At its inception, drawing from the ancient practice of listing names on memorial tombstones, the Yad Vashem launched the project Pages of Testimony, a one-page form allowing the submission of names and biographical information of Holocaust victims. In 1968, the Yad Vashem created a Names Room storing nearly 800,000 names and testimonies organized in alphabetical order. A decade later, the Yad Vashem dedicated the Hall of Names building featuring the names of nearly one million victims of the Holocaust, which in the following years were gradually added to a database. Although not necessarily having inspired other memorials around the world, the Yad Vashem is among the very first large initiatives using the names of victims as an instrument to memorialize a human atrocity.[38]

But probably the most iconic and influential memorial featuring walls of names is the Vietnam Veterans Memorial opened in 1982. Conceived by a group of US Vietnam veterans through the Vietnam Veterans Memorial Fund, the memorial occupies a two-acre area at the National Mall, a vast zone at the heart of Washington DC, the capital of the United States, where many other national memorials, monuments, and museums are also established. The memorial embraces a more conventional approach to commemoration through an abstract structure that evokes a tombstone. The memorial comprises two black granite walls of nearly three meters high cut into earth. The two walls form a V of approximately seventy-five meters in length, divided into seventy-two panels, currently listing 58,220 names of US Vietnam War veterans according to the date they were declared dead or missing, even though specific criteria excluded a number of names from the memorial.[39] Podiums placed at both sides of the memorial also allow visitors to identify specific names. Although its location in the National Mall gives it the highest national official status, the memorial is not visible from a distance. Likewise, its horizontal shape and black color contrast with many other nearby vertically oriented memorials and monuments.[40] Still, visitors to the memorial who include many US veterans who travel to Washington DC on annual basis, especially to participate in the activities of the Veteran's Day, can personally engage with the deceased veterans whose names are engraved on the walls by seeing their own image reflected on the bright granite's surface.[41] They can also leave notes, flowers, and other mementos at the memorial's foot. Nearly three million tourists visit the memorial every year. Yet international tourists without any personal connections with American citizens killed during the war can hardly create a link of empathy with the deceased veterans.

Alternative memorials also incorporated a variety of versions of the "wall of names" as mnemonic devices to honor victims of war and other human atrocities. Starting in 1992, the German artist Gunter Demnig developed the project *Stolpersteine* (literally translated as "stumbling stones").[42] Again, borrowing from the prophet Isaiah (8:14), a *Stolperstein* refers to "a symbolic stone over which a wrongdoer or an entire people living in violation of God's law must stumble is a reminder to live life in fear of God and a gauge that tells whether one has lived a proper life or not."[43] Contrasting with state-sponsored robust memorials like the Yad Vashem's Hall of Names, a *Stolperstein* is a simple device paying homage to a single individual.[44] It consists of a concrete cube bearing a brass plate memorializing a victim of the Holocaust and placed near the individual's last place of residence or work. Although the project started in Berlin and Cologne, to this day Demnig laid nearly 70,000 brass plates in more than 280 cities across Europe. Containing the victim's name as well as the date of birth and death, the plates fulfill the function of tombstones to murdered men, women, and children who never had access to a proper burial service.

In the twenty-first century, ordinary citizens and governments sponsored many other initiatives incorporating the idea of walls of names to pay homage to victims of atrocities. Several African countries created memorials to remember victims of racial violence and genocide. Following the formal end of the Apartheid in 1994, a number of state-sponsored museums and memorials honoring its victims were unveiled in South Africa.[45] In 2001, the Apartheid Museum opened in Johannesburg. An entire alley of the museum lists the names and death dates of 115 people who died in detention between 1963 and 1990 in South African prisons, whereas another panel lists dozens of people who were executed for political reasons between 1962 and 1989. In 2004, a wall of remembrance dedicated at the Kigali Genocide Memorial Centre in Rwanda featured some of the names of the more than half a million victims of the Hutu genocide against the Tutsi. In 2007, the Freedom Park unveiled in Pretoria, South Africa, also included a circular memorial structure comprising a wall of names measuring 697 meters.[46] The memorial pays tribute to South Africans who died in conflicts that shaped the South African nation, listing the names of 75,000 men and women who lived during slavery and indentured servitude, who died during the genocide imposed by European colonial rule, who fought the various wars in which South Africa participated as well as those who struggled for liberation during Apartheid. Likewise, European countries continued to fully embrace the listing of names to memorialize victims of war and genocide. Bosnia and Herzegovina established walls of names as part of memorials paying homage to the victims of the Bosnian War. Opened to the public in 2003, the Srebrenica-Potočari Memorial features a large white-stone circular platform displaying the names of more than 8,000 Bosnian Muslims massacred in Srebrenica. Inaugurated in 2010, the Kozarac Central Memorial honoring the city's citizens killed during the war also displays their names on its circular walls.

Coinciding with the sixtieth anniversary of the liberation of Auschwitz-Birkenau extermination camp, new memorials unveiled in Paris, Berlin, and Jerusalem feature different versions of the walls of names to pay homage to the victims of the Holocaust. In January 2005, the Shoah Memorial (Mémorial de la Sohah) in Paris dedicated its wall of names listing 76,000 Jewish victims, including 11,000 children, who were deported from France during the Second World War. Located at Marais neighborhood, the initiative is an extension of the Memorial to the Unknown Jewish Martyr Memorial unveiled in 1956. Composed of three massive limestone walls, the wall of names displays the victims' first names, surnames, and dates of birth, inscribed on both sides of each wall, which are all divided into thirty rectangular sections organized by year of deportation.[47]

In March 2005, the Yad Vashem was renovated and expanded, incorporating a new Hall of Names to its Holocaust History Museum. Entering the memorial, visitors reach a circular ramp. The space below the ramp has a curved design carved in the mountain bedrock. The ceiling over the ramp, a ten-meter conical structure, displays portraits of six hundred victims of the Holocaust along with fragments of the Pages of Testimony. Filled with water, this pool-like structure reflects the pictures displayed on the upper conical ceiling. The memorial's outer walls consist of shelves holding the physical copies of Page Testimonies covering information for nearly four of the six million Jewish victims of the Holocaust. At the exit of the circular ramp, visitors reach a computer center where they can consult the entire collection of Page Testimonies by accessing the Central Database of Shoah Victims' Names.

This new Hall of Names introduces at least two new dimensions to the conventional wall of names. If genocides are characterized by their massive scope through the killing of large groups of nameless individuals usually belonging to the same ethnic group, the memorial subverts this logic by identifying each victim with a name and a portrait, as in an identity card.[48] Accompanied by their profiles, Holocaust victims regain the humanity that was taken from them. Moreover, the memorial also complexifies and expands the notion of wall of names by offering the visitors a physical repository of biographical information as well as a digital archive accessible via the online database. In a similar fashion, Berlin's Memorial to the Murdered Jews of Europe (the first Holocaust memorial sponsored by the German government), composed of 2711 concrete blocks whose format evokes gravestones, was unveiled in May 2005. Its subterranean Information Center includes a Room of Names. In contrast with other similar memorials, the room does not simply display victims' names. Like the Yad Vashem, each murdered Jewish person is individualized in dynamic ways. Here not only each Holocaust victim's name and date of death is projected on the four walls of the empty dark room, but visitors can also listen to the audio records of the various short biographies.[49] This theatrical display of the wall of names is an effort to humanize the victims who never received a proper burial service while encouraging visitor's engagement.

In the Americas, several other memorials commemorating victims of atrocities were also unveiled during the same period. After years in planning, the city of Buenos Aires dedicated the Monument to the Victims of State Terrorism in 2007. The memorial is located at the Memory Park (Parque de la Memoria), along the River Plate boardwalk in the Argentinean capital of Buenos Aires. It honors men, women, and children who were killed or disappeared during the civil-military dictatorship that ruled Argentina from 1969 to 1973, the governments of Juan Perón and Isabel Perón (1973–1976), but especially the victims of the Dirty War launched during the latest Argentine military dictatorship (1976–1983). Consisting of four concrete walls, symbolizing a wound emerging between the bank and the river, the memorial features 30,000 Patagonian porphyry plates, of which 9,000 are currently engraved with the names of victims, displayed in alphabetical order according to the year they were killed or disappeared.[50] The plaques also indicate the victims' ages and if they were pregnant. Like in the Yad Vashem's Hall of Names, the memorial leaves space for the inclusion of thousands of additional names and comprises a database allowing the visitors to find additional information about the victims.

In 2008, the Pentagon Memorial, honoring 184 victims of the terrorist attack of September 11, 2001, was dedicated in Arlington, Virginia. The memorial, located at the southwest area of the Pentagon (headquarters of the US Department of Defense), occupies a landscaped area of 7,800 square meters. Here the wall of names concept is expanded over 184 illuminated benches (made of stainless steel and decorated with smooth granite) built over a lighted shallow pool. Each bench is engraved with the name of a victim and placed along the memorial according to age.

If more than one family member was killed in the attack, their names are also engraved in the pool under the bench.

Likewise, in 2011, the World Trade Center Memorial was dedicated in Lower Manhattan in New York City to remember the victims of the terrorist attack against the two towers of the World Trade Center on September 11, 2001.[51] Occupying the area where the twin towers were once located, the memorial commemorates the 2,977 victims killed in 2001 and the six victims of the site's bombing carried out on February 26, 1993. Reflecting Absence, as the memorial was named, it consists of two reflecting pools, each one measuring nearly 4,000 square meters. The two pools are placed within the footprint of the two destroyed towers, and their edges are composed of bronze panels where the engraved names of each person killed during the attacks offer a different format for the wall of names, where general visitors, relatives, and friends can pay homage to the victims. Correspondingly, in 2011, the Flight 93 National Memorial located at the site of the crash of Flight 93 of United Airlines hijacked in the attacks of September 11, 2001, was dedicated in Stonycreek Township, Pennsylvania. The memorial site encompasses an area of 8,900 square meters. One of its main features is a wall of names composed of forty individual marble panels, each of them displaying the name of one of the forty victims of the terrorist attacks.

Wall of Names and Cultural Memory of Slavery

During the second half of the twentieth century, embodying the idea of multidirectional memory that recognizes the transnational dimension of memory, the commemoration of slavery and the Atlantic slave trade evolved by embracing elements of the memorialization of the Holocaust and other atrocities.[52] As naming became a major trend in memorials installed during the second half of the twentieth century, memorials, museums, and heritage sites associated with slavery and the Atlantic slave trade embraced walls of names as mediums by which to pay homage to enslaved Africans and their descendants.[53] Paradoxically, in the context of the Atlantic slave trade the act of naming was also a dehumanizing practice. Slave merchants and slave owners stripped the original names of African-born enslaved individuals by imposing on them new Christian names. Likewise, the practice of recording names of slaves reinforced dehumanization. Listed as ordinary commodities in ship manifests and farm books, different enslaved men, women, and children very often carried the same names. Many times, written records show nameless enslaved individuals, identified only by their physical characteristics. Yet lists of names of enslaved men, women, and children do appear in Catholic Church's baptism books and death records.

Likewise, in both Europe and the Americas, a small number of vaults of enslaved individuals are marked and include tombstones identifying their names. The grave of Sambo, an enslaved African boy brought from West Indies to England and deceased in 1736, is still featured at Sunderland Point, near Lancaster, the third British slave port. As Alan Rice explains, because he was not baptized, Sambo was buried in secular ground, in a remote grave near the beach. In 1796, a plaque memorializing Sambo was placed on his tomb. Vandalized during the 1990s, a new plaque replacing the old one reproduces the original inscription that reads: "Here lies poor SAMBOO, A faithful NEGRO, Who (attending his Master from West Indies) DIED on his arrival at Sunderland," and is followed by a poem. Recurrent visitors to Sambo's grave depose on it flowers, painted stones with dates and their names, and other mementos to pay homage to the enslaved boy.[54] Although not common, like Sambo's tomb, a few graves of enslaved men and women who labored in New England in the United States (such as those of the enslaved couple Adjua and Pauledore D'Wolf owned by the DeWolfs (examined in Chapter 1) are decorated with carved gravestones that display their names, occupations, and year of death.[55]

Despite the problems associated with naming enslaved persons, the establishment of walls of names as commemorative devices of slavery carries a sacred dimension.[56] These initiatives emerged as a response to social actors who demanded to make slavery and their enslaved ancestors visible in the public space. Problematizing long-lasting historical narratives in which enslaved men, women, and children have been portrayed as nameless victims, public historians, designers, curators, heritage site managers, and docents labored to acknowledge the presence of slavery emphasize the humanity of enslaved individuals and perpetuate their memory in slavery heritage sites, memorials, and museums. Yet, only in some cases the descendants of the enslaved (when they are known) have actively participated in the creation of these wall of names.

The UK is among the first European countries to confront and engage with its Atlantic slave-trading and slave-owning past. The prosperity of British economy was deeply associated with the wealth produced by the work of enslaved men, women, and children, especially in the West Indies, and the British slave ships transporting the second largest number of enslaved Africans to the Americas, which were behind in number only to those transported by the Portuguese and the Brazilian merchants together. During the 1990s, when the public memory of slavery surfaced in more visible ways in societies involved in the Atlantic slave trade, black British citizens and city representatives pressured the city councils of Liverpool and Bristol to put in place initiatives aimed at acknowledging the city's involvement in the human trade. In 1997, the efforts of these black residents led to the opening *Slavery and John Pinney*, a small six-panel exhibition. Conceived by David Small, a history teacher, the exhibition occupied one room of the Georgian House Museum, housed in the old residence of John Pinney (1740–1818), a merchant, who was also the owner of several plantations and human chattel in Nevis, a Caribbean island.[57]

British tourists and Bristolians are the main visitors of the Georgian House Museum, whose slavery exhibition was updated in 2018. The redesigned space consists of one long horizontal panel displaying texts and images that narrate Pinney's involvement in the Atlantic slave trade. Two images reproduced in the panel call the visitor's attention. The first image is the iconic photograph of Gordon, a black man who escaped slavery in the United States in 1863. Represented from behind with his face barely discernible, what is visible is his deeply scarred back resulting from whipping. A quintessential image representing the dehumanization of an enslaved individual, the photo circulated the world during anti-slavery campaigns. The second image features the actor Tim Wesley in the role of Pero Jones (*c*.1753–1798), an enslaved man owned by Pinney (played by the actor Jon Price, also featured in the panel), in a living history recreation of life in the Georgian House, held in 1999. At the other side of the room, near the window, a recently added long vertical panel "Enslaved People of the Pinney Plantation" features the names of 903 enslaved individuals who between 1670s and 1834 lived in Pinney's estate (also known as Mountravers plantation) in the island of Nevis in the West Indies. Intended to acknowledge the crucial role of slavery in building Pinney's wealth, the decontextualized list of names is rather an inventory of first names and unnamed individuals that can hardly pay homage to men, women, and children who lived in slavery.

Similarly, during the 1990s, well-known freedmen were honored in other European memorials featuring walls of names. Among these ventures France's Pantheon in Paris is probably the most prominent. In 1998, the year marking the sesquicentenary of the abolition of slavery in France, an inscription commemorating the leader of the Saint-Domingue Revolution Toussaint Louverture (1743–1803) was added to the Pantheon. This highest honor was a long overdue posthumous recognition. In 1802, during the ongoing insurrection that ended slavery and broke Saint-Domingue's colonial ties with France, Louverture was captured by the troops of Napoleon Bonaparte. Deported to France, he was imprisoned at Fort-de-Joux, in Doubs, that functioned as a state prison. Died in prison on April 7, 1803, Louverture's body was interred in the fort's chapel that was destroyed in 1879. The human remains found in the sanctuary's site are said to have been deposed on the fort's grounds. In 1901, a first plaque paying tribute to Louverture was unveiled at the fort. Only in 1954, did the Embassy of Haiti in France unveil a memorial, exactly like a tomb, commemorating Louverture at Fort-de-Joux. Although his body was never found or exhumed, Louverture was memorialized in the Pantheon with an inscription that reads: "To the memory of Toussaint Louverture: Combatant for liberty, artisan of the abolition of slavery, Haitian hero died in deportation at Fort-de-Joux in 1803." Unlike fellow enslaved persons whose names appear in farm books of plantations in the Americas, there is a wealth of information about Louverture's life, and his story has been the object of biographies, novels, and films. Yet, in contrast with other figures added to the French building, because his remains were never transferred to France, his plinth remained empty.[58]

In the United States, other heritage sites created spaces to honor the enslaved people who lived and worked in their premises. The Royall House and Slave Quarters in Medford, Massachusetts, is one of these sites. A National Historic Landmark transformed into a museum, the mansion is the only surviving structure comprising an adjacent building with urban slave quarters in the North of the United States. The property was part of a farm owned by Isaac Royall, a British planter established in Antigua, who moved to the United States in 1737, bringing with him twenty-seven slaves. Royall's son, Isaac Royall Jr, inherited his father's assets and bequeathed Harvard University with land. Inside the mansion, one entire room honors Belinda, the first known freedwoman to petition the state to obtain financial reparations for slavery.[59] The building that once housed the slave quarters features a large panel displaying the names of the nearly sixty slaves who lived and worked on the property. Still, like many other heritage sites and museums in the United States exhibiting similar panels that play the role of wall of names, this display rather reinforces the inventory format of farm books. Although it gives bondspeople an individual identity, this kind of representation does not provide a deeper look into the trajectory of these individuals. Despite honoring the enslaved by recognizing their work in the Royall's property, the setting is not intended to disrupt the overall framework of white supremacy that dehumanizes enslaved people.

At the end of the 1990s, South Africa's institutions gradually started incorporating the history of the slave trade and slavery as part of the democratization process that emerged with the fall of the Apartheid and the development of the UNESCO Slave Route Project.[60] The new international interest in slavery and the work of scholars on slavery in South Africa impacted Cape Town's National Cultural History Museum, renamed Slave Lodge Museum on Heritage Day, in 1998. The museum occupies a seventeenth-century building where the Dutch East India Company accommodated its slaves. Although Cape Town did not export slaves to the Americas, the colony was not dissociated from the pathways of the Atlantic slave trade.[61] In 2006, the museum opened its permanent exhibition *Remembering Slavery* exploring the local history of slavery. The new exhibition showcases the Column of Memory, one of the first existing displays of names memorializing bondspeople, consisting of an interactive lit cylindrical structure composed of several rings bearing the names of most of the enslaved men, women, and children who were held at the Slave Lodge. The text on an adjacent panel explains that the column evokes the form of a tree under which the slave auctions were held, and its rings symbolize life "passing of centuries and 'holding' of memories." The panel also exposes how naming enslaved persons was a problematic process. It indicates that upon their arrival at Cape Town enslaved individuals carried their original names but were later renamed by the colonists, even though the slaves kept at the Slave Lodge could keep their first names.[62] Likewise, on the Church Square, just behind the museum, nine blocks of black granite of different heights commemorate slavery by presenting various dimensions of the life under slavery. Again, two additional granite blocks pay homage to bondspeople kept at the Slave Lodge by displaying their names. Either in the column of names or the granite blocks, wall of names is readapted to introduce the presence of enslaved individuals in a space where their presence was erased for a very long time.

Beyond these early smaller initiatives, the United States also witnessed the creation of wall of names honoring the victims of slavery. The Whitney Plantation Museum in Wallace, Louisiana, nearly thirty-five miles from New Orleans, is the first and most significant US private venture featuring not one but three walls of names honoring enslaved people. Originally named Haydel Plantation, its first owner was the German planter Ambrose Heidel (1702–1778), who settled in Louisiana in 1721. His family owned the property until the Civil War, but in 1867 his descendants sold it to Bradish Johnson (1811–1892) of New York, who renamed it Whitney to honor his grandson Harry Payne Whitney (1872–1930).[63] In 1999, John Cummings, a retired trial lawyer and real estate magnate of Irish descent from New Orleans purchased the property to diversify his investments. In the next few years, he made a total investment of more than $8.5 million to restore buildings and purchase artifacts in order to transform the estate into a plantation museum. Cummings also fostered research about the site, with the support of historian Ibrahima Seck who became director of research of Whitney Plantation Museum.[64]

The Whitney Plantation Museum opened to the public on December 7, 2014.[65] Two years before its unveiling, large audiences became familiar with the site because it served as the setting for some scenes of *Django Unchained*, Quentin Tarantino's motion picture released in 2012. The site comprises several original and newly built structures, including a visitors' center, a big house, several pigeonniers, a kitchen, a barn, a blacksmith shop, a reconstructed church, and slave cabins brought from other plantations. Like other southern plantations, Whitney Plantation Museum targets an audience of white tourists. As shown in a recent survey, the typical visitors to the site are white college-educated women in their forties.[66] Still, African Americans also visit it in school groups or with family members and very often leave testimonies on social media about these excursions.

Between 2014 and 2017, the plantation welcomed 110,000 visitors, but today an average of 11,000 tourists visit the site every month. Contrasting with other sites that glorify wealthy planters and very often present a nostalgic narrative of the US South slave past, Whitney Plantation Museum seeks to represent bondage from the point of view of enslaved children, who in this context become the "special carriers" of cultural memory of slavery.[67] To achieve this goal, Cummings and his staff used the *narratives* of former slaves from the Federal Writers' Project, a choice justified because these interviewees experienced slavery when they were still children. Hence, upon arrival visitors to Whitney are assigned a card displaying the name of a freedperson who was interviewed as part of the Federal Writers' Project as well as a picture of one of the various clay sculptures representing children spread along the site, a strategy attempting to create empathy among racist and white supremacist visitors.[68] Yet, this approach is not new. Each visitor to the United States Holocaust Memorial Museum in Washington DC receives one of the six hundred identification cards, a strategy that allows each person to identify with one Holocaust victim. This narrative tool is based on the idea that "behind every name there is a story," an effort to write biographical essays of each of these victims that ultimately recognizes that names are crucial but not sufficient to give back the humanity stripped from victims of human atrocities.[69] Basically, by assigning visitors with a name, Whitney Plantation Museum engages in a process of multidirectional memory in which the memorialization of the Holocaust shapes the ways slavery is memorialized.[70]

Carrying an identity card bearing the name of an enslaved person, visitors to Whitney must follow the plantation guided tour that covers the various sites of the property, including three memorials featuring wall of names. The first of these memorials is the Wall of Honor (Figure 2.2).

FIGURE 2.2 *The Wall of Honor, Whitney Plantation Museum, Wallace, Louisiana, United States. Photograph by Elsa Hahne, 2016. Courtesy: Whitney Plantation Museum.*

A two-sided cement wall of nearly two meters high, it pays tribute to the 350 enslaved men, women, and children who labored in the plantation. One side of the wall contains names of African-born enslaved persons, distributed along thirteen vertical panels in black granite. A vacant space is left for an additional panel as a reminder of the names that remain unknown. The opposite side of the wall displays fourteen panels with names of enslaved individuals born in the United States. In addition to the first names (in English, Spanish, and French), further information provides the jobs they performed, date of birth, and region of provenance, especially for African-born individuals. Both sides of the wall also contain passages taken from the slave narratives of the Federal Writers' Project, even though none of the interviewees were ever enslaved at Whitney Plantation Museum. Some engravings and photographs depicting slaves also illustrate the panels. Although several newspaper articles reported that the Wall of Honor was inspired by the design of the Vietnam Veterans Memorial, Cummings claims that he took inspiration from the graves of slaveholders in Louisiana cemeteries that according to him carry similar formal elements.[71]

The second memorial presenting names of slaves is the Allées Gwendolyn Midlo Hall (Figure 2.3), named after the historian who created the Afro-Louisiana History and Genealogy database. The memorial is composed of eighteen cement L-shaped wall segments of nearly two meters each, evenly placed on both sides of a rectangular grass field. Each section contains twelve horizontal black granite panels that together display the names of 107,000 men, women, and children enslaved in Louisiana and currently stored in the database. This memorial draws from sources stored in physical and digital

FIGURE 2.3 *Allées Gwendolyn Midlo Hall, Whitney Plantation Museum, Wallace, Louisiana, United States. Photograph user Redditaddict69, 2018/ cc-by-4.0.*

archives. But unlike these repositories that very often represent nameless and faceless enslaved individuals referred to as commodities, the Allées seek to give them back their humanity and make them permanently visible.

The Field of Angels (Figure 2.4) is the third memorial featuring a wall of names at Whitney Plantation Museum. The memorial pays homage to enslaved children by following a trend visible in other initiatives such as the Memorial to the Murdered Children of Besieged Sarajevo. The emphasis on enslaved children at Whitney Plantation Museum, whose statues are spread along the estate and especially inside a reconstructed church to tell the story of slavery at the property, is an approach designed to move white and black audiences. The memorial covers a quadrangle area surrounded by a low wall. Carrying formal features much like that of the two previous memorials, this third wall of names honors 2,200 children who were born in slavery in Louisiana and died before the age of three. The names engraved on the memorial's granite plaques were registered in birth records of the Archdiocese of New Orleans. A bronze statue occupies the middle of the memorial's quadrangle area. Created by Rod Moorhead, the sculpture depicts a bare breasted black female angel carrying a baby in her arms, evoking angel figures found in opulent southern tombstones.

Whitney Plantation Museum introduces walls of names to honor enslaved men, women, and children in unprecedented ways, by destabilizing the usual racialized structure of plantation heritage sites that reinforce white

FIGURE 2.4 *Field of Angels, Whitney Plantation Museum, Wallace, Louisiana, United States. Photograph by Elsa Hahne, 2016. Courtesy: Whitney Plantation Museum.*

supremacy. Yet, from the perspective of cultural memory as commemoration, the three walls of names still pose two problems. Only the Wall of Honor pays homage to the actual men, women, and children enslaved at Whitney Plantation Museum. This strategy tends to create a certain confusion between the names of those enslaved in the site and the thousands of individuals enslaved in Louisiana. As put by Michelle Commander, establishing these memorials is certainly "a gesture of recognition that is unique given the dearth of records kept by those who bothered to refer to human property by name."[72] Still, as commemoration devices to rehumanize enslaved people, the walls of names solely derive from the work of historians, in a process that did not include the participation of groups with ancestral connections with the men and women enslaved in the plantation. Naming the enslaved repeatedly in three walls of names certainly counters the ways white supremacy frames the work of cultural memory that made bondspeople invisible. But are these walls of names alone successful in humanizing enslaved individuals and in creating empathy among visitors? Apparently not. Despite privileging naming as a memorial device, both the Wall of Honor and the Field of Angels also incorporate figurative images of enslaved individuals, suggesting that naming alone may not be sufficient to allow visitors to create an emotional bond with the victims of the Atlantic slave trade. Also, because the plantation is a private site, several additional factors limit visitors' engagement with the walls of names as commemorative devices allowing the engagement of descendants of enslaved people. Tourists must purchase a ticket (whose cost in 2019 was $23 and can only visit the plantation by following the ninety-minute guided tour, a period allowing them to spend only a few minutes seeing each memorial. Still, visiting the Whitney Plantation's Museum walls of names is also a ritualized experience. The visits led by a trained guide follow a preestablished path, and visitors are not allowed to move around the memorials as they wish. Of course, the way tourists engage with the three walls of names also largely depends on whether the tour guide can elicit emotions in them. However, the widespread use of smartphones allows many visitors to expand their experiences beyond the time spent on the site by posting their personal reviews, photographs, and videos on social media, especially Facebook, YouTube, and Instagram.

Other recent projects in the United States are using walls of names to pay homage to enslaved people. Unveiled on September 24, 2016, in Washington DC, the National Museum of African American History and Culture (NMAAHC) is a Smithsonian Institution administered by the Government of the United States. The museum features the permanent exhibition *Slavery and Freedom* curated by Nancy Bercaw and Mary N. Elliott, which I explore in more detail in Chapter 5. Chronologically and thematically organized, the exhibition starts in the African continent with the first contacts between Africans and Europeans, then explores the period of the Atlantic slave trade, and slavery in the thirteen colonies of what would become the United States.

FIGURE 2.5 *Thomas Jefferson, statue. Exhibition* Slavery at Jefferson's Monticello: Paradox of Liberty, *National Museum of American History, Washington DC, United States. Photograph by Michael Barnes, 2012. Courtesy: Smithsonian Institution.*

Following the section on the American Revolutionary War, visitors enter a great hall titled "The Founding of America" that underscores the persistence of slavery despite the Declaration of Independence. The exhibition is inspired by one section of *Slavery at Jefferson's Monticello: Paradox of Liberty*, an older traveling exhibition that opened in 2012 in the National Museum of American History (NMAH) in Washington DC, four years prior to the NMAAHC's inauguration, and which continues to travel around the United States. This earlier exhibition, curated by Rex Ellis and Elizabeth Chew, focuses on the lives of the enslaved individuals who labored in Monticello. Its opening section features a full-body size sculpture of Jefferson in the middle of a circular platform. Behind Jefferson's statue is a large panel listing the names of nearly 600 enslaved persons (Figure 2.5) who lived and worked in Monticello, obtained from Jefferson's farm books and other records. The panel also acknowledges the existence of enslaved individuals whose names remain unknown. However, Jefferson is at the center of the display and the wall of names honoring Monticello's enslaved people is limited to the background. This section of the exhibition subverts the idea of a wall of names as a privileged instrument to give humanity to bondspeople. By reaffirming the slaveholder's centrality and maintaining the invisibility of enslaved men, women, and children, this display utilizes the wall of names device to reinstate racialization and reinforce white supremacy.

The section "The Founding of America" of NMAAHC's exhibition *Slavery and Freedom* recreates the idea of wall of names initially presented in the exhibition *Slavery at Jefferson's Monticello: Paradox of Liberty*. With its high open ceiling, the great hall contrasts with the previous dark and narrow rooms exploring the Atlantic slave trade and slavery. The segment focusing on the newly independent United States provides visitors with the illusion of grandness. A huge wall displays the words "The Founding of America" and reproduces a passage of the Declaration of Independence, with an emphasis on slavery's survival and expansion after the end of British colonial rule. Across from the great wall, a rectangular platform titled "The Paradox of Liberty" features a life-size full-body statue of Jefferson facing the visitors who enter the room. Distant from Jefferson, statues of Benjamin Banneker (1731–1806), Phillis Wheatley (1753–1784), Elizabeth Freeman (*c.* 1742–1829), and Toussaint Louverture also occupy the other section of the display. Behind Jefferson is a wall of bricks (Figure 2.6), where each brick is engraved with the name of one enslaved person owned by the founding father. Although the structure evokes the idea that bondspeople built Jefferson's wealth, visitors can barely see any of the names featured on the brick wall. In addition, this unusual wall of names remains in the background of Jefferson's figurative representation, in a setting that resembles plantation displays that still privilege slave owners instead of the enslaved.[73] Almost imperceptible to the many visitors who usually visit the exhibition, the bricks carrying the names of Monticello's enslaved population once again fail to place enslaved men and women in a central position, by clearly reaffirming that what prevailed in the creation of the new nation was not freedom but rather the big wall of white supremacy that relied on the exploitation of black bodies by ensuring their invisibility.

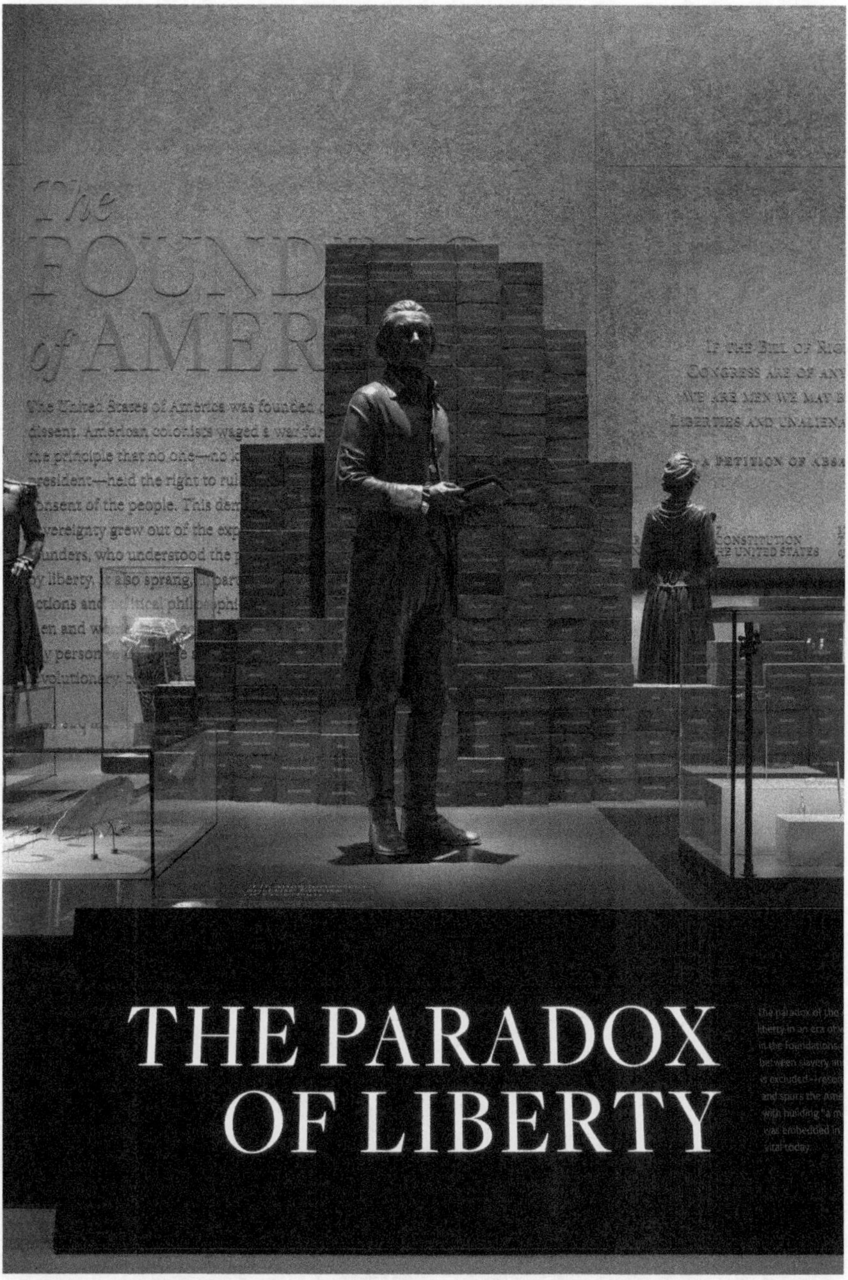

FIGURE 2.6 *Exhibition* Slavery and Freedom, *National Museum of African American History and Culture, Washington DC, United States. Photograph by Josh Weillep, 2019. Courtesy: National Museum of African American History and Culture.*

Yet the approach of the section "The Founding of America" is not unique by suggesting that when founding fathers are involved curators and public historians still have a hard time breaking existing structures of white supremacy that shape the conception of museum exhibitions. In 2016, a new exhibition *Lives Bound Together: Slavery at George Washington*'s *Mount Vernon* was unveiled in Mount Vernon, the home and plantation of the first US President George Washington. At the entrance of the exhibition, a transparent glass panel (Figure 2.7) through which the visitors can see what is exposed in the galleries lists the names of the slaves who lived and worked in the plantation. Again, a full-body life-size statue of Washington is overseeing the glass wall of names. Shadowed by Washington, the wall of names is not effective in paying homage to Mount Vernon's enslaved population. Like in other initiatives, the founding father remains the main protagonist, supporting the typical persistent invisibility of bondspeople whose names are not clearly discernable because the panel is translucent. Despite the rise of the wall of names as an exemplary device to commemorate slavery in the United States, white supremacy remains the leading force guiding the representation of the country's founding fathers. Hence, enslaved people are destined to always remain in the background.

FIGURE 2.7 *Exhibition* Lives Bound Together: Slavery at George Washington's Mount Vernon, *Mount Vernon, Virginia, United States. Photograph by Ana Lucia Araujo, 2019. Courtesy: George Washington's Mount Vernon.*

Beyond recognition, writing and reading the names of enslaved people aloud give them the humanity once stripped from them in the holds of the slave ships. Therefore, the principle behind the establishment of wall of names is not dissociated from the present struggles against the legacies of slavery. The movement Black Lives Matter, an African American-led international movement that emerged in the United States in 2013 to campaign against violence and racism against black people, largely employed the hashtag #sayhername on social media as an instrument to resist police violence against black women.

In a similar fashion, imprinting the names of bondspeople on commemorative walls also reached audiences beyond museums and heritage sites. In 2016, the Slave Route Challenge, a race covering heritage sites in Cape Town in South Africa, paid homage to enslaved individuals when each runner was given one of the 8,000 names of enslaved people displayed on the Iziko Slave Lodge Museum's Column of Memory. Likewise, South African artist Sue Williamson, whose work addresses issues of memory of colonization and Apartheid, explores in her work individual stories of enslaved men, women, and children who were shipped by the Dutch East India Company from Kochi in India to Cape Town in South Africa. Her art installation titled *One Hundred and Nineteen Deeds of Sale* at the Kochi Biennale of 2018 displayed 119 clothes symbolizing these bondspeople. On each garment, she wrote details about one enslaved person, including name, sex, age, buyer, and price as well as date and place of the sale.[74]

New community and official projects continue the construction of walls of names to memorialize slavery. In 2017, a partnership between educators, historians, and local nonprofits launched the Witness Stones Project in Guilford, Connecticut, United States. Inspired by the *Stolpersteine* project, the initiative aims to recover the memory of enslaved people in Guilford by "installing a marker which recalls an enslaved individual at a site of significance, such as where they lived, worked, or prayed." Another expression of multidirectional memory of the Holocaust and Atlantic slavery, the initiative follows the leads of the *Stolpersteine* project: each plaque contains the name of an enslaved person, his or her profession, and "whether they were emancipated or died enslaved with corresponding dates."[75]

Similar ventures also emerged in Europe, once again highlighting the multidirectional dimension of the memory of Atlantic slavery and the Holocaust. In 2018, French President Emmanuel Macron confirmed his intention to create a Foundation for the Memory of Slavery, similar to the Foundation for the Memory of the Shoah, whose headquarters includes a wall of names. The idea of this institution derived from an old proposal advanced by French poet, writer, and philosopher Édouard Glissant (1928–2011). In a long essay-report published in 2006, Glissant recommended the establishment of a National Center for the Memory of Slaveries and Their Abolitions.[76] More than a traditional cultural center, Glissant conceived the new institution also as a "repository for material relating to the afterlives of slavery and abolition" including "museums, centres, memorial sites, and other institutions."[77] Macron also announced his intention to create a wall of names to commemorate the victims of slavery at Tuileries Garden in Paris. The project is in dialogue not only with the existing wall of names at the Shoah Memorial but also with other two walls of names unveiled in Sarcelles and Saint-Denis (suburban region of Paris), on May 23, 2013. The Committee of May 23 March, 1998 (Comité Marche du 23 mai 1998), CM98, a black organization gathering members of Caribbean heritage that "emphasizes French citizenship, slave ancestry, and shared historical heritage of plantation culture and colonization," sponsored both initiatives based on genealogy work undertaken by the group over the last three decades.[78] Each memorial displays the first and last names along with registration numbers of 213 enslaved persons who were freed in Guadeloupe and Martinique in 1848. Jean-Claude Nasso who is racialized as black conceived the wall of names of Sarcelles, a rectangular marble structure decorated with the image of a globe. Nicolas Cesbron who is identified as white created the wall of names of Saint-Denis, consisting of a spherical metal sculpture from where hanging metal medallions display the engraved names. Likewise, Macron's planned wall of names to be unveiled in Paris is a response to the demands of these organizations and according to him a way to "show that there are lives, biographies, people behind this reality, these numbers."[79] Eventually, as the new Foundation for the Memory of Slavery was launched on November 12, 2019, under the presidency of former French Prime Minister Jean-Marc Ayrault, the wall of names remains to be created.

In the United States, as many universities started uncovering their ties with slavery and the Atlantic slave trade, similar initiatives emerged. In 2003, Brown University's President Ruth Simmons (the first African American president of an Ivy League institution) appointed a Steering Committee on Slavery and Justice to study the institution's ties with slavery and the inhuman commerce. Three years later, and endorsed by the university in 2007, the committee released a report with several recommendations that included various measures such as the creation of a memorial to the Atlantic slave trade, a center on slavery and justice, and a variety of measures to support public schools of Rhode Island.[80] As the work of historians such as Craig Wilder revealed the involvement of Ivy League institutions with slavery and the Atlantic slave trade, many other universities established similar projects and commissions over the last decade.[81] In 2014, the University of Virginia initiated discussions that led to the creation of Universities Studying Slavery (USS), an organization intended to gather the universities investigating their ties with slavery and the Atlantic slave trade. Today, this consortium comprises more than sixty institutions in the United States, Canada, England, and Scotland that are developing a variety of projects to bring to light their involvement with slavery and the Atlantic slave trade.[82]

The University of Virginia, conceived by Thomas Jefferson, created a working group that produced a long study of the role of slavery in its development as an institution. One of the outcomes of this initiative was the creation of a memorial honoring the nearly 5,000 "enslaved laborers" who lived and worked at the university between 1817 and 1865. The memorial's approved design comprises a circular structure with an interior granite wall nearly 2.5 meters high where the known names of enslaved men and women will be inscribed.[83] Also in Virginia, the College of William and Mary created the Lemon Project: A Journey of Reconciliation with the goal of addressing and coming to terms with its historical ties with slavery.[84] After almost a decade of work, like the University of Virginia, the institution approved the creation of a memorial honoring the enslaved people who labored in the college by opening a contest to select the memorial design. The wining proposal by William Sendor is titled "Hearth" and evokes a brick fireplace, where bondspeople worked and gathered. Made of brick, material visible in most university buildings, the new memorial will highlight the names of William and Mary's enslaved workers.[85] In all these initiatives, the inclusion of wall of names in slavery memorials differs from the early cases studied in this chapter, because they are rather a clear response to the demands of communities of descendants of enslaved persons who after consultation have determined that this kind of device is the most appropriate to reinstate humanity to their ancestors. This very new trend suggests that when walls of names to commemorate slavery and the Atlantic slave trade emerge from calls made by local black communities, they can be conceived as a form of symbolic reparation.

Burial Grounds and Naming as Cultural Memory of Slavery

Especially in the aftermath of the Second World War and the revelation of the horrors of the Holocaust, memorial projects increasingly embraced the idea of wall of names. Writing the names of the deceased on memorial walls not only recognized the humanity of millions of victims of human atrocities but also conferred them a permanent presence among the living ones. As the commemoration of the Atlantic slave trade and slavery gained ground over the last thirty years, monuments and memorials paying tribute to enslaved men, women, and children adopted various versions of the wall of names. Although these early ventures drew from quintessential dehumanizing sources such as slave ship manifests and farm books, they were the first step to gradually make bondspeople visible in public spaces where white supremacy has always prevailed.

Yet the proliferation of walls of names as memorialization devices can trivialize the Atlantic slave trade and slavery in contexts where it remains difficult to tell the stories of enslaved men, women, and children behind the displayed names. Unlike other memorials, Whitney Plantation's Museum three walls of names follow a conventional design. Moreover, they do not stand alone. Not only do they heavily rely on the use of visual images and narratives from enslaved people whose names are not exhibited on the walls, but their impact greatly depends on the tour guide's words. In addition, despite Whitney Plantation's Museum excessive use of walls of names, visitors to the site are not given time to freely contemplate and interact with the memorials. Despite these limitations, the three walls of names disrupt the traditional plantation heritage setting intended to assert white supremacy through the emphasis on the lives of slaveholders while making enslaved people invisible. Still, in some ventures instead of humanizing enslaved men, women, and children, walls of names have been used as mere textured backgrounds, therefore reinforcing white supremacy embodied by founding fathers such as Jefferson and Washington who are presented as powerful slaveholders, even in the scale of their sculptural representations. Despite these failed initiatives, new emerging projects suggest that naming remains the most influential device to pay homage to individuals whose humanity has been historically denied.

3

Battles of Public Memory

Public memory of slavery is a permanent battleground. Surely, slave-trading activities in ports of Europe, Africa, and the Americas were never a secret. But in the early 1990s, during the period that followed the end of the Cold War, this painful past was brought to light like never before. Many cities and former slave ports in the Atlantic world encompass sites attesting their involvement in slavery and the slave trade. In some cases, these structures, such as wharfs, slave markets, and slave cemeteries, were abandoned. In other cases, they were deliberately destroyed and made invisible. As black social actors continue to fight against racism and police violence, they also reclaim these urban spaces by demanding the recognition of these sites as places associated with the Atlantic slave trade and slavery. Whereas organized groups demanded that urban landmarks such as buildings and streets named after pro-slavery individuals, slave traders, and slave owners to be renamed to honor enslaved people, other groups also fought to take down public monuments representing men involved in slave-trading activities and who supported slavery. Drawing from the notion of public memory and using examples from England and the United States, I explore how different citizens and groups engaged in debates associated with the Atlantic slave past of their societies. Regardless of historical evidence, for social actors, communities, associations, and other organized groups seeking to memorialize slavery, what is at stake is whose views win and prevail in the public space. In this struggle, men and women demanding the preservation of heritage sites associated with the Atlantic slave trade, or the removal and renaming of tangible markers commemorating pro-slavery individuals, and, in turn, the construction of monuments honoring enslaved historical actors are not simply the act of engaging with the slave past. Indeed, they are also decrying entrenched structures of white supremacy that perpetuate racial inequalities and racism that insist in remaining alive in former slave societies and societies where slavery existed. Still, although their interventions are shaped by local and national contexts, in societies shaped by white supremacy, not only are their actions and discourses carrying similar elements, but the responses to their activism by governments, institutions, and elite groups designated as white also present significant similarities.

Colston Must Fall

Africans set foot in Britain as early as AD 253.[1] In the early sixteenth century, well before the British involvement in the Atlantic slave trade, descendants of Africans had lived in Tudor England. As historians David Olosuga and Miranda Kauffman have shown, the traces of this very early presence can be found not only in archaeological sites, paintings, and artworks but also in written archival documents.[2] Likewise, over the last fifty years, in several scholarly works and projects, historians have shed light on how Britain at large benefited from the wealth generated by the Atlantic slave trade and slavery in Caribbean colonies.[3] Despite abundant evidence, this ancient history of black presence in Britain has been largely ignored. Also until recently British involvement in the Atlantic slave trade has been concealed from the public landscape of its former slave ports. Port cities became the quintessential examples of this active participation in the inhuman trade.

Despite this long-lasting deliberate denial, of the European nations involved in the Atlantic slave trade, Britain is among the first ones to begin highlighting its slaving past in the public sphere. Organized groups of black residents of former British slave ports such as Liverpool, Bristol, and London, as well as other cities like Nottingham, Bath, and Birmingham, with the support of some academics and other activists, exerted pressures on public authorities and institutions that gradually started acknowledging the nation's nefarious involvement in the trade of enslaved Africans.

Bristol's active participation in the Atlantic slave trade is well documented.[4] More than 2,000 slave voyages departed from Bristol transporting nearly 565,000 enslaved Africans to the Americas.[5] During the eighteenth century, the city was the first British slave port, active for two decades (1723–1743), even though during the overall era of the Atlantic slave trade it remained the second slave port in Britain, following Liverpool. Black Bristolians descend from immigrants of former British colonies in Africa and the Caribbean islands, where their ancestors were enslaved. During the 1970s, Bristol's black population remained economically excluded, facing growing rates of unemployment and deteriorating housing conditions.[6] Under section 4 of the Vagrancy Act 1824 (still in force), the police could stop, search, and arrest vagrant individuals who were suspected of criminal activity.[7] As poverty remained largely concentrated in neighborhoods where most residents were black and immigrants of African descent, law enforcement increasingly targeted these citizens, contributing to upsurge in racial tensions.

On April 2, 1980, suspecting drug dealing activity, Bristol police officers raided Black and White Café in St. Paul's, a neighborhood of nearly 7,000 residents where half were of black Caribbean descent. As they dragged customers outside the premises, a growing crowd of hundreds gathered in the streets and reacted against the police. While tensions escalated, St. Paul's insurgent residents looted Lloyds Bank and various shops in the neighborhood while also setting fire to several cars. The incident resulted in thirty-three people injured, including twenty-one police officers and three firefighters, and twenty-one individuals arrested, though none were convicted. St. Paul's incident left deep scars in Bristol's black community. As other smaller incidents followed, excessive use of force proved to be ineffective, therefore leading the city authority and members of the civil society to engage in public debates about racism and racial inequalities.[8]

Drawing from these earlier conflicts motivated by existing racial tensions, Bristol's public memory of slavery emerged in the early 1990s. According to the Census of 1991, 376,113 people resided in Bristol, including 6,000 African Caribbean residents (about 1.5 percent), 106 black African residents, and another 861 residents individuals recorded as "other black."[9] In the Census of 2011, Bristol's population was 428,234 people, including 6,727 identified as African Caribbean and 12,085 as black Africans, both groups summing up nearly 4 percent.[10] Although only citizens of Caribbean descent have direct ties with slavery, these two groups are linked to Britain's colonial history, having been impacted by the legacies of slavery and colonialism, especially racism and racial disparities.

Debates about Bristol's slave-trading past became prominent during and following the *Festival of the Sea*. During this event, held at the historic harbor from May 24 to May 27, 1996, the city administration clearly failed to mention Bristol's leading role in the Atlantic slave trade.[11] Black residents and their allies, with the support of academics, publicly reacted to this omission. They reached the public sphere and started exposing Bristolian families who inherited wealth generated by slave-trading ventures.[12] As underscored by Christine Chivallon, this initial process of memorialization of the Atlantic slave trade was accelerated by other events. In 1995, British novelist Philippa Gregory, who is identified as white and who spent her childhood in Bristol, published the historical novel *A Respectable Trade*.[13] Set in Bristol at the end of the eighteenth century, the book explored the story of the city's slaving activities by centering its narrative around a prosperous slave owner and Mehuru, an African-born enslaved man.[14] The novel was soon transformed into a television series. At the end of 1997, an advance screening was presented to a Bristolian audience. Aired in 1998, the series' success contributed to bringing Bristol's involvement in the Atlantic slave trade to the public space and propelled an avalanche of commemoration activities. Also in that same year, with the goal of highlighting the city's participation in the infamous commerce, city councilors, council officers, members of Kuumba (a community center oriented toward Bristol's black population), representatives of the Commission for Racial Equality, and other residents of black Caribbean and African origin created the Bristol Slave Trade Action Group (BSTAG).[15] This initiative led to the creation of a small exhibition at the Georgian House Museum (as discussed in Chapter 2), the house of the merchant, planter, and slave owner, John Pinney, who owned several sugar plantations and enslaved people in the island of Nevis, in the Caribbean. These debates had a public impact and propelled more concrete actions. On December 12, 1997, during the European year against racism, Ian White, member of the European Parliament for Bristol, sponsored a plaque to honor the victims of the Atlantic slave trade. Unveiled by the novelist Philippa Gregory, the marker that reads "In memory of the countless African men, women, and children whose enslavement and exploitation brought so much prosperity to Bristol through the African slave trade" was placed at the city docks on the exterior wall of the then Bristol Industrial Museum.

Whereas the growing recognition of the city's involvement in the Atlantic slave trade made the descendants of slave merchant families and some ordinary Bristolians uncomfortable, black citizens and other supporters made distinctive efforts to gradually appropriate the city's space by exposing its slave-trading past through tangible markers. Black and white women were crucial actors in this process. After holding consultation sessions with black Bristolians in 1998, academic historian Madge Dresser along with Caletta Jordan and Doreen Taylor (who had been providing guided tours exploring the city's slave trade sites) released the booklet *Slave Trade Trail around Central Bristol*.[16] Sponsored by the Bristol City Council and the Society of the Merchant Venturers, the brochure mapped the locations associated with the history of the Atlantic slave trade.[17] Starting at Bristol Industrial Museum at Prince's Wharf, just beside the floating harbor, the trail highlights forty-two sites, including buildings, wharfs, pubs, squares, streets, and churches that were associated, directly or indirectly, with the city's slave-trading activities.

Bristol's black citizens supported by academics continued fighting to memorialize the Atlantic slave trade in the following years. In March 1999, the city inaugurated Pero's Bridge in the docks area. Spanning St. Augustine's Reach in Bristol's floating harbor, the pedestrian bridge was named after Pero Jones, an enslaved man owned by the merchant John Pinney who was brought by him from the island of Nevis to Bristol and who lived in the Georgian House.[18] Almost hidden, on the left side of the bridge's entrance, a plaque whose engraved letters are fading reads:

> Pero's Bridge: This bridge is dedicated to the memory of Pero, an enslaved man of African origin who was brought from the Caribbean island of Nevis to Bristol in 1783. He was a servant of the Pinney family who lived in what is now the Georgian House Museum in Great George Street. He died in the city in 1798.

While various organized groups, gathering activists, city representatives, and academics supported and pushed the emergence of all these initiatives, some white members of the civil society remained strongly opposed to proposals that would expose in the public space the city's controversial past. At that point, such divergent views were articulated through letters published in local newspapers.[19]

In the same period, Bristol Museums and Art Gallery and the University of West England produced the exhibition *A Respectable Trade? Bristol and Transatlantic Slavery*. Curated by Sue Giles, the show was held at the City Museum and Art Gallery from March 6 to September 2, 1999. The political debates about the city's participation in the Atlantic slave trade shaped the approach of the exposition that counted on a wide range of advisors, including academics and citizens such as Bristol councilors, associations representing ethnic minorities, teachers, and community workers, who called local black citizens to participate in the consultation process.[20] Although members of the black community initially joined the efforts, their participation gradually decreased. Yet, during the six months it remained in view, the show attracted 160,000 visitors, confirming that public engagement could produce positive results.[21] When the exhibition ended, some of its displays were transferred to the then Bristol Industrial Museum to compose the new permanent gallery titled *Bristol and Transatlantic Slavery: The Story of the City's Role in the Eighteenth-Century Slave Trade*, addressing the city's involvement in the transatlantic slave trade. Although imperfect, the new space came to stay. Despite the closure of the Bristol Industrial Museum in 2006, the new museum M Shed that replaced it in 2011 maintained the old display. Likewise, during the commemoration of the bicentennial of the British abolition of the slave trade in 2007, Bristol unveiled *Breaking the Chains*, an exhibition that occupied six galleries of the entire third floor of the British Empire and Commonwealth Museum.[22]

In the last thirty years, Bristol's social actors waging battles for the public memory of Atlantic slave trade also engaged with existing monuments and markers honoring individuals who supported the inhuman trade. Edward Colston (1636–1721) has been the most controversial historical character at the center of these disputes. Although residing in London, Colston, a native of Bristol, is still considered the city's father. He belonged to a family of merchants, and his father had an important role in the Society of Merchant Venturers, a charitable entity that played an important role in the expansion of the British Empire. When Bristol entered the Atlantic slave trade, many members of the society made profits from the infamous commerce and from slavery, especially through investments in West Indies sugar production.

Colston joined the Court of Assistants of the Royal African Company in 1680, an entity that until 1698 detained the English monopoly of the commerce with Africa. His trading activities comprised imports of goods in ships owned by his father and brother, including the trade of sugar with the West Indies, which along his participation in the ownership of a sugar house at St. Peter's churchyard in Castle Park greatly contributed to his wealth.[23] According to Kenneth Morgan, it is unknown to what extent Colston directly profited from the selling of enslaved Africans, even though he underscores that he was paid to occupy positions in different committees of the Royal African Company.[24] Yet historian Madge Dresser has emphasized Colston's direct participation in the trade of enslaved Africans, activity documented by the existence of numerous written records attesting his presence in meetings of the Royal African Company that "approved the sale and transport of Africans to the Caribbean."[25] In 1710, as a member of the Church of England and a Tory, Colston was also an elected Member of Parliament for Bristol.

Like other merchants whose activities derived from the enslavement of Africans and the use of enslaved workforce, Colston utilized part of his profits to finance schools, churches, almshouses, and other charitable ventures not only in his hometown but also in London and surrounding areas. Therefore, between the eighteenth century and the end of the twentieth century, the collective memory of white Bristolians embraced the depiction of Colston as a philanthropist who contributed to many important charitable causes. But as racial consciousness started emerging and uncovering the city's memory of slavery, a variety of black and white citizens along with scholars increasingly denounced Colston's involvement in the commerce of enslaved Africans. Like in other Atlantic societies that participated in the slave trade and where slavery existed, place names are crucial reminders of the city's slave-trading past. Indeed, to this day many Bristol sites still carry Colston's name. The booklet *Slave Trade Trail around Central Bristol* already identified three of these landmarks. First, the Colston Hall, on Colston Street, surrounded by Colston Yard and Colston Avenue. The building is located where the city's first refinery of Caribbean sugar stood. In 1708, the warehouses were converted into Colston's hospital that was later renamed Colston's Boys' School. The Colston Hall was constructed in 1867 to house an auditorium, yet, Colston's name remained attached to it. Second, the trail highlights All Saints' Church, an Anglican temple on Corn Street. The church houses Colston's opulent Baroque tomb, designed by the famous British architect James Gibbs (1682–1754). The marble tombstone consists of a vertical panel structure, framed by two Greco-Roman columns, listing Colston's charitable ventures in London, Mortlake, East Sheen, Tilerton, and Manchester, and concludes with the following words: "This great and pious Benefactor was known to have done many other excellent Charities, and what He did in Secret is believed to be not inferior to what He did in Public," which blatantly failed to mention that Colston benefited from slave-trading ventures. Colston's marble life-size statue carved by the Flemish sculptor John Michael Rysbrac (1694–1770) rounds out the tomb at the front of the panel. The sculpture represents Colston reclined in left lateral position. With both legs flexed, and with his left hand touching the right side of his chest, the drapery of his clothes gives the sculpture a sense of movement. Other sites named after the slave merchant but not comprised in the trail include two schools, Colston's School and the Colston's Girls' School.

The booklet *Slave Trade Trail around Central Bristol* also highlights the infamous bronze statue paying homage to Colston (Figure 3.1). Created

FIGURE 3.1 *Colston statue, Bristol, UK. Photograph by Ana Lucia Araujo, 2018.*

by sculptor John Cassidy (1860–1939), the monument was unveiled on November 13, 1895, by the Lord Mayor of Bristol W. Howell Davies (1851–1932). The sculpture was commissioned by a committee led by Bristol book printer and publisher James William Arrowsmith (1839–1913), who promoted the Industrial and Art Exhibition of 1893–1894, held in the city's downtown area, in the same zone where the monument stands (Colston Avenue, not far from Colston Hall).[26] The statue measures nearly eight feet and is placed on a pedestal of approximately ten feet, and each corner of the plinth is decorated with sculptures depicting bronze dolphins. In the full-body statue Bristol's iconic city father is represented like he appears in images of the seventeenth and eighteenth centuries. The statue shows Colston in his middle age. Wearing a long curly wig, he appears in a meditative attitude. The right arm is crossed in front of his body and the right hand holds a long stick. The left elbow is pressed into the palm of his right hand, while the left hand supports his head. The bronze plaque adorning the pedestal reads "Erected by citizens of Bristol as a memorial of one of the most virtuous and wise sons of their city." Not surprisingly once again, the text excludes any references to Colston's association with the trade and exploitation of enslaved bodies. But as Madge Dresser points out, such suppression is a relatively recent occurrence. Indeed, until the first years of the twentieth century, Colston's involvement with slavery and the slave trade was quite visible in municipal printed materials. For example, the city's official guide published in 1908 mentioned Bristol's slave-trading activities and consisted of not only textual references to Colston but also the reproduction of the painting *The Death of Edward Colston* (1844) by Richard Jeffreys Lewis (*c.* 1822–1883).[27] This rendering of Colston's death shows him in his deathbed, attended by a vicar, an unidentified relative or friend, and a black female servant who is kneeling and kissing his hand, in a position of submission and alleged gratitude.[28] However, in its edition of 1934 (centennial of the British Slave Emancipation Act), the official municipal guide no longer made references to Colston. The change may be related to the publication of Colton's biography by Reverend H. J. Wilkins that presented evidence of his membership in the Court of Assistants of the Royal African Company.[29] But despite these developments, Colston continued to be commemorated in ceremonies and the numerous Bristol landmarks named after him.

As the battles of public memory of slavery surfaced in the 1990s, black Bristolians started protesting Colston's omnipresence in the city's landscape. In 1998, Bristol's musical group *Massive Attack* (of which two of its members are black Bristolians) pledged to not perform at Colston Hall until the name of the building changed and continued campaigning to rename the concert hall.[30] In a press statement, the group also demanded the construction of a statue honoring the "Unknown Slave," a request that to this day has not been fulfilled.[31]

Colston's statue on Colston Avenue did not escape the storm. In January 1998, its pedestal was painted with the words "slave trader." The event gained visibility in the national press, exposing the persistent racialized debates wherein black activists and other social actors involved in the process of memorialization of Bristol's slave past supported either the removal of the sculpture from the city center or the addition of a plaque acknowledging Colston's participation in slave-trading ventures.[32] Still, white Bristolians opposed these proposals in public demonstrations and in the local newspapers *Bristol Evening Post* and *Western Daily Press*, defending that the statue should be preserved whereas "malcontented ethnics" should return to their "ancestral homelands."[33] Like any battles of public memory of slavery, when one group demands the removal of a statue or renaming a landmark, individuals with opposing views immediately respond in the public sphere to defend it. Colston became the symbol of Bristol's slave-trading history that survived over the centuries among a population identifying as white. For these groups, protecting Colston's statue is part of how white supremacy operates in Bristol. Keeping the statue is synonymous with preserving a white Bristolian identity as opposed to that of Bristol-born black residents who are still considered "foreigners" by the local white population.

Two decades after these debates started, Colston continues to be a central symbol of Bristol's involvement in the Atlantic slave trade. During the commemoration of the bicentennial of the British abolition of the slave trade, black residents persisted in their demands to topple Colston's sculpture. The statue's pedestal was painted with red in December 2007, calling attention to the city father's "bloody involvements in the slave trade."[34] Although protestors persisted in demanding the statue's removal, the city public authority continued ignoring these calls. In this context, over the last ten years, activists, ordinary citizens, academics, and artists engaged in what Alan Rice appropriately characterized as "guerrilla memorialization" by developing alternative and creative ways to contest the infamous monument. As argued by historian Olivette Otele, Bristolian activism has specifically focused on "the visual representation of this common history" of slavery and colonialism, in line with other movements such as Rhodes Must Fall in South Africa and the wave of protests that demanded the removal of statues honoring Confederate generals in the United States.[35] On the eve of the bicentennial of the British abolition of the slave trade, artist Graeme Mortimer Evelyn, who is racialized as black, developed *The Two Coins Project*, a visual sculpture and moving image installation that would be projected in several sites of memory of slavery around the world, including Bristol's Colston's statue on Colston Avenue.[36] Although the project was not approved, artists and citizens committed to making Bristol's slave past visible in the public space led many other "unauthorized" interventions.

The launch of Countering Colston in 2016 helped the movement to acknowledge Bristol's role in the infamous trade gain additional strength. The public campaign gathers academics, concerned residents, one city councilor, and members of the board of Colston Hall. The group's goal is to tell the history of Colston as a slave trader and demand the removal of his name from all of Bristol's premises. On November 9, 2016, posters placed around the pedestal of Colston's statue displayed the terms "human trafficker," "kidnapper," "murderer," and "slave trader."[37] In August 2017, a plaque reading "Unauthorized Heritage: Bristol: Capital of the Atlantic Slave Trade, 1730–1745, commemorating the 12,000,000 enslaved of whom 6,000,000 died as captives" was placed on the plinth of Colston's monument. The plaque, whose creation has been attributed to British sculptor and street artist Will Coles (identified as white), followed the model of Bristol's official heritage plaques displayed on heritage buildings and remained attached to the monument for almost two months before its removal by the city authority.

On May 6, 2018, protestors appended a red yarn ball and chain to the feet of Colston's statue. Although not as explicit as previous manifestations, the subtle intervention is a reference to his slave-trading activities.[38] On the date designated as anti-slavery day in Britain (October 18, 2018) another intervention occurred: one hundred figurines representing human bodies were displayed in front of the statue. The lying white statuettes evoked the image of the *Brookes*, the iconic eighteenth-century British slave ship whose diagram was extensively used in abolitionist propaganda.[39] Surrounding the statuettes were rectangular blocks whose surfaces were painted with the words "here and now," underscoring the idea that slavery still exists. Other blocks indicated the professions of present-day individuals submitted to forced labor: "nail bar workers," "sex worker," "car wash attendant," "domestic servant," "fruit picker," "kitchen worker," and "farm worker."

Although its visual impact was undeniable, this intervention poses several problems for the study of public memory of Atlantic slavery. First, unlike previous social actors organized around groups with an anti-racist agenda, the authors of the action concealed their identities. Were they just a group wanting to call attention to the issue of modern-day slavery, or did they situate themselves in the long struggle to recognize Bristol as a city that largely benefited from the trade on human beings and where black citizens are still victims of racism? Second, by highlighting present-day human trafficking, a problem that affects peoples of all origins in various parts of the globe, instead of underscoring Colston's participation in the inhuman trade, the creators of the installation evacuated the racialized dimension that marked the Atlantic slave trade and continues to determine its legacies, therefore distancing themselves from the approach that since the 1990s has led Bristol's debates. To this day, as no second plaque was added to the monument, these interventions at Colston's statue contribute to the ongoing pressure on the municipality to officially recognize the city's involvement in the Atlantic slave trade.

Despite resistance, there are new developments. For example, after two decades without official acknowledgment or revision, in April 2017, Bristol Music Trust, the charity that manages Colston Hall, announced it will change the building's name after the end of renovation works expected to be completed in 2020. In 2018, Cleo Lake, a city councilor and member of the Green Party, former actress and activist, who is also a member of the movement Countering Colston became Bristol Lord Mayor.[40] Lake identifies herself as a black Bristolian: "I was born in Bristol. I am first-generation Bristolian. My father was a proud African man born in Jamaica and my mother is of Scottish heritage, so I am Campbell by clan on my mother's side."[41] In a powerful symbolic gesture, she decided, in July 2018, to remove Colston's large painted portrait that was prominently displayed in her office. Despite these pulverized initiatives and the widespread media coverage of the protests to remove Colston's name from the city's landmarks, institutions such as the Colston's Girls' School decided to keep its designation. Hence, movements such as Countering Colston continue to evolve and the demands to publicly recognize Bristol's slave-trading past in the public space persist. Yet, despite the specific local context, Bristol's battles of public memory of slavery are in dialogue with similar movements demanding the removal of statues of individuals who supported slavery and colonialism around the world.

Whose Streets?

Liverpool shares a similar slave-trading history with Bristol. In the 1730s, the city became the largest British slave port, passing Bristol and London. In the last two decades of the eighteenth century, the city's docks developed extensive shipbuilding activity. Nearly 4,972 slave voyages started in Liverpool, which transported approximately 1,337,530 enslaved Africans to the Americas.[42] Obviously, a great part of Liverpool's economic activity and wealth derived from its slave-trading interests during the eighteenth century until 1807, when the British slave trade was outlawed.

After the passing of the Slavery Abolition Act of 1833 legally ending slavery in the British colonies, the ways slavery has been memorialized in the public spaces of former British slave ports changed. Because of the massive abolitionist movement that emerged in Britain toward the end of the eighteenth century and because of its colonial role in Africa, at various moments British public commemoration basically emphasized the role of white savior abolitionists instead of honoring the victims of slavery and the slave trade.

Liverpool was not remarkable in its abolitionist activities. After the legal ban of the British slave trade in 1807, and especially between the 1820s and the 1830s, a greater number of organizations supporting the end of slavery emerged in the city. Still, this new trend contradicted the fact that in the decades that followed the British abolition of slavery Liverpool's economic activities greatly relied on cotton grown by enslaved men and women in the United States.[43] Liverpool was the biggest cotton port in the world, and its merchants "traded raw cotton, shipped cotton goods, and financed both cotton agriculture and cotton manufacturing."[44] These interests explain why the city was the "most pro-Confederate place in the world outside the Confederacy itself."[45] In the early 1860s, on the eve of the US Civil War, Liverpool economically supported the Confederate states in a variety of ways such as warship building, as well as credit and military equipment.

The marks of this special relation with the Confederacy remain visible in the city's built heritage. For example, Charles K. Prioleau (1827–1887), a Confederate businessman from South Carolina, was married to the daughter of a Liverpool's shipowner. Naturalized British citizen, he became the representative of the merchants and bankers Fraser, Threholm, & Co, who had privileged ties with the Confederacy and therefore made possible the transactions between Liverpool's businessmen and the Confederates. Prioleau's residence at number 12, Rumford Place (today's 19, Abercromby Square, building of the University of Liverpool) became known as the Charleston House in a reference to his Confederate home state.[46] A fresco depicting a palmetto tree, symbol of South Carolina, decorated the walls of the building, erected to house an unofficial embassy of the Confederacy.[47]

Despite growing self-criticism, Liverpool's slave-trading past and its later support of pro-slavery Confederacy survived in commemoration activities and accounts published during the nineteenth and twentieth centuries. These memories drew from a nostalgic view of slave labor, when Britain made its wealth on the slave trade and slavery. As late as 1907 (the 700th anniversary of Liverpool and the centennial of the British abolition of the slave trade) commentators had no objections to the evocation of the memory of the city's cotton trade with the US South.[48] Three decades later, the British landscape of commemoration of slavery had barely changed, and the same trend continued. In 1934, Britain timidly observed the first centennial of its abolition of slavery. Reinforcing white supremacy, William Wilberforce (1759–1833) was consolidated as a central figure symbolizing British humanitarian vein, a tendency that persisted during the entire twentieth century.[49] Overall, Britain's active participation in the Atlantic slave trade and its support of slavery were absent from the festivities that instead emphasized its role in promoting abolitionist ideals, an accent that also justified the continuation of British imperialism in Africa, the Caribbean, and Asia. Likewise, as sociologist Mark Christian has emphasized more than two decades ago, the city of Liverpool also made efforts to conceal its crucial involvement in the Atlantic slave trade.[50] Like in the United States, during the period that immediately followed the end of the First World War (1914–1918), Liverpool witnessed the emergence of white mobs targeting black seamen and black British veterans.[51]

Although Britain passed racial equality legislation in the 1960s, it was not until the end of the 1980s that a variety of groups whose origins are associated with British colonial rule in Africa, Asia, and the Caribbean started demanding central and local governments to take official measures to address the problem of racial inequalities affecting the country. These actions entailed an ethnic monitoring system to collect racial and ethnic statistics, and the creation of antiracist programs.[52] This new nationwide trend coincided with the end of the Cold War, a period that favored the assertion of national and collective identities of historically oppressed groups in societies involved in the Atlantic slave trade and wherever slavery existed.[53]

Like in Bristol's case, historians have largely studied Liverpool's involvement in the slave trade.[54] Yet the city's recognition of its slave-trading past presented specific challenges. The economic recession in 1981, during the government of Margaret Thatcher (1925–2013), impacted the city's working class, and its black community witnessed a dramatic rise in unemployment. In this context of racial disparities and growing police violence against black residents, Liverpool police stopped and arrested a motorcyclist in Toxteth, a low-income neighborhood, on July 3, 1981. The incident led residents to respond violently to police truculence, provoking an insurrection that lasted many hours and then remerged twenty days later. Although Liverpool black social actors did not typically lead movements to remove statues honoring slave traders and pro-slavery individuals, during the insurgence, residents pulled down the statue of William Huskisson (1770–1830), a Member of Parliament for Liverpool, mistaking him for a slave merchant. This spontaneous intervention forced the city to remove the statue from its plinth.[55] The Toxteth protests also led to the production of the Gifford Report examining the city's race relations and influenced later developments on memorialization of the Atlantic slave trade in the city.[56]

In the early 1990s, despite its ancient presence in Liverpool, the city's black population remained socially and economically excluded.[57] Today estimated at 4 percent, the city's population of African descent includes men and women whose ancestors settled in the city as early as the eighteenth century, as well as the descendants of immigrants from British colonies in Africa and the Caribbean who established themselves in the city starting in the nineteenth century. During the 1980s and the 1990s, residents identified as black consisted of "formerly colonized and currently racialized groups" such as Asians, Chinese, and Arabs.[58] In other words, being black was and still is a political identity, associated with the lived experience of racism and exclusion. But for men and women of African descent, this black identity is intrinsically related to the history of slavery and the Atlantic slave trade. Anthropologist Jacqueline Nassy Brown showed how in the early 1990s, black residents of Liverpool carried a collective memory of slavery and even without being asked they associated their experiences of racism to specific urban sites linked to slave-trading activities.[59]

A Liverpool black resident, Eric Scott Lynch evoked the slave past at least since 1980 to decry the persistency of racism in Liverpool. Asserting a "Liverpool-born-black" identity, he denounced how whites continued manipulating the divisions among black populations to support white supremacy and racism in the same way "White slave owners put Black over-seers over the slaves."[60] In the years that followed, Lynch started interpreting the city built heritage linked to the Atlantic slave trade by leading the Liverpool Slavery Trail, a tour highlighting the sites and buildings that witnessed Liverpool's history of the Atlantic slave trade and black population.[61]

This process that brought the slave-trading past of British ports to the public space produced various initiatives. In 1994, after a three-year-long process involving the consultation of the local black community, the Merseyside Maritime Museum in Liverpool opened in its basement the permanent exhibition *Transatlantic Slavery: Against Human Dignity*, or simply *Transatlantic Slavery Gallery*.[62] Academics and members of the city's black community were crucial players for the creation of this new exhibition space embracing the history of slavery and the Atlantic slave trade.[63] Curated by Anthony Tibbles, the show consisting of forty text panels, video displays, audio recordings, artifacts, and artworks, as well as a replica of the hold of a slave ship, established Liverpool's first permanent display telling the history of slavery.[64] In 1997, UNESCO passed a resolution making August 23 (the day that marked the beginning of the Saint-Domingue slave insurrection in 1791) the International Day of Remembrance of the Slave Trade and Its Abolition. On August 23, 1999, Liverpool commemorated the first Slavery Remembrance Day, a date that since then has been celebrated with a parade, a ceremony at Canning Dock as well as lectures and symposia. On that occasion, Member of Parliament Bernie Grant (1944–2000), who had been a central leader in the African Reparations Movement, unveiled a plaque at the docks acknowledging Liverpool's role in the infamous commerce. Later that year, on December 9, 1999, the Liverpool City Council voted on a text addressing an apology for the city's participation in the Atlantic slave trade. These measures, along with the creation of a *Transatlantic Slavery Gallery* in the Merseyside Maritime Museum that gave birth to the International Slavery Museum (see Chapter 4), were very significant. However, they were not accompanied by other tangible initiatives effectively interfering in the urban space.[65]

Nevertheless, black concerned citizens and their allies were demanding more than the simple recognition of Liverpool's slave-trading past in the confined space of the museum. Although a plaque is a concrete marker, most passersby do not see it in the middle of the touristic paraphernalia that since the turn of the twentieth century has been installed along Liverpool's renovated docks. In this context, activists also wanted to address the city's slave past through interventions that would alter the city's landscape. Evidently, like in Bristol, addressing this problem was and remains a major challenge because the marks of Liverpool's slave-trading activities are present nearly everywhere in its houses, churches, streets, squares, and cemeteries.[66] In this urban landscape embedded in white supremacy, many plaques identify different buildings around the city, especially those where male prominent figures were born and lived. Yet, because no inscriptions indicate the sites associated with the slave trade, the connections between these places and the city's slave-trading past remain invisible to tourists, outsiders, and newcomers.

One of the most prominent constructions in the city's downtown area is the Liverpool Town Hall. The eighteenth-century neoclassic building stands in High Street at the intersection with Dale Street, Castle Street, and Water Street. Part of the National Heritage List for England, its high dome is adorned with a statue of Minerva, the Roman goddess of wisdom and patron of arts, trade, and strategy. The building's large rooms and ballrooms feature decoration of the late Georgian period. Built at the height of the British involvement in the Atlantic slave trade, between 1749 and 1754, the building is a slave-trade heritage site, because most of the city's mayors between the eighteenth century and 1807 (date of the British abolition of the slave trade) were directly or indirectly connected to the infamous commerce of human flesh. Not surprisingly, at least twenty-five lord mayors of the Borough of Liverpool during the period between 1700 and 1820, along with many councilors and Liverpool's Members of Parliament, had interests in the infamous commerce.[67]

The Liverpool Town Hall offers guided tours twice a month. On an annual basis, during the summer, the building is open to public visitation as well. In addition to exploring the building's architecture, lavish furniture, crystal chandeliers, and collection of artworks, local visitors and tourists can have tea with live piano music in the Lord Mayor's Parlor. In the two floors of the building, the rooms and ballrooms are decorated with objects, sculptures, and paintings, many of them associated with the slave trade. Under the sumptuous staircases, on the first floor, two glass displays exhibit the Liverpool Town Hall's silver collection consisting of a variety of objects given as gifts to the city over the centuries. Among these objects, there is a George III oval silver cake basket (by silversmith Robert Hennell, 1780) offered in homage of Thomas Golightly Esq. (1732–1821). Golightly, whose painted portrait is featured in the International Slavery Museum, was elected member of Liverpool Town Council in 1770, and in 1772 he was the city's mayor, having served the city in various capacities until his death. A wine merchant and shipowner, he financially participated in the Atlantic slave trade until its abolition. Opposed to the abolition of the slave trade, as late as 1807, Golightly's name appeared in the list of the Company of Merchants Trading to Africa.[68]

Nearly two dozen painted portraits of former Liverpool mayors are exhibited all over the rooms of the second floor of the Liverpool Town Hall, but the explanatory labels attached next to the paintings omit the term "slave trade." In one of the rooms, for example, hangs a full-body oil portrait of slave trader George Case (1747–1836), by artist Sir Thomas Philips (1770–1845). Case was a member of the Town Council for forty-five years and Mayor of Liverpool in 1781–1782. However, the label describing the painting does not include one single word regarding his active participation in the Atlantic slave trade. It also omits that Case along with his father-in-law William Gregson (1721–1809), who in 1762 had also been the Mayor of Liverpool, was member of the syndicate that owned the infamous slave ship *Zong*.[69] In 1781, while the *Zong* was heading to Jamaica and ran out of water, the crew threw overboard 133 enslaved persons to cash in the insurance taken on their lives. The *Zong* became known worldwide as one of the bloodiest massacres in the history of the inhuman trade. As underscored by historian James Walvin, the *Zong*'s atrocious incident did not discourage Gregson from continuing to engage in the slave trade. Between 1781 and 1790, his slave ships transported 8,018 enslaved Africans from the Gold Coast region to be sold in various Caribbean islands. Between 1780 and 1800, Gregson's ships transported 34,931 slaves, half of whom were disembarked in Jamaica.[70] Obviously, references to these atrocities are nowhere to be found in the Town Hall building.

Likewise, one of the ballrooms features another smaller oil painting portraying Peter Whitfield Brancker (1750–1836), who is described in the label as "a merchant, trading with the West Indies." Indeed, Brancker was a captain in the slave trade, who during the period 1784–1799 was also a slave merchant, an information that is not displayed in the labels explaining the painting. In the various labels associated with the displayed portrait paintings the only one that includes the term "slavery" is the tag describing the portrait of William Wallace Currie (1784–1840), Mayor of Liverpool in 1835–1836, who is referred to as a man who "devoted much of his time to the anti-slavery cause."

Like the Liverpool Town Hall, other iconic sites are associated with the city's slave-trading past. But with few exceptions, most of them remain unmarked. In 2001, during the construction works to build the new shopping center Liverpool One at Canning Place, across from the Canning Dock, workers discovered the structure of the old wharf, buried since 1826. Constructed in 1715, at the height of the British participation in the Atlantic slave trade, the dock became the point of departure of ships that would sail to African ports to exchange a variety of products for enslaved men, women, and children that were subsequently sold in the Americas. The National Museums Liverpool (a group of museums and galleries) offers one-hour tours of the dock three times a day on Mondays, Tuesdays, and Wednesdays. The dock's composition is visible through a porthole, a glass cylindrical structure at Canning Place (Figure 3.2), at which the following words are displayed: "The Old Dock was designed and built by Thomas Steers between 1709 and 1715." The term "slave trade" is absent not only from this marker but also from the website that announces the tours.[71] Only by reading the bar

FIGURE 3.2 *Display of the Old Dock. Canning Place, Liverpool, UK. Photograph by Ana Lucia Araujo, 2017.*

code, exhibited on the display, with a smartphone can visitors see the digital artwork *Layers of the Old Dock* that provides decontextualized references to the slave trade, including the iconic image of the kneeling enslaved man "Am I not a Man and a Brother," a quotation by Frederick Douglass, and a 1799 engraving depicting the old dock, connecting them with the more recent history of the dock.[72]

Approximately 1,500 feet from Canning Place, almost across the Princess Dock, stands Our Lady and Saint-Nicholas Church. Although the original temple dates to the thirteenth century, the church was reconstructed by the middle of the eighteenth century at the height of the Atlantic slave trade. Honoring Saint-Nicholas, the patron saint of sailors, visitors to the building can see sculptures and stained glass depicting ships that conjure the decades during which the city slave-trading activity flourished. Likewise, other churches such as the Saint-James Church at the corner Upper Parliament Street and Park Road still display its connections with the inhuman commerce of human flesh. Opened on June 4, 1775, this Anglican church is among Liverpool's oldest churches. Although closed since 1971, under the protection of the Churches Conservation Trust, the temple was returned to the Diocese of Liverpool in 2010, when safeguarding works to recuperate the building started. The church contains nineteen monuments to slave traders, its archives comprise baptism records of slave owners and slaves, and although not confirmed by evidence, its graveyards are said to hold the remains of enslaved individuals.[73] Nevertheless, only locals and informed tourists visit the church, located outside the city's main touristic area.

Years of black activism in Liverpool impacted official initiatives that eventually had to highlight the city's links with the Atlantic slave trade. At the turn of the twenty-first century, several British institutions started preparing for the commemoration of the 2007 bicentennial of the abolition of the British slave trade.[74] This context made possible the organization of several exhibitions and conferences in various British cities, including London, where the Museum of London Docklands opened its first permanent gallery examining the city's involvement with the Atlantic slave trade, titled *London, Sugar, and Slavery*.[75]

Meanwhile, Liverpool's memory of slavery landscape continued evolving. In 2004, UNESCO added Liverpool Maritime Mercantile City to its World Heritage List. One of the three criteria for the city's inclusion in the list referred to the central role of Liverpool in the Atlantic slave trade.[76] Whereas creating permanent markers for slave trade heritage sites and conceiving monuments to honor those who fought against slavery was a project hard to achieve, after the addition of Liverpool to the World Heritage List there was additional pressure on heritage institutions to provide more information about urban structures named after slave merchants and planters.

In July 2006, Councilor Barbara Mace submitted a proposal to the Liverpool City Council regarding renaming streets that carry names of slave traders such as Ashton Street, Blundell Street, Bold Street, Cropper Street, Gladstone Road, Parr Street, Tarleton Street, Rodney Street, Cunliffe Street, Earle Street, Earle Road, Sir Thomas Street, and Penny Lane. Mace, who is categorized as white, recommended renaming the streets after British abolitionists such as William Wilberforce (1759–1833). In response, black educator Gloria Hyatt, a founding member of the organization Merseyside Campaign Against Racist Terrorism who was born in Toxteth, defended a proposition to rechristen the streets with the names of successful black individuals.[77] But opponents to the proposal quickly emerged. Although several contributors to the public debate argued that renaming the streets would "whitewash history," one of the greatest obstacles to the project was the inclusion of Penny Lane among the streets to be renamed.[78] Immortalized in the *Beatles*' homonymous song, the street is said to have been named after the slave merchant John Penny, and renaming it would directly affect the city's image and tourism industry that largely relies on the *Beatles*, whose members were born and raised in Liverpool. Without large popular support, the proposal was eventually dismissed. In 2007, the Historic Environment of Liverpool Project released a modest sixteen-page booklet, authored by historian and television presenter Laurence Westgaph, listing the streets associated with the infamous commerce.[79] Despite all the debates surrounding Liverpool's slave-trading past and the city's UNESCO World

Heritage status, only the permanent exhibition of the International Slavery Museum opened in 2007 underscores the connections between street names and the slave trade. To this day, there are no plaques or signs explaining to the city's visitors and residents how and why the names of these streets are associated with the slave trade. Yet, by their own initiative, Liverpool black citizens continue leading the battles of public memory through a variety of tools, including tours exploring the history of the city's involvement in the Atlantic slave trade. As late as in 2017, legendary Eric Scott Lynch was still taking visitors in his Liverpool Slavery History Trail. Likewise, Laurence Westgaph, now a very well-known public figure, leads The Liverpool and Slavery Walking Tour, a popular tour highlighting the city's slave-trading past. Despite these major developments, slavery memorialization remains largely confined to the International Slavery Museum. Indeed, to this day, Liverpool failed to approve the construction of a memorial or monument commemorating its involvement in the abominable commerce.

The White Tide

In the United States, like in Britain, black social actors have demanded for very long time the removal of monuments and the renaming of urban landmarks paying homage to pro-slavery individuals. These struggles of public memory are racialized and hence closely associated with the fight against racism, especially police violence against African Americans who symptomatically grew during the two terms (2009–2016) of Barack Obama presidency. In July 2013, Black Lives Matter occupied the streets of several US cities after George Zimmerman (a member of a community watch in Sanford, Florida, who killed the seventeen-year-old African American Trayvon Martin) was acquitted. Between 2014 and 2015, demonstrations continued evolving when, among others, police officers killed Eric Garner (1970–2014) on Staten Island, New York; unarmed teenager Michael Brown (1996–2014) in Ferguson, Missouri; twelve-year-old Tamir Rice (2002–2014) in Cleveland, Ohio; and Freddie Gray (1989–2015) in Baltimore, Maryland.

On June 17, 2015, a group of twelve African American men and women gathered to attend a Bible study group, as they did every week at the Emanuel African American Methodist Episcopal Church in Charleston, South Carolina. The church was no ordinary building. Among its founders was Denmark Vesey (*c.* 1767–1822), a freedman accused and convicted of plotting a slave rebellion, who was sentenced to death along with more than thirty other black men. In the aftermath of the plot, a mob of whites burned down the church building, which was only reconstructed after the end of the Civil War.

Despite this tragic legacy, nothing in that evening seemed to evoke that distant past. Since 2009, the first black president of the United States was in office and Vesey, who for many years was referred to as a "would-be killer" by several Charleston white residents, was now memorialized in a statue unveiled in the previous year at Hampton Park.[80] But that Wednesday evening, Dylann Roof, a twenty-one-year-old white man joined the Emanuel African American Methodist Episcopal Church's Bible study group. One hour later, he took his handgun and opened fire against the attendees. Witnesses reported that Roof said "I have to do it. You rape our women and you're taking over our country. And you have to go," before shooting nine African American men and women.[81]

The investigation that followed the killing uncovered the path that transformed the young man into a domestic terrorist, including several pictures featuring him in various slavery heritage sites in Charleston, such as Sullivan Island where newly arrived enslaved Africans and crew members were put into quarantine aboard ships or in pesthouses upon their landing in South Carolina, the slave cabins of Boone Hall Plantation and Gardens, and Magnolia Plantation and Gardens.[82] In one picture, he is posing holding a gun and a Confederate battle flag, which during the Civil War and still today is a symbol associated with the heritage of those who fought against the union to preserve slavery. The pro-slavery symbol has been appropriated by white nationalists who, during the twentieth century, persisted in promoting racial hatred.

Irrespective of these heinous events, the Confederate battle flag continued flying on the grounds of South Carolina statehouse in Columbia. But honoring their long tradition of protest, African American women responded to it. In the early morning of Saturday, June 27, 2015, Bree Newsome, a fearless educator, artist, and activist of Charlotte, North Carolina, climbed the thirty-foot flagpole and took down the flag. In a public statement, she declared: "We removed the flag today because we can't wait any longer. We can't continue like this another day. It's time for a new chapter where we are sincere about dismantling white supremacy and building toward true racial justice and equality."[83]

Newsome's action was neither a new nor isolated event. Ethan J. Kytle and Blain Roberts explain that as early as in the second half of the nineteenth century, African Americans have contested monuments honoring pro-slavery white supremacist individuals such as John C. Calhoun (1782–1850), the South Carolina politician who served as the seventh vice-president of the United States (1825–1832).[84] Karen L. Cox also underscores that in 2000 the Confederate battle flag that flew atop the South Carolina state capitol was removed from the building, even though it remained in the capitol's grounds.[85]

In the months that followed Charleston's terrorist attack, black residents and activists along with other anti-racist allies organized demonstrations demanding the removal of the Confederate battle flag and monuments honoring military leaders and other individuals who fought the Civil War to defend slavery, but who lost their fight. White nationalists and white supremacists immediately responded to the protests by occupying the public space to reclaim these symbols. Bringing back the old flawed argument that the Confederate statues and battle flag honored their alleged ancestors who died fighting for the Confederacy, these extremists argued that removing them was erasing "history," as if the statues built several decades after the end of the war constituted some kind of contemporary historical record of the Civil War. Still, neither these monuments nor any other statues derive from the work of history. They are rather part of the realm of public memory, which in this context is a reconstruction of the past that aims to fulfill the present-day political agenda of a specific group of white individuals who pretend to claim the legacy of those who fought to keep slavery alive. As part of this context, public memory of slavery and emancipation once again emerges as a racialized process. On the one hand, white individuals embrace the Confederate flag as a quintessential symbol of white supremacy. But on the other hand, as historian Kevin Levin has demonstrated, to accomplish their political project, especially starting in the 1970s, these white conservative groups also needed to fabricate the idea that black individuals not only supported the Lost Cause of the Confederacy but also joined the Confederate army not as "camp slaves" but as "soldiers."[86] Likewise, Confederate monuments are commemorative devices built nearly four decades after the end of the Civil War as part of the battles of public memory to reinforce the position of Southern whites who with the end of slavery continued promoting racial violence against African Americans in order to prevent them from acquiring economic and political power. Ultimately, Confederate monuments are devices produced by white supremacists to perpetuate white supremacy as a system intended to annihilate and make black subjects invisible.[87]

The debates and rallies around Confederate markers are useful examples of the ongoing battles of public memory of slavery, which like in Britain are intrinsically related to the dominance of white supremacy that marginalizes black subjects in urban settings, while promoting the representations of pro-slavery white men as righteous. Whereas white supremacists continue to appropriate devices commemorating Confederates, whether or not their ancestors fought in the Civil War, black activists, ordinary citizens, and their white allies appealed for the removal of these monuments because not only did they memorialize men who took arms to defend slavery, but also these statues and memorials erected during the Jim Crow era when African Americans were victims of racial hatred and denied civil rights remain quintessential symbols of white supremacy.

Tension increased when, in November 2016, Donald Trump was elected president of the United States. His discourse fomenting hate against immigrants was supported and disseminated by white supremacist and white nationalist men and women. More than ever before, these groups instrumentalized Confederate monuments by organizing demonstrations in various US cities where the municipalities voted to remove them. On August 11 and 12, 2017, the Unite the Right rally gathered in Charlottesville, Virginia, the home of University of Virginia, founded by Thomas Jefferson, a few dozens of neo-Nazis, neo-Confederates, and Klansmen. The alleged reason for the meeting was the municipality decision to remove the statue of Robert E. Lee (1807–1870), the slave owner and general who commanded the Confederate Army during the Civil War. On the night of August 11, prevented from convening in the now Emancipation Park, where Lee's statue was covered while awaiting a decision from the city council, hundreds of extremists marched throughout the campus of University of Virginia. Carrying torches, the group freely walked around the university Rotunda and congregated at Jefferson's statue chanting slogans such as "blood and soil" and "Jews will not replace us." The following day, the far-right participants armed with assault guns, shields, and clubs were met by counter-protesters. One white terrorist drove his car in high speed over the counter-protesters killing Heather D. Heyer (1985–2017), a thirty-two-year-old paralegal from Charlottesville, leaving dozens of people injured.

The next two days after this tragedy, the movement to take down Confederate monuments gained new force. In some cities, such as Durham, North Carolina, citizens took these actions in their own hands and tore down a statue representing a Confederate soldier.[88] Following this trend, several cities in Missouri, Virginia, Florida, Texas, Maryland, Ohio, North Carolina, New York, Wisconsin, Louisiana, Kentucky, and even California decided to remove their Confederate monuments, sometimes during the night to avoid turmoil. As of 2019, nearly 1,700 Confederate markers remain standing in the United States, including nearly 780 monuments.[89] Yet, as statues were removed, various associations of descendants of Confederate soldiers started erecting new monuments in private-owned spaces around the country, suggesting that the battles of public memory of slavery and its legacies are far from over.[90]

Whereas Black Lives Matter activism evolved, similar debates and actions continued emerging in various universities in the United States. As discussed in Chapter 2, at the turn of the twenty-first century, many universities started launching initiatives to study their links with the Atlantic slave trade and slavery. During the last five years, university students, and especially black students, several of whom joined Black Lives Matter or at least sympathized with the movement, also protested the existence of markers named after slave merchants and pro-slavery individuals in university campuses. Charleston's terrorist attack impacted these debates. At Yale University, students, faculty, staff, and alumni started once again to demand the institution change the name of Calhoun College, named after John C. Calhoun, the infamous pro-slavery South Carolina politician and vice-president of the United States who graduated from the university in 1804. The pressure produced initial results. On August 29, 2015, during his address to the incoming class of 2019, Yale University president, Peter

Salovey, decried Charleston's tragedy. By acknowledging that one of the university's colleges was named after the notorious white supremacist who defended slavery, Salovey called the community to debate the issue. As the new academic year began, students organized protests denouncing long-lasting racist practices in the university, described by the protesters as an unwelcome environment for black and minority students, faculty, and staff.[91] In April 2016, Salovey declared the university's intention to examine Calhoun's legacy and develop initiatives to encourage diversity. Yet the announcement also stated that Calhoun College's name would be preserved: "More than a decision about a name, we must focus on understanding the past and present, and preparing our students for the future."[92]

While demonstrations for the removal of Confederate monuments spread all over the country, Yale University's students continued protesting. Pressed by the demonstrations, Salovey appointed a Committee to Establish Principles on Renaming, in August 2016, to determine standards for renaming university buildings. Along with community leaders and nonprofit organizations, students formed the Change the Name Coalition. After numerous rallies, including occasions when students were arrested by the police, on February 11, 2017, Yale University president announced that Calhoun College would be renamed to honor Grace Murray Hopper (1906–1992), a computer scientist and US Navy rear admiral and alumna.[93]

Outside university campuses in other northern cities of the United States, a variety of black citizens and activists also demanded the renaming of buildings associated with the Atlantic slave trade. By the middle of the eighteenth century, Boston had 16,000 inhabitants, of which nearly 10 percent were bondspeople.[94] Enslaved men worked on a variety of tasks associated with the city's mercantile economy, including shipbuilding, blacksmithing, coopering, and printing. Most enslaved women performed domestic work, even though in some rich households enslaved men were also coachmen and butlers. Slaves could work directly for their owners, but some owners hired out their human property, and in some cases allowed them to hire themselves out.[95]

Peter Faneuil (1700–1743) was probably Boston's richest merchant and slave trader, the son of a French Huguenot (Protestant) couple who fled Catholic France to escape religious persecution and settled in New Rochelle, New York.[96] After the death of his parents, Faneuil and his siblings moved to Boston to live with his uncle Andrew Faneuil, a wealthy merchant, landowner, local slave trader, and owner of Boston's Merchant Row where he bought and sold enslaved people. Faneuil inherited a large part of his uncle's assets and participated in the Atlantic slave trade through the commerce of tobacco, produce, rum, molasses, and fish, as well enslaved Africans. He owned at least one slave ship, the *Jolly Batchelor*, which on November 23, 1741, sailed from Boston to Sierra Leone. On August 15, 1743, after Faneuil's death, the slave ship disembarked twenty enslaved individuals in Newport, Rhode Island.[97]

To respond to its great trading activity, Boston opened a public market in 1733 at Dock Square, but four years later a mob opposed to trade regulation destroyed the facility. In 1740, Faneuil offered to pay for the construction of a new hall market in the same location where the previous market was located.[98] The town accepted the offer and voted in favor with the declaration, "in testimony of the town's gratitude to Peter Faneuil, Esq. and to perpetuate his memory, that the Hall over the Market place, be named Faneuil Hall, and all times hereafter, be called and known by that name."[99]

Unveiled in 1742, Faneuil Hall functioned as a marketplace and meeting hall, and quickly became one of the most important of Boston's landmarks (Figure 3.3). Over more than two centuries of its existence, the building has been the stage of several important events associated with the history of the United States. When Samuel Adams (1722–1803) was invested as president of the United States, a banquet celebrating him was held at Faneuil Hall, and later the site was also the place where William Lloyd Garrison (1805–1879) delivered passionate speeches demanding the end of slavery.[100] Although Faneuil's connections with the Atlantic slave trade are well documented, until recently the iconic building carrying his name has been remembered as a "cradle of liberty."[101] But Charleston's tragedy and the movement to take down Confederate monuments have impacted the city of Boston, where 25 percent of its overall population (estimated at 694,583) identifies as black or African American.[102]

FIGURE 3.3 *Faneuil Hall, Boston, Massachusetts, United States. Photograph by Robert Linsdell, 2013/cc-by-2.0.*

Faneuil's connections with the infamous trade were never a secret, especially for those who take the guided tours of the building provided by the rangers of the National Park Service. Likewise, on August 23, 2015, the National Park Service and the Museum of African American History commemorated the Day of Remembrance of the Middle Passage and its Abolition that acknowledged the role of Boston in the Atlantic slave trade.[103] Still, the city historically failed to make any significant effort to bring to light its connections with the slave trade and slavery. This erasure, combined with the racial tensions that emerged all over the country during the wave of protests to take down Confederate monuments, led Boston's concerned black residents to occupy the public space in unified demand, calling for the city to rename Faneuil Hall and to acknowledge the building's links with the history of the slave trade. In August 2017, the New Democracy Coalition, led by Kevin C. Peterson, challenged the city to officially change the name of the building. In a public statement, the Mayor of Boston Marty Walsh responded negatively to the request, arguing that instead of renaming he preferred to add more information about Faneuil's past to the site.[104]

But the movement to rechristen Faneuil Hall persisted. Peterson called for a boycott of the building in August 2018, along with other actions including a picket line and a sit-in.[105] Meanwhile, African American artist Steve Locke proposed the construction of a memorial consisting of a bronze plate representing an auction block embossed with the map of the Atlantic slave trade. The memorial proposal was supported by Boston's mayor, but the New Democracy Coalition criticized the project and accused the artist of undermining the demands to rename the building, as according to the group no black leader has requested a memorial.[106] On November 10, 2018, as part of a larger demonstration against racism in Boston, Peterson and other activists reenacted a slave auction at the entrance of Faneuil Hall: "I would like the community to understand that slavery was a reality in Boston, and I would like the community to connect the fact that what happened in the 1740s, in terms of the denigration of black people, continues into 2018."[107] As debates on Faneuil Hall persisted, the National Association for the Advancement of Colored People (NAACP) Boston Branch eventually opposed the project by arguing that the community had not "been given enough of a voice in the selection of the location and proposal." Reacting to this position, Locke decided to withdraw his proposal of a slave memorial on July 16, 2019.[108] In an op-ed justifying his decision, he stated that the purpose of his project "has been mischaracterized and maligned by people who have other agendas."[109] Like in other cities involved in the Atlantic slave trade where the battles of public memory are in play, the calls for renaming of Faneuil Hall are deeply associated with how over the last two centuries the tentacles of white supremacy spread throughout the urban fabric by making Boston's black population invisible, while perpetuating long-lasting racial inequalities.

Public Memory in Black and White

This chapter shows how public memory of slavery is a specific modality of memory carried out by living groups who fight to occupy the public space and have their political views prevail. Like collective memory, public memory of slavery is racialized and gendered, and fueled by the structures of white supremacy. In the second half of the twentieth century, especially after the end of the Cold War, Britain and the United States became the ground of continuous fights between racialized groups with opposing views about the Atlantic slave trade and slavery. Either in Britain or in the United States, the battles to make these atrocities visible in the public spaces of port cities such as Bristol, Liverpool, Charleston, and Boston cannot be dissociated from the ways white supremacy has operated on both sides of the Atlantic Ocean. Despite different contexts, many decades after the end of the slave trade and slavery, former slave ports continued to actively promote the memory of slave merchants, slaveholders, and pro-slavery social actors as benefactors and philanthropists by maintaining multiple tangible markers paying homage to them. But this hegemonic perspective never remained unchallenged. Black activists and other racially oppressed groups, along with white allies, have led various kinds of actions to oppose the public memory of pro-slavery historical actors. Individually represented or organized in associations and coalitions, these citizens use a variety of strategies such as demonstrations, performances, and works of art to bring to light the history of the Atlantic slave trade and slavery. By contesting the public memory of slave merchants, slave owners, and white supremacists, these social actors denounce the persisting structures that maintain black individuals and other minorities economically and socially excluded in former slave societies and societies that participated in the inhuman trade. Their fight shows, to the degree that racism and white supremacy remain alive, the painful past of slavery is doomed to echo in the present, thus propelling the battles of public memory of slavery to endure.

4

Setting Slavery in the Museum

Battles of public memory are always in progress, but from time to time, groups or associations with concerted political agendas obtain enough support to officially validate their views in the public space. Endorsed by legislative bodies such as town councils, state assemblies, national congresses and parliaments, or federal governments they succeed in making their claims recognized by eventually leading to the establishment of official dates, holidays, institutions, and programs, as well as the creation of monuments, memorials, and museums commemorating slavery and the Atlantic slave trade. Yet, although general international trends influence local contexts, making sure the memory of slavery is officially recognized through permanent initiatives always depends on complex dynamics involving diverse groups at the municipal, state, and national levels. However, even after reaching a more permanent status through formal recognition, these initiatives are not forever set in stone. As time passes and the waves of public memory battles continue evolving, monuments can be removed, holidays cancelled, museum exhibitions dismantled.

How is the memory of slavery officially incorporated into the public space? In this chapter, I explore how national, state, and municipal governments as well as institutions have embraced demands of social actors to recognize slavery as a human atrocity that contributed to build and enrich societies in Europe, Africa, and the Americas. With the purpose of introducing the reader to the problem of official memory of slavery, the chapter examines case studies in which slavery was incorporated into formal initiatives carried out by recognized institutions. I explain how official memory of slavery shares the public and private spheres with other modes of memory. First, I discuss how slavery and the Atlantic slave trade were memorialized through commemoration activities, the preservation of heritage sites, and the creation of monuments and memorials in France and England. Second, I explore the development of permanent exhibitions and museums dedicated in part or entirely to address the problem of slavery in England, at the International Slavery Museum in Liverpool; in France, at the Nantes History Museum (Musée d'histoire de Nantes) and the Museum of Aquitaine (Musée d'Aquitaine); and in the United States, at the National Museum of African American History and Culture, in Washington DC. I insist that the official memory of slavery is shaped by other modalities of memory (collective, cultural, and public) but in various nations it also depends on government involvement in publicly and privately funded initiatives. Therefore, although official, these memories are not static and are affected by national, regional, and international contexts. They remain dynamic like the societies from where they emerge.

Slavery in Two French Museums

Like other European nations, until the late 1980s, France resisted giving any kind of recognition to slavery and the Atlantic slave trade as part of its past. In 1935, this refusal was already visible during the celebration of the three hundredth anniversary of the annexation of the French West Indies and French Guiana to France, a commemoration intended to highlight and convince the colonial populations of the benefits of French colonization.[1] In 1948, the commemoration activities of the centenary of the French abolition of slavery continued to perpetuate the myth of Victor Schoelcher (1804–1893) as the great emancipator. Although timid in scope, the centennial commemoration included the participation of black intellectuals and politicians from French Guiana, French West Indies, and Senegal, such as Gaston Monnerville (1897–1991), Aimé Césaire (1913–2008), and Léopold Sedar Senghor (1906–2001). Invited to give lectures at Sorbonne University on April 27, 1948, the trio emphasized the horrors of slavery and its persisting legacies, although within the context of praising Schoelcher.[2] In the years that followed, Césaire became a central actor in interpreting France's relation with its past associated with slavery. When France commemorated the bicentennial of the French Revolution in 1989, official initiatives continued omitting the fact that the French Revolution did not extend to its colonies its principles of *égalité, fraternité*, and *liberté*.[3] On February 4, 1794, although the Convention passed the end of slavery, France failed to implement it, a context that in 1802 allowed Napoléon Bonaparte to reinstate slavery in the French colonies.

Christine Chivallon has argued that unlike British ports such as Bristol, where memory of slavery emerged in the early 1990s, during this period France continued developing a self-celebratory narrative of the nation that concealed slavery to highlight and celebrate abolition. But one initiative held in Nantes, France's largest slave port, was probably an exception to this general trend. In 1992, on the eve of the commemoration of the quadricentennial of the arrival of Columbus in the Americas, there were growing public debates associated with the role of Africa and enslaved Africans in the construction of the New World, a dimension embraced by UNESCO in 1994, when the institution launched the Slave Route Project. Nantes, France's largest slave port, was the first French city to lead initiatives to make the country's slave past visible in the public space. In 1991, the lawyer and unionist Yvon Chotard, who is categorized as white, created the working group Nantes-Africa-Americas (Nantes-Afrique-Amériques) aimed at studying the history of this French port and its connections with the Atlantic slave trade. Based on this initial work, Chotard's group created the association Shackles of Memory (*Anneaux de la mémoire*). Gathering many members, the organization aimed at contributing to the elaboration of a homonymous exhibition. Meanwhile black social actors joined other groups that carried sometimes opposing views. With the support of the city council that worked in close collaboration with the association and other committed citizens, the Nantes History Museum conceived the show *Shackles of Memory* that was presented at the Castle of the Dukes of Britanny (Château des ducs de Bretagne) from December 5, 1992, to February 4, 1994.[4]

Shackles of Memory was the first international exhibition focusing on the Atlantic slave trade held in Europe, attracting at least 300,000 visitors. The exhibition, displaying four hundred objects, briefly contextualized the history of Africa by showcasing various artifacts held in French collections.[5] The show not only described the dynamics of the Atlantic slave trade, the terrible conditions of transportation of enslaved Africans, the dreadful working environment in the plantations in the Americas, but additionally explained how Nantes made profits from slave-trading activities.[6] *Shackles of Memory* also presented innovative elements such as the recreation of a slave ship's hold. While attempting to provide an accurate historical account and balancing the use of figurative elements, the exhibition also sought to evoke emotions among the visitors.[7] Although held in Nantes, and not in Paris, the exhibition had a national and international impact and was largely covered by the media.[8] *Shackles of Memory* became a reference for a variety of black and white residents, activists, concerned citizens, and academics, helping foster further discussions on Nantes's slave-trading past and the need of national recognition of slavery and the Atlantic slave trade as part of French history.[9] But even though the black and white social actors who contributed to the exhibition *Shackles of Memory* continued pushing for the creation of a slavery museum, the city refused this proposal.

In 1998, the sesquicentennial of the abolition of slavery whose slogan was "All born in 1848" (*Tous nés en 1848*) emphasized abolition as the genesis of the French Republic, reinforcing an existing trend that presented France as the nation that promoted liberty, while at the same time concealing its long history of slavery and participation in the Atlantic slave trade.[10] Yet by the time of the commemoration French black social actors mobilized to denounce this persistent silence. Together they created the

Committee of May 23, 1998 (CM98), and along with other groups such as the Committee of the Daughters and Sons of Deported Africans (COFFAD), and Collectif-DOM, gathering French citizens from the DOM (French Overseas Departments), they organized a march gathering 40,000 men and women, who identified themselves as "descendants of slaves" to protest the commemoration activities surrounding abolition by simultaneously claiming the memory of bondspeople.[11]

Black activism and debates surrounding the reemergence of the memory of slavery in France led to the passing of legislation officially recognizing slavery as part of French history. In 1999, Deputy Christiane Taubira, representing French Guiana and who is racialized as black, introduced a bill recognizing the transatlantic slave trade and slavery as a crime against humanity, which the senate eventually adopted on May 10, 2001 (Law number 1297). The new "Taubira Law" also included provisions for the creation of a committee to establish the guidelines to commemorate and promote the memory of slavery in France. On January 5, 2004, an official decree established the Committee for the Memory of Slavery. The committee presided by Maryse Condé, officially launched in April 2004, included other intellectuals such as François Vergès as well as academics like Nelly Schmidt and Marcel Dorigny. On April 12, 2005, the committee's first report established as a goal "making the shared memory of slavery an integral part of the national memory."[12] Other recommendations included the development of teaching methodologies for the history of slavery, further research in the field, and as briefly discussed in Chapter 2, the creation of a National Center for the History and the Memory of the Slave Trade, Slavery, and Its Abolition.[13] The committee also proposed the development of an inventory of the objects related to the slave trade present in the national and regional collections. These initiatives were justified by the need to break France's silence regarding its involvement in slavery and the slave trade. According to the committee, although the "singular and collective memories of slavery orally survived through myths, tales, and rites, this irreplaceable memory started to be explored and reconstituted just about twenty years ago."[14] In this same report, the committee ended by proposing May 10, the date of passage of the Taubira Law, to be the official national day of commemoration of the abolition of slavery in metropolitan France. In 2006, the National Day of Memories of the Slave Trade, Slavery and Their Abolition was commemorated in metropolitan France for the first time. Earlier, in 2005, a bill regarding the recognition of the nation and national contribution in favor of French repatriates was introduced in the French Parliament. The bill included a controversial article stating that French school curricula should recognize the positive role of the French that faced fierce opposition by associations as well as academics and intellectuals.

French President Jacques Chirac (1932–2019) repealed the polemic article four of the Law no. 2005–158, but the wounds of slavery and the French colonial past remained exposed. In October 2005, Zyed Benna and

Bouna Traoré, two teenage residents of Clichy-sous-Bois, a Paris suburb, died by electrocution when escaping police persecution. The case brought to light again how the social and economic exclusion of younger generations of immigrant descendants from the old French colonies remained alive in the continuous and persistent state of social exclusion, fueling an insurrection in the suburbs of several French cities. Like the British experience in the 1980s, the insurrections in neighborhoods with predominantly black and other minority residents exposed endemic racism and racial inequalities affecting immigrants and their descendants in France, debates that could not be dissociated from the discussion about the country's past marked by slavery, slave trade, and colonialism.

Despite the Taubira Law, either in Paris or in former slave ports such as Nantes and Bordeaux, black groups also demanded the construction of tangible markers acknowledging the country's history of slavery, slave trade, and colonialism. In response to these demands, on May 10, 2007, the city of Paris unveiled at the Jardin du Luxembourg the monument *Le cri, L'écrit* (The Cry, Writing) (Figure 4.1), a twelve-feet-high bronze sculpture by French artist Fabrice Hyber, who is characterized as white. This artwork represents a broken chain composed of broken rings. One side of the sculpture reveals a network of red and green lines painted on a white background, evoking tree branches like the real ones surrounding the artwork. Although not including names, Hyber embraces the use of the written word in his work. The surface of the other unpainted side of the bronze sculpture reveals engraved words such as *libre* (free), *mort* (death), *inhumain* (inhuman), and *souvenir* (remembrance).

The enactment of the Taubira Law was a major step to officially recognize the memory of slavery in France. But as bearers of national narratives, museums also became central spaces to address this difficult and usually avoided dimension of the country's past. However, this slave-trading and pro-slavery past was not addressed in national museums in the French capital but was rather restricted to the museums of history located in its main former slave ports, Nantes and Bordeaux. In 2004, the Nantes History Museum, which in the previous decade had led a successful experience with the exhibition *Shackles of Memory*, started planning a permanent exhibition exploring the city's slave-trading history.

The permanent exhibitions of the Nantes History Museum are housed in the site of Château des ducs de Bretagne, an opulent castle, whose construction dates to the fifteenth century. The museum that welcomed nearly 56,463 visitors in 2017 also includes an adjacent building, hosting temporary exhibitions.[15] In 1915, the French state sold the castle to the city of Nantes which, in turn, transformed it into a city history museum in 1924. Its collections derive from six different museums that over the twentieth century closed their doors. Following the exhibition *Shackles of Memory*, the museum underwent renovation works for nearly fifteen years. During this period, with the aim of filling the gaps of the main major sequences

FIGURE 4.1 Le cri, L'écrit *(The Cry, Writing), bronze sculpture by Fabrice Hyber. Jardin du Luxembourg, Paris, France. Photograph by Ana Lucia Araujo, 2017.*

proposed in its exhibitions, the museum launched an ambitious acquisition plan, increasing its collections nearly 25 percent. Today, the Nantes History Museum houses nearly 32,000 items, of which more than 1,150 are on display. Most objects in its collections were obtained from private collectors, including local families with a documented history of involvement in the slave trade. In 2016, the museum opened new rooms, with new themes, and three hundred additional objects.

Housed in the castle main building, the permanent exhibitions of the Nantes History Museum provide an account of the history of Nantes from its origins to the present as well as an overview of the castle's history, whose imposing architecture also orient the ways the various displays are presented to the public. The exhibitions are organized into seven major sequences that follow thematic and chronological order. Visitors are expected to cover the thirty rooms in three hours, but the museum also suggests a briefer ninety-minute visit covering only sixteen rooms and other shorter visits covering specific themes and periods. For example, the museum's printed guide suggests itineraries of forty-five or ninety minutes to cover the theme "Slave Trade and Slavery." Yet the most logical way to visit the permanent exhibition focusing on Nantes's slave-trading past is to follow the long itinerary throughout the castle that requires visitors more time walking and stair climbing.

The first proposed sequence "The Castle, Nantes, and Brittany until the Seventh Century," distributed in six rooms, retraces the history of Nantes, which from its inception has been referred to as a "merchant city." The second track "Daughter of the River and the Ocean" is spread into four rooms and represents Nantes as a woman, first as "a city of estuary," then as a "siren city," and then as an "open city." Eventually the third proposed path "The Business and the Black Gold in the Eighteenth Century," exhibited throughout seven rooms, explores the role of the Atlantic slave trade in building Nantes's wealth. Other sequences cover Nantes and the French Revolution, Nantes as "A Colonial and Industrial Port (1815–1914)," Nantes during the two great wars, and Nantes as an Atlantic city today and tomorrow.

Although Nantes's involvement in the slave trade is discussed in the third sequence (composed of seven rooms), the topic is also addressed in the thematic track spread across twelve rooms of the first three sequences that visitors can identify, thanks to the signs displaying the image of a shackle that reads "thematic itinerary: the slave trade and slavery." A printed calico produced in 1795 at the Petitpierre Frères et Cie (a Nantes's factory of textiles) is one of the first selected objects of this thematic path. The label explaining the printed motifs on the piece of cloth explains that "the slave trade favored their development, as certain printed calico fabrics were used as currency along the African coasts, whereas others were sold to the European colonizers established in the West Indies or decorated refined French interiors."[16] Calling attention to "Neptune or the Sea's Empire" as the main theme of the printed motif, the description emphasizes that other elements of the cloth's design evoke Nantes's colonial vocation. However, the label fails to mention one of the central images printed on the cloth that clearly portrays a conflictual scene whose protagonists are bondspeople. Surrounding a palm tree are three enslaved persons. On the left side is an enslaved woman who, while carrying her baby on her back, is kneeling in a supplicant position (perhaps demanding to purchase her freedom) before a white colonizer dressed in European attire and holding a bag and a written document. On the right side of the palm tree, one enslaved man is holding another bondsman who seems to be attempting to intervene in the scene.

The first room of the third sequence "The Business and the Black Gold in the Eighteenth Century" tells the history of Nantes's slave trade by using various displays with artifacts, paintings, and replicas of slave ships, as well as textual panels that focus on Nantes's maritime history, especially shipbuilding. Barely visible, references to slavery and enslaved individuals appear in two paintings by Pierre-Bernard Morlot (1716–1784). Dated 1753, the paintings portraying the wealthy Nantes's merchant and shipowner (who occasionally traded in slaves) Dominique-René Deurbroucq (1715–1782) and his wife Marguerite-Urbane Deurbroucq (1715–1784) were commissioned to celebrate the couple's ten-year marriage anniversary. The first portrait depicts the Nantes's merchant as a distinguished businessman working at his desk. The background, filled by an opulent red curtain and a large collection of books, features an enslaved boy, elegantly dressed and wearing a silver necklace. The second oil painting portrays Marguerite-Urbane Deurbroucq in a lavish embroidered silk dress and comfortably seated. On a table next to her lies a cup of hot chocolate, a rare and expensive commodity derived from cocoa produced by enslaved people in the Americas. The wealthy lady is attended by an enslaved woman, wearing a white dress, a headscarf, earrings, and a pearl necklace, and holding a tray with a bowl and sugar cubes, also produced by slaves in the French West Indies. Likewise, a gray parrot, a bird native to equatorial Africa, perched on the left side of the armchair's backrest, suggests the tropical environment where the Deurbroucqs conducted their trading activities. Despite the presence of the two enslaved persons in these imposing portraits, the labels accompanying the paintings say very little about these two coadjutant characters. Yet an additional glass vitrine displays several artifacts associated with the production and consumption of sugar, described as a "luxury product from the colonies." Among the objects showcased are a sugar axe, a sugar hammer, and pottery articles. Other items exhibited in this section include maps, visual images describing the living and working conditions in the plantations of French West Indies, *manillas* (horseshoe-shaped bracelets), glass beads, fire guns, and other articles that were exchanged for slaves during the era of the Atlantic slave trade. The section also incorporates a replica of the Nantes's slave ship Aurore as well as a scale model of La Solitude, a Saint-Domingue's sugar plantation owned by Jérôme Maré (1702–1760). The maquette is placed on a platform (Figure 4.2) surrounded by a structure made of wooden beams, once again conjuring the slave ship, through which viewers can see the rest of the room. On one side of the wooden beam structure, a video screen projects an animation using nineteenth-century engravings portraying enslaved people working and being punished. On the other side, a large reproduction of the photograph *Negro Bozales, Zaracunde* (taken at Villa

FIGURE 4.2 *Replica of La Solitude, Saint Domingue's sugar plantation and* Negro Bozales, Zaracunde, *photograph by Charles Fréger. Permanent exhibition, Nantes History Museum, Nantes, France. Photograph by Ana Lucia Araujo, 2019. Courtesy: Nantes History Museum.*

de los Santos, Los Santos, Panama) by French photographer Charles Fréger (who is identified as white) evokes the term *bozal* given to enslaved men and women born in Africa and who were said to be more inclined to resist slavery. The portrait represents a black man wearing a straw costume and a mask with a muzzle that was used to punish enslaved individuals. By using this portrait to establish a dialogue with the plantation's maquette and the nineteenth-century images, the exhibition highlights how memory of resistance against bondage remains alive today in societies where slavery existed.

In different displays of "The Business and the Black Gold in the Eighteenth Century" the experience of bondspeople is associated with physical punishment and rarely with rebellion and agency. Wood-covered walls simulating a slave ship characterize one of the rooms of the segment "A Slave-Trading Capital." One wall showcases an eighteenth-century iron neck shackle, used to punish enslaved people who attempted to escape. The label next to the artifact explains that "neck shackles like this one were probably worn by 'maroon' slaves, name given to those who attempted escaping." The description is not entirely accurate. Although "petit marronage" often referred to enslaved who escaped for short periods of time and returned to the plantations, the term "grand marronage" describes the activity of slaves who ran away and, along with other fugitive slaves, formed independent communities. Next to the neck shackle, on the left, a glass vitrine exhibits "a slave presenting a tray of cigars." This cigar tray in the form of a bare-chested slave, an object from the former Salorges Museum, reinforces the idea of accommodation as opposed to rebellion and can hardly relate to the vitrine's title "Showing One's Social Success." However, displayed on the right side of the iron necklace is another photograph by Charles Fréger. The staged photograph portrays *Neg Gwo Siwo*, a character of Martinique carnival, whose body is covered with molasses produced from a mixture of syrup and soot. *Neg Gwo Siwo* is a small reproduction of one of the several photographs in Fréger's temporary exhibition *Cimarron*. This show, comprising photographs that explore masquerades practiced in the Americas by the descendants of enslaved Africans, was presented in the Nantes History Museum's exhibition building from February 2 to April 14, 2019. During this period, six of these photographs, reproduced in smaller sizes, were also displayed throughout the permanent exhibition on slavery and the slave trade, interrogating the artifacts held in the museum's collection.

The two rooms "In the Homes of the Trade's Gentlemen" and the other two rooms "The City of Traders" exhibit a variety of eighteenth-century objects found in the homes of Nantes's slave merchants including silverware, tea sets, Chinese porcelain teapots, jars, plates, vases, and sculptures, as well as mahogany furniture. Also, on display are primary documents, paintings, and additional artifacts attesting to Nantes's participation in the Atlantic slave trade. If all these eighteenth-century artifacts that once belonged to the families of colonial merchants and slave traders tell the history of the infamous commerce from the point of view of Nantes's slave-trading elites, the fourth proposed sequence, "Nantes and the Revolution," housed in one single room, briefly presents slave resistance through one single display consisting of three artworks focusing on the Saint-Domingue Revolution. But again, the scope is limited. Three images are displayed on the wall: a reproduction of the eighteenth-century engraving *View of the 40 Days of Fire of the Plain's Houses at Cap-Français* (Vue des 40 jours d'incendie des habitations de la plaine du Cap Français), a portrait of Toussaint Louverture, and another contemporary photograph by Charles Fréger portraying the leader of the revolution, Jean-Jacques Dessalines (1758–1806). In addition, a glass vitrine features documents and one painting depicting a young enslaved man. Loyal to its collection of eighteenth-century artifacts and primary documents, the Nantes History Museum was successful in incorporating an accurate account of the Atlantic slave trade and slavery in the city's official history. But as argued by Renaud Hourcade, by leaving out the perspective of enslaved subjects and by not engaging with any dimensions of present-day legacies of slavery, especially racism, the permanent exhibition only makes official the memory of Nantes's slave-trading social actors, failing to establish a dialogue with the city's black community whose ancestors were enslaved.[17] This overemphasis on the city's slave-trading elites represented in all sections of the slavery exhibition tends to reinforce a narrative where white supremacy not only remains unchallenged but is also reinforced. Although problematic, this approach is not crystallized. The introduction of contemporary artworks in the permanent exhibition destabilizes the official view centered around Nantes's traders and slave merchants by temporarily adding to it the missing dimension of the experience of enslaved people and their descendants.

Nantes History Museum's exhibition does not stand alone. In 2012, the municipality of Nantes unveiled the Memorial to the Abolition of Slavery (Figure 4.3), which to this day is the only French memorial to the Atlantic slave

FIGURE 4.3 *Memorial to the Abolition of Slavery (Mémorial de l'abolition de l'esclavage), interior. Nantes, France. Photograph by Ana Lucia Araujo, 2019.*

trade. The idea of erecting a memorial dated back to the commemoration of the sesquicentennial of the French abolition of slavery in 1998. Sponsored by the city of Nantes, Mémoire de l'Outre-Mer (Overseas Memory), an association created in 1989 with the goal of memorializing slavery and its abolitions and of promoting world and overseas cultures, along with several other groups, embraced the mission of organizing a series of activities. Seeking a public impact, Mémoire de l'Outre-Mer commissioned the young artist Liza Marcault-Dérouard for the creation of a statue representing an enslaved person breaking chains attached to her wrists. Titled *Délivrance* (Deliverance), the ephemeral sculpture made of concrete iron and cement was unveiled during a ceremony held at the Quai de la Fosse on April 27, 1998. But a few days later, the statue was vandalized.[18] The act of vandalism generated outrage among politicians and members of local black associations.[19] Whereas the statue was relocated at the Nantes History Museum where it remains on display, the various organizations gradually agreed on the need of creating a permanent memorial to commemorate the Atlantic slave trade.

Conceived by the artist Krzysztof Wodiczko and the architect Julien Bonder, both identified as white and based in the United States, the memorial is an extension of other initiatives that bring Nantes's slave-trading past to the public space in a permanent fashion.[20] Located at Quai de la Fosse, on the bank of the Loire River, near the location where the slave ships were anchored during the era of the Atlantic slave trade, and facing the luxurious buildings that once served as residences of Nantes's shipowners, the memorial occupies an area of 23,000 square feet. Horizontally oriented, the structure consists of two parts. The first is a promenade along the river on which 1710 small glass plaques display the names of the slave vessels and the dates of slave voyages that departed from Nantes, whereas 290 plaques indicated the names of slave ports in Africa, West Indies, the mainland Americas, and the Indian Ocean. Two sets of stairs allow the visitors to access an underground passage where the Universal Declaration of Human Rights as well as the word "freedom" in forty-seven languages of the present-day countries that participated in the slave trade are featured. Along one side of the underground cement corridor, glass panels display images, maps, and several quotes from laws, literary works, and especially abolitionist texts mainly authored by male historical actors. At times replicating the confined space of a slave ship, while engaging with this cacophonic "archive of slavery," when looking at the other side of the underground cement structure, visitors can see the river and listen to the noise of its waves.[21]

In the heart of the city, the Memorial to the Abolition of Slavery is totally integrated to Nantes's urban landscape. The format and distribution of its glass plaques displaying the names of the slave ships that departed from Nantes greatly evoke the concept of *Stolperstein* (examined in Chapter 2). The plaques can rarely go unnoticed for everyday joggers, tourists, schoolchildren, and passersby who walk along the memorial promenade.

Along the way attentive observers can read the lovable names given to the slave ships (*La Reine*, *La Princesse d'Angola*, *Les Deux Amis*, and others) that departed from Nantes to procure tropical commodities in the French West Indies and to purchase enslaved men, women, and children along the West African and West Central African coasts. Here, however, unlike the original *Stolperstein* and other conventional walls of names created to honor victims of wars and atrocities such as the Vietnam War in Washington DC and the Shoah Memorial in Paris, instead of paying homage to the enslaved victims by naming and humanizing them, the creators of the memorial honored the vehicles that transported them through the Atlantic Ocean into slavery in the Americas. Reverberating the permanent exhibition of the Nantes History Museum, the approach developed in the memorial is intimately linked to the city's maritime history but not focused on the experience of the victims of the Atlantic slave trade.[22] Despite this approach that emphasizes the abolition of slavery through the display of the slave ships' names instead of highlighting the names of the victimized enslaved Africans, Nantes made consistent choices for the development of its official memory of slavery and the Atlantic slave trade.

Bordeaux was the second largest slave port in France. During the era of the Atlantic slave trade the city launched 437 slave voyages that transported to the Americas approximately 135,000 enslaved Africans. Like Nantes, during the 1990s Bordeaux started to gradually incorporate the history of slavery and the Atlantic slave trade in its Museum of Aquitaine. Unveiled in 1962, this city museum covers multiple dimensions of the history of Bordeaux region from prehistory to the present. In 1981, the institution addressed for the first time the role of Bordeaux in the Atlantic slave trade in the temporary exhibition *Bordeaux, Rum, and the West Indies* (Bordeaux, le Rhum et les Antilles). But despite this first attempt, its permanent exhibition dedicated only two vitrines to the city's maritime history and slave-trading activities were barely represented.[23]

In the 1990s, this context started changing. The publication of a history monograph in 1995, exploring the city's involvement in the Atlantic slave trade, gained attention from the local press contributing to highlight Bordeaux's slave past in the public sphere.[24] On the eve of the commemoration activities of the sesquicentennial of the France's abolition of slavery, the rise of new black organizations around the country encouraged the emergence of black activism in Bordeaux. In 1998, black university students created the association Diverscités with the aim of making the city's slave past visible in the public space. In addition, a major donation to the Museum of Aquitaine motivated the inclusion of slavery in the official historical narrative provided by the institution. In 1999, Marcel Chatillon (1925–2003), a white French surgeon who made his career in French Guiana and Guadeloupe where he became a collector of West Indian artifacts and artworks, donated his collection to the Museum of Aquitaine. The gift included six hundred maps, paintings, engravings, drawings, and artifacts mainly associated with the history of the French West Indies and its connections with the African continent during the eighteenth and nineteenth centuries.[25] Between September 23, 1999, and January 16, 2000, part of the collection was presented for the first time at the museum as part of the temporary exhibition *Look at the West Indies* (Regard sur les Antilles) curated by Hélène Lafont-Couturier, the museum's director at the time. Although the public memory of slavery was gradually emerging in France during this period, and despite the importance of the collection's objects and artworks for telling the history of slavery in the French West Indies, the show failed to critically discuss how Bordeaux participated in the Atlantic slave trade, how the city benefited from slavery in the Caribbean, and how the present legacies of these atrocities remain alive.[26]

In the next decade, this context continued to evolve. By 2005, the Museum of Aquitaine started discussing the renovation of its exhibitions covering the eighteenth and the nineteenth centuries. Haiti gave to the city of Bordeaux a bust of Toussaint Louverture (1743–1803) in 2005, which was placed at the Square Toussaint Louverture, across the Botanic Garden, at Quai de Queyries. On May 10, 2006, when Bordeaux celebrated the National Day of Memories of the Slave Trade, Slavery and Their Abolition for the first time, Mayor Hugues Martin unveiled at Quai des Chartrons a small bronze plaque acknowledging the role of Bordeaux in the Atlantic slave trade. As explained by Renaud Hourcade, the inclusion of Bordeaux's history of slavery in the Museum of Aquitaine's permanent exhibition was partly inspired by the development of the International Slavery Museum of Liverpool. Yet as organized groups such as the association DiversCités demanded the construction of a slave trade memorial, the museum exhibition could be conceived as a viable political alternative to avoid these requests.[27]

Eventually, on May 10, 2009, the Museum of Aquitaine opened its permanent exhibition on slavery and the Atlantic slave trade, curated by the museum's director François Hubert and Christian Block (assistant curator of modern collections), who are both identified as whites. The new exhibition space is oriented by the engravings from the Chatillon collection complemented by objects that help to elucidate the city's participation in the Atlantic slave trade, including elements of Bordeaux monumental architecture, artifacts reflecting the history of African and Pre-Columbian civilizations, objects that illustrate the contact between Europeans, Africans, and Native populations, in addition to maps, audiovisual elements, extracts of motion pictures, and numeric images to add "a more emotional dimension" to the exhibition.[28]

The new displays "Bordeaux in the Eighteenth Century: The Atlantic Trade and Slavery" (Bordeaux au XVIIIe siècle: Le commerce atlantique et l'esclavage) were incorporated into the museum's large permanent exhibition, which is organized chronologically starting in the prehistory, passing through the Antiquity, Middle Ages, until the present. The exhibit, spanning

2,500 square feet, is divided into four thematic rooms. The first room "A City of Stone, Standing Proud" (La fierté d'une ville de pierre) occupying an area of nearly 820 square feet explores the emergence of Bordeaux as an Atlantic port in the eighteenth century. Large red panels displaying texts in French, translated into English and Spanish, explain how the French colonies in the West Indies fueled the development of Bordeaux. Although mentioning commercial exchanges, sugar production, and Bordeaux's important industry, in the section's opening panel and the four following panels ("A Controlled and Structured Hinterland," "Town Planning and Monumental Architecture in the 18th Century," "Bordeaux, a Provincial Capital," "Bordeaux's Fortunes") the words "slave," "slavery" or the term "slave trade" are not mentioned and consequently no connections are established between the city's increasing wealth and the use of slave labor in the French colonies of the Americas. Despite this important omission, the sixth panel titled "Black Africans and Mixed Race People in Bordeaux" refers to 4,000 blacks and *gens de couleur* (free mixed-race individuals of African ancestry) who "come to Bordeaux in the eighteenth century. Most of them were domestic servants following their masters, slaves sent to learn a trade, and mixed-race children who come to finish their training." The ambiguous panel fails to explain that the presence of people of African descent in Bordeaux was not the result of voluntary migration but associated with slave ownership in metropolitan France and the West Indies. Such an omission reveals how France shapes its own version of white supremacy that, as argued by Crystal M. Fleming, is characterized by the "denial of race as an extant phenomenon" and "anti-communitarianism, which refers to the idea that French people should not emphasize their group membership in civil society."[29] Yet the room displays a consultable inventory of enslaved individuals as well as an eighteenth-century painting Portrait of Princess Rakoczi and Her Negro (*Portrait de la princesse Rakoczi et de son négrillon*) by Nicolas Largillière (1656–1746). However, both the inventory and the painting are not contextualized within the history of Bordeaux's slave-trading activities. Also featured in the room are mascarons, painted portraits of elite city's residents, and ornamental ironwork that witness the city's wealth in the eighteenth century. Further segments include a set of scales made in Bordeaux, barrels, and a large panel reproducing a ship's profile cross-section, whereas another section discusses demographic growth and the city's religious life. Overall, not a single section of the first room discusses Bordeaux's role in the Atlantic slave trade and slavery.

The opening panel of the second room of the permanent exhibition titled "Bordeaux: Gateway to the Ocean" (Bordeaux: porte océane) clearly mentions for the first time the city's involvement in the slave trade by stating that "the West Indian colonies' demands for slave labour incited the shipowners of Bordeaux to develop the 'triangular' slave trade." Yet it emphasizes that this "represented less than five percent of the city's colonial expeditions on average during the eighteenth century." Other panels

FIGURE 4.4 *Permanent exhibition, Museum of Aquitaine, Bordeaux, France. Photograph by Ana Lucia Araujo, 2019. Courtesy: Museum of Aquitaine.*

underline Bordeaux's direct trade with the West Indies, while additional displays showcase paintings, maps, trunks, and ship replicas. A section focusing on the West Indies before the arrival of the Europeans displays pre-Colombian ceremonial artifacts from the nineteenth and twentieth centuries.[30] This room (Figure 4.4) also includes glass displays combining images from eighteenth-century travel accounts depicting the African continent as well as torture devices such as iron shackles and chains. The room also contains rifles and ammunition, which Europeans exchanged for enslaved Africans. To explain the dynamics of the Atlantic slave trade from a variety of points of view, glass panels and displays feature maps illustrating a range of slave trade routes, the names of slave ships, slave ships logbooks, extracts of slave narratives, and photographs of the late nineteenth century portraying enslaved individuals in Africa.

Also displayed in this section are two ritual objects (*bocio*) from the southern region of present-day Republic of Benin.[31] The introduction of these artifacts, described according to the European colonial vocabulary as "fetishes," may have been an unsuccessful attempt by the curators to provide an "African" point of view of the Atlantic slave trade.[32] One figure, wearing an iron necklace, is described as: "A fetish used in the Voodoo cult. The iron collar suggests that it was used in a cult linked to slavery."

In addition to referencing the Vodun religion in a derogatory manner, the label fails to explain how allusions to enslavement appeared in an object produced several decades after the end of the Atlantic slave trade. A second *bocio* is described as covered with "authentic and very old slave chains and adorned with two crocodile skulls" used to deliver mentally ill individuals from evil spirits who needed to be restrained in chains. Likewise, several other decontextualized objects from "French West Africa" or from the Democratic Republic of the Congo such as knives decorated with cowry shells, a carved tusk, and an Akan prestige stool are also displayed in vitrines. Not surprisingly, perpetuating the silences that shape white supremacy, these labels neither address the connections between the slave trade and European colonialism nor explain how these artifacts ended up in a French museum.[33]

The third room, "The Aquitanians' Eldorado" (L'Eldorado des Aquitains), largely based on the work of historian Jacques de Cauna, underscores the privileged economic, social, and cultural connections between Bordeaux and Saint-Domingue. This room is mostly illustrated with engravings and paintings from the Chatillon collection portraying the life in sugar plantations in the West Indies. One section includes a film, engravings, and terracotta sugar loaf molds to explain the process of sugar production. Another display features a maquette of the sugar plantation Nolivos in Croix-des-Bouquets in Saint-Domingue. Other vitrines showcase expensive furniture and bibelots representing enslaved people that decorated the homes of rich residents of Bordeaux. Finally, the fourth room "Heritages" (Héritages) briefly focuses on the abolition, slave revolts, and the present-day legacies of slavery. Through a small selection of objects conveying derogatory representations of black individuals, this segment fails to properly call attention to the evident racism of these depictions. Instead, the display problematizes racial mixture by using additional paintings and engravings from the Chatillon collection that portray the relations between whites and the enslaved, freed, and free population of the French West Indies. Eventually, the exhibition features a final panel largely inspired by a similar display of the International Slavery Museum in Liverpool.[34] The panel, occupying an entire wall, includes two video displays and a mosaic of black-and-white photographic portraits of black citizens of Bordeaux accompanied by various quotes underscoring the idea of racial and cultural mixture (*métissage*). In this last section of the permanent exhibition the city's heritage of slavery is characterized by harmonious cultural and racial relations. While avoiding the discussion about racism, this "happy conclusion" remains totally dissociated from the next segment of the museum's permanent exhibition exploring Bordeaux as a colonial port. In the end, despite shedding light on the long-standing involvement of Bordeaux and France in the slave trade and slavery, the Museum of Aquitaine fails to connect these atrocities with the rise of French colonialism, therefore never confronting white supremacy as a system that continues promoting the invisibility of black subjects in the city and in the overall country.

In 2017, 143,449 people visited the Museum of Aquitaine.[35] But the institution's representations of slavery are not immutable and have been contested in the public sphere. As recently as May 2019, a group of writers led by Anne-Marie Garat, who is identified as white, denounced the ambiguous language of the panel "Black Africans and Mixed Race People in Bordeaux" displayed in the first room "A City of Stone, Standing Proud." In a letter published in the newspaper *Le Monde* the group condemned the museum's word choice for suggesting that blacks voluntarily migrated to Bordeaux and for promoting a revisionist history of the city's slave-trading history.[36] The letter did not remain unanswered. A few days later, the museum director Laurent Védrine, who is characterized as white, responded to the letter in the same newspaper. He agreed to the need to update the exhibition and reported that the panel using ambiguous language had been removed from the permanent exhibition.[37] Using few textual references and many artifacts and artworks, the memory of the Atlantic slave trade and slavery made official in the Museum of Aquitaine remains that of Bordeaux's elites, and despite some concessions it only scarcely disrupts the narrative of white supremacy that associates the city's slave-trading activities with a glorious past. Still, as public memory of slavery is gradually legitimated as official memory, both in the museum and in Bordeaux's public space, the director's response to the *Le Monde*'s letter suggests a growing dynamic dialogue between the museum, black social actors, and academics, as other recent developments seem to confirm.

On May 11, 2019, one day after the National Day of Memories of the Slave Trade, Slavery and Their Abolition the city of Bordeaux inaugurated a statue (Figure 4.5) at the Quai des Chartrons, the same site where a small plaque was unveiled in 2006. The initiative resulted from the work of the Commission to Reflect on the Slave Trade and Slavery in Bordeaux established in 2016. Its final report, released in 2018, included ten recommendations, including the proposal to create a monument paying homage to Marthe Adélaïde Modeste Testas (1765–1870).[38] This choice was justified not only because Testas was an enslaved woman, but also because she was sold to the brothers and planters François Testas (1737–1795) and Pierre Testas (1756–1785), both from Bordeaux, and then sent into slavery to Saint-Domingue, the largest slave society under French domination during the colonial period, which later liberated itself through an insurrection led by enslaved people. Conceived by Haitian-born black sculptor Woodly Caymitte (alias Filipo), unlike the monument *Le Cri, L'écrit* or the abstract and imposing structure of the memorial unveiled in Nantes, this life-size bronze sculpture is a figurative representation of the body of an enslaved woman. In all her humanity, facing the Garonne River, with the imposing eighteenth-century buildings constructed with the wealth made by the slave trade stand as a background, Modeste is now part of Bordeaux's postcard view. In this context, official memory of slavery takes gendered contours, as to this day,

FIGURE 4.5 *Marthe Adélaïde Modeste Testas. Bronze sculpture by Woodly Caymitte (alias Filipo). Bordeaux, France. Photograph by Carole Lemée, 2019. Courtesy: Carole Lemmée.*

the statue is very likely the only official public monument paying homage to an enslaved woman unveiled in Europe.

The processes that led Bordeaux to officially start coming to terms with its active participation in the Atlantic slave trade continue evolving. On

December 2, 2019, the United Nations International Day for the Abolition of Slavery, the municipality unveiled a new sculpture commemorating Bordeaux's slave-trading past at the gardens of the City Hall. The sculpture was conceived by Sandrine Plante-Rougeol, a French artist whose father was born in the Reunion Island (a former colony and present-day region and overseas department of France), who identifies herself as a descendant of slaves. The monument represents a metal tree with three branches evoking the Atlantic slave trade, from where hang three wine barrel rings, elements that evoke Bordeaux's main colonial produce and the hold of slave ships. Within each of the metal rings, there are three metal sculptures representing men heads, "blindfolded to show their loss of identity, represent fear, pain and abandonment."[39] At the same occasion, resulting from enduring debates among citizens, politicians, local associations, and academics, the city of Bordeaux revealed new street name plaques for Rue Gramont, Passage Feger, and Rue Desse, which will replace the current signs whose names are associated with individuals involved in the Atlantic slave trade. Despite a recommendation to name various streets after enslaved persons and abolitionists who lived in Bordeaux, the Commission to Reflect on the Slave Trade and Slavery decided to not change the existing names, but rather to create new plaques providing a description of the participation of these wealthy men in the Atlantic slave trade. Each plaque also displays a bar code sending passersby to the website Memory of Slavery and the Slave Trade (Mémoire de l'esclavage et de la traite négrière), showing a map with a "memorial itinerary," a list of several associations involved in the process of memorializing slavery and the Atlantic slave trade in Bordeaux, as well as "portraits" of abolitionists, shipowners, slave traders, and black social actors who resided in the city.[40]

Slavery in the International Slavery Museum

As part of the process that led to the emergence of the public memory of slavery in Liverpool, as discussed in Chapter 3, the Merseyside Maritime Museum created the *Transatlantic Slavery Gallery* in 1994. The new gallery was conceived to specifically focus on the city's slave-trading activities, a dimension that during those years not only became part of international debates but also was recognized in official initiatives led by international institutions such as UNESCO. Also in 1994, UNESCO launched its Slave Route Project and only three years later made August 23 (the day marking the beginning of the Saint-Domingue slave rebellion that ended French colonial rule and abolished slavery in what became Haiti) the International Day of Remembrance of the Slave Trade and Its Abolition. Starting in 1999, every August 23, Liverpool organizes a Walk of Remembrance that departs from the city's downtown area, passing through the historic Old Dock and finishes at the Royal Albert Dock, where speeches, music, and libations mark the end of the ceremony.

At the turn of the twenty-first century the *Transatlantic Slavery Gallery* was nearly ten years old. Britain, and especially Liverpool, prepared for the commemoration of the bicentennial of the abolition of the British slave trade in 2007, a year that also marked Liverpool's 800th anniversary.[41] Favored by the international context, debates about the creation of a slavery museum eventually took form. On August 23, 2007, under the leadership of Richard Benjamin, who identifies as a descendant of "Africans sold as slaves," the International Slavery Museum opened in Liverpool.[42] Unlike Bordeaux and Nantes, which had just started integrating slavery and the slave trade in its existing history museums by this date, Liverpool created a new independent institution. International in its scope, the museum was funded by the Heritage Lottery Fund, the Department of Culture Media and Sport, and the North West Regional Development Agency. Unlike any other museum, the International Slavery Museum engaged the city's black community during the process of conceiving its permanent exhibitions. At the time of its creation, the institution was the only robust slavery museum in the world and still today remains the sole publicly funded institution of its kind.[43]

The International Slavery Museum occupies an area of 3,280 square feet and is two and a half times bigger than the previous Transatlantic Slavery Gallery. Housed on the third floor of the Merseyside Maritime Museum at Liverpool's Royal Albert Dock, the museum's building is located in a heritage site associated with the Atlantic slave trade. The opening panel of the permanent exhibition acknowledges that the history of slavery and the Atlantic slave trade have been neglected for too long. It also clearly conveys its mission to explore "how millions of Africans were forced into slavery; the crucial part that Liverpool played in this process; and how there are permanent consequences for people living in Africa, the Caribbean, North and South America, and Western Europe." This mission aimed at an exploration into the history of slavery and its present-day legacies is reflected in the museum's organization. Divided into three galleries, the first segment examines "Life in West Africa," the second one is titled "Enslavement and the Middle Passage," and the third and last one is titled "Legacy." In addition, the museum also includes an education center to host conferences and workshops, a temporary exhibition space, a campaign zone that hosts initiatives related to contemporary slavery, and a community space.

Before the entrance of the first segment on African history, two panels feature quotations by Abraham Lincoln and Frederick Douglass. Glass vitrines with red backgrounds display a variety of West African artifacts including musical instruments, masks, and carved wooden sculptures. One of the first panels displaying text is intended to respond to the question "Why Africans," explaining to the visitors that "Europeans began exploring West Africa during the fifteenth century, even before they discovered the Americans." Excluding any information about the context of these first encounters, the panel states that the "enslavement of Africans by Portuguese traders began more or less immediately." Without mentioning specific regions, states, and peoples, the display fails to explain how these captives were procured. Instead, it concludes that because Europeans were unfamiliar with African societies and cultures, they "denounced the continent as barbaric." In a curious shortcut, the text ends by stating that these racist beliefs later led to colonization but does not point out that the enslavement of Africans was primarily motivated by economic profits, which afterward was justified by racism. Another panel entitled "African Pasts" also conflates the period of the Atlantic slave trade and colonialism by featuring a quote by Patrice Lumumba in which he states, "Africa will write its own history, and it will be, to the north and to the south of the Sahara, a history of glory and dignity." Despite Lumumba's tragic fate the panel highlights that Africa is a "vast continent... full of rich and diverse cultures." Yet the panel erroneously asserts that West Africa is the region from where "Europeans seized and trade most Africans for the transatlantic slave trade," even though the region that provided the largest number of captives to the Atlantic slave trade was West Central Africa.[44]

Another display examines "African origins" by featuring tools from the Early Stone Age (2.6 million to 300,000 years ago), the Middle Stone Age (300,000 to 50–25,000 years ago), and the Late Stone Age (50–25,000 years ago). One glass display exhibits pottery, knives, cloths, shoes, iron tools, and additional masks, dating between the late nineteenth century and the second half of the twentieth century. This first segment also proposes an interactive experience by presenting a "family compound of a titled Igbo man." The gallery "Life in West Africa" provides an idyllic image of Africa. Lacking nuances of the internal dynamics of West Central African and West African societies that also contributed to the development of the Atlantic slave trade, this representation tends to avoid addressing the layers found in the accounts of the period, suggesting that Africans were absolute passive victims in their interactions with Europeans. Yet the International Slavery Museum is the first to include the African continent in the narrative of the Atlantic slave trade by dedicating to it an entire gallery totaling almost one-third of its total space.

The second gallery "Enslavement and the Middle Passage" is the central and most robust space of the International Slavery Museum. The gallery's opening panel provides the visitor with an authoritative statement: "This is the story of how the transatlantic slave trade operated. It shows what happened to enslaved Africans—their sufferings on the Middle Passage across the Atlantic, and the lives they led in the Americas. It tells how Europeans have benefited from slavery." Unlike the Nantes History Museum and the Museum of Aquitaine, the International Slavery Museum clearly addresses European responsibility in the Atlantic slave trade. With panels presenting very concise texts, its displays emphasize the victims of the horrendous commerce of human flesh. The exhibition spaces are conceived as dark and saturated. Its several segments mixing sound and images appeal to the visitors' emotions, inviting them to establish a link of empathy with the victimized African men, women, and children.[45]

Several sections of this gallery focus on the history of slavery and the slave trade. A large panoramic screen projects a poignant film evoking the

Middle Passage. Next to it, an exhibit combines a painting, a small replica of a Liverpool slave ship, and other artifacts such as a Flintlock blunderbuss to illustrate how Europeans purchased and transported enslaved Africans. Combining panels with text and illustrations from nineteenth-century travel accounts, one vitrine portrays the arrival and sale of enslaved Africans by expounding instruments of torture such as a punishment collar, iron shackles, a hand whip, a muzzle, and a branding iron. Another display features artifacts employed as currency during the slave trade such as glass beads and *manillas*. In the background, large panels show a mosaic of black-and-white reproductions of lithographs and drawings depicting life under slavery not only in the British colonies but also in other areas of the Americas, such as Brazil. Intercalated with these large images are glass displays including metal tools and archaeological findings witnessing the few material possessions by enslaved individuals.

In contrast, a few vitrines illustrate the economic benefits generated by slavery and the slave trade by exhibiting paintings representing Liverpool port and a few portraits of city officials such as Thomas Golightly, a Liverpool councilor who served as mayor (1772–1773) and treasurer (1789–1820), who participated in the slave trade and who, until 1807, appeared in the list of the Company of Merchants Trading to Africa. Other artifacts exhibited include luxury objects such as cutlery, teapots, sugar bowls, coffee cups, and coffeepots found in the homes of the city's slave-trading elites. Also attached to these displays are drawers that allow the visitors to explore written documents associated with the Atlantic slave trade. Other figurines representing enslaved individuals are on view along with porcelain plates and bowls featuring the abolitionist representation of the kneeling slave along with other abolitionist slogans. Acknowledging the role of Liverpool elites in slave-trading activities, one exhibition panel titled "Reminders of Slavery" informs the visitor that many streets in the city were named after merchants in the slave trade. Next to it, a panel with interactive cylindrical plaques lists the names of these streets, including Tarleton Street, Rodney Street, Earle Street, and Penny Lane.

In this second gallery, Liverpool is presented as the capital of the transatlantic slave trade. Yet a screen shows an animated map of the Atlantic world that chronologically presents the ports of departure in Africa and the ports of arrival in the Americas. One panel acknowledges the presence of black residents in eighteenth-century Liverpool. Illustrated with the advertisement of a slave sale, an engraving, and a photograph, the panel underscores that "some Africans were sold in the town in the 1760s and 1770s but very few enslaved Africans were brought to Liverpool directly from Africa." Merchants also brought enslaved men, women, and children from the West Indies "to work as servants in their homes" and by 1790s, there were fifty children of African rulers studying in Liverpool schools. In addition, the painting *The Black Boy* (1844) by William Windus (1822–1907) represents a black boy who may have traveled from West

Africa to Liverpool as a stowaway and who is said to have been later reunited with his parents after the painting disseminated his image.

A central element of this second gallery (Figure 4.6) is an interactive table showcasing the maquette of a sugar plantation along with a mosaic of illustrations of travel accounts depicting slaves at work and scenes of physical punishment. Around this structure lightboxes feature more information about the plantation system and three computer stations offer the visitors access to more information. Through objects and images, the museum gives a prominent place to slave resistance while insisting on the museum's international scope. One entire panel highlights Zumbi of Palmares (leader of the larger runaway slave community in seventeenth-century Brazil), as well as eighteenth-century rebellions in Saint-Domingue, Jamaica, New York, Antigua, and South Carolina. For example, the objects showcased behind glass reflect this emphasis, with names such as "maroon earthenware bowl," a "maroon amulet or obia," and a "maroon wooden knife" from Suriname.

The third and last "Legacy" room surveys the long-standing impacts of slavery on populations of African descent around the globe. A mosaic panel with text, images, and video features a chronology marked by the rise of the abolitionist movement starting in the late eighteenth century

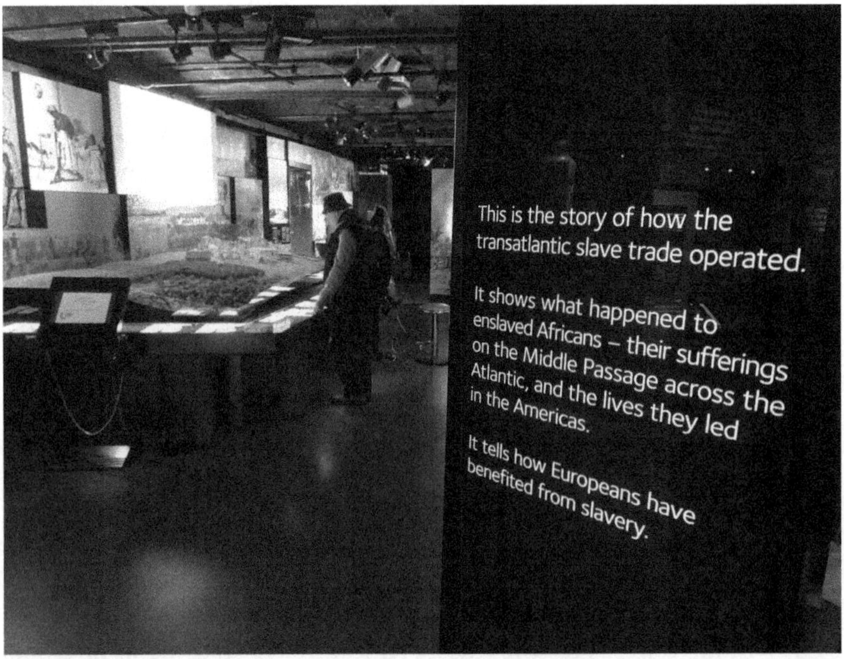
This is the story of how the transatlantic slave trade operated.
It shows what happened to enslaved Africans – their sufferings on the Middle Passage across the Atlantic, and the lives they led in the Americas.
It tells how Europeans have benefited from slavery.

FIGURE 4.6 *Permanent exhibition, International Slavery Museum, Liverpool, England. Photograph by Adam Jones, 2016, cc-by-sa-2.0.*

until the present. It highlights emancipation in various parts of the world, including the French colonies, the United States, and Brazil. The path to the emancipation in the United States is underscored with a panel honoring Harriet Tubman and visitors are invited to join the underground railroad: "Do you want to catch the Underground Railroad to escape from slavery? Look out for and listen to the coded messages. These will guide you to Freedom. You are a slave. You hear stories about a Freedom Train…and someone called 'Moses.'" Additional sections on this same panel also explore other events that took place in the second half of the nineteenth century, including the rise of Ku Klux Klan in Tennessee, the Berlin Conference that divided the African continent among European powers, the Pan-African Congress in London, the rise of the Civil Rights Movement and Black Power in the United States, and the 2001 World Conference against Racism held in Durban, South Africa. The next section "Racism and Discrimination" addresses the evolution of racism in the British colonies, the United States, and South Africa, and concludes by exploring the case of Liverpool. In this segment, one display showcases a Ku Klux Klan outfit donated by "an American citizen living in the United Kingdom who wished to remain anonymous."[46] Close to this display is the gallery's central and concluding section "Wall of Black Achievers," a large panel presenting pictures of W. E. B. Dubois (1868–1963), Frederick Douglass (1818–1895), Pelé, Oprah Winfrey, Frantz Fanon (1925–1961), Stokely Carmichael (1941–1998), and many others. One of the concluding panels of the "Legacy" gallery focuses on the contemporary demands of reparations. Highlighting a citation by Frantz Fanon stating that the "wealth of the imperial countries is our wealth too," the panel explains that reparations are a "call for compensation to be paid to descendants of enslaved Africans by the United States and European governments." Despite delimiting the movement demanding reparations mainly to the United States, the International Slavery Museum is the only institution to give this debate a prominent place in its exhibits.

The museum's innovative approach in treating the problem of slavery and the Atlantic slave trade continues to evolve. Over the last few years, the International Slavery Museum added a new dimension that was not contemplated in its original mission through the organization of several temporary exhibitions featuring the works of contemporary visual artists dealing with issues of slavery, memory, and reparations. Among these artists are Laura Facey, Rachel Wilberforce, and François Piquet (whose work is discussed in Chapter 6). Beyond the traditional, historical approach combining text, images, and artifacts, the museum's director and curators understood that art is a creative and provocative way to invite visitors to engage with sensitive issues for which there are no simple answers.

A popular venue for tourists and locals, in 2018, the International Slavery Museum was visited by 393,380 people.[47] Yet its restricted space poses challenges for further growth. In 2008, the museum purchased the Dock Traffic Office (an adjacent building to the Merseyside Maritime

Museum) on the Royal Albert Dock.[48] Renamed Dr. Martin Luther King Jr, the building (intended to become the new museum's entrance) will include an education and exhibition center to foster the development of educational and community activities such as archival research. But despite this purchase, lack of additional funding has kept the museum's expansion plans on hold. In 2011, not far from the International Slavery Museum, the new Museum of Liverpool was unveiled. Its various galleries, distributed on three floors, tell the city's history including a black community trail, therefore demonstrating that despite the long battles of public memory, Liverpool is fully incorporating its slave-trading past into its official history and memory.[49]

Slavery in the National Museum of African American History and Culture

Although many museums in the United States discuss the Atlantic slave trade and slavery in permanent exhibitions, a few private small museums such as the Slave Mart in Charleston, South Carolina, the Slave Relics Historical Museum in Walterboro, South Carolina, and the George and Georgianna Campbell Sandy Spring Slave Museum and Africana Art Gallery, in Sandy Spring, Maryland, are specifically dedicated to present this history. Yet, since the end of the 1980s, exhibitions focusing on slavery, such as those of the exhibition *Back of the Big House: The Architecture of Plantation Slavery*, unveiled at the Library of Congress (Washington DC) in 1995, and *Of the People: The African American Experience*, the permanent exhibition of the Charles H. Wright Museum (Detroit, MI) unveiled in 1997, generated hostile reactions.[50] At the time and still today, many African Americans rejected these representations of slavery that tended to convey victimizing images of enslaved Africans and their descendants placing them in a position of inferiority. In other words, the stance against the construction of a slavery museum in the United States has been historically related to the resistance of white public authorities and the population they represent in recognizing these atrocities as part of the country's official history and also associated with African Americans' rightful refusal to make slavery the central place of their historical experience.

After several decades in planning, on September 24, 2016, the Smithsonian National Museum of African American History and Culture, set in a five-acre site on the National Mall in Washington DC, opened its doors. With a total area of 400,000 square feet the museum occupies a newly constructed ten-floor building (five above and five below ground). Half of the budget for the museum's construction and exhibition (estimated at $500 million) was provided by the Congress of the United States, whereas the other half was raised through gifts from private donors. Without a preexisting collection, the curators acquired a variety of items among African American citizens and members of the African diaspora. In 2019, these artifacts, documents, photography, and media, most of which entered the museum collections through donations, amounted to nearly 37,000 items.[51] With a total exhibition space of 57,000 square feet, nearly 3,500 items are on display in the various galleries of the museum.

The National Museum of African American History and Culture is composed of three underground galleries covering four hundred years of history of the United States, a contemplative court, a heritage hall, an education center, one café, a museum store, as well as two other above-ground thematic galleries. The institution is not a slavery museum, but its first permanent exhibition *Slavery and Freedom 1400–1877* explores the history of the Atlantic slave trade and slavery until the Civil War and the period of Reconstruction. Curated by Nancy Bercaw, who is identified as white, and by African American curator Mary N. Elliot, this first historical exhibition is located in the Concourse 3 gallery. Spread over nearly 18,000 square feet, the exhibition space is almost six times larger than the entire International Slavery Museum. Following chronological order, the exhibition is centered on the history of slavery, emancipation, and the ten years that followed the end of slavery in the United States. Yet there are occasional efforts to establish transnational connections with other regions of the Americas where slavery existed.

Slavery and Freedom is where the visit to the museum starts. Visitors take an escalator to an elevator that brings them to the lowest underground level where the exhibit begins. While waiting in the line in a dark hallway, visitors listen to the music coming from the gallery and can have a few glimpses of what is displayed in the exhibition. Inducing the idea of moving back in time, the elevator is an important stage of the exhibition experience. As the elevator goes down, visitors can see through its glass windows a chronology, from 1440 to the abolition of slavery, displayed on the external wall. During the ride, the operator underscores some of the most important dates that mark the forthcoming exhibition.

Exiting the elevator visitors are introduced to the first segment of the exhibition. This segment features a large screen projecting a video alternating images, maps, and quotes associated with the history of Africa and its significance to the African Americans. On the left, the opening text printed on a metal-clad wall introduces an exploration of "Europe and an Emerging Global Economy." The text and visual images enclosed in the glass display present fifteenth-century Iberian Peninsula (present-day Portugal and Spain) as societies marked by cultural and religious diversity that were already seeking to expand their influence across the Atlantic Ocean. The same design is mirrored on the right side of this introductory room, titled "Africa and an Emerging Global Economy." Likewise, the script introducing this section emphasizes that in the 1400s "Africans did not see themselves as 'African.' The continent included many city- and nation-states, and like Europe, it was made up of diverse societies. The people of one region might have little in common with their neighbors." The written segment remains very general by stating that the "majority of enslaved Africans came from the western coast of the continent. These regions were known for their centers of learning, military prowess, vast empires, and diverse faiths. They traded with societies as far away as Asia and Europe." The panel concludes by underscoring four elements that characterized "The World in 1400: slavery was everywhere; the trade in gold, salt, and spices far exceeded the trade in slaves; slavery was not based on perceptions of race; and slavery was a temporary status." Despite being general, the glass vitrines explain in more detail the broad outline by using maps, manillas, cowry shells, and glass beads that served as currency in the trade, fifteenth-century images depicting the encounters of Capuchin missionaries with West Central Africans, and nineteenth-century visual representations of slave coffins. In addition, a central display in the middle of the room showcases Queen Njinga who ruled the Kingdom of Ndongo-Matamba in the seventeenth century in what is present-day Angola. It also discusses the "Atlantic Creoles," a term coined by historian Ira Berlin (1941–2018) to designate cosmopolitan African-born individuals who navigated between European, African, and American cultures.[52] Like the gallery "Life in West Africa" of the International Slavery Museum, the exhibition gives equal space to both Africa and Europe in its displays. But in contrast with Liverpool's museum, *Slavery and Freedom* does not provide a romanticized image of the African continent in the moment of the first encounters with Europeans. *Slavery and Freedom* also better conveys the diversity of African societies. By avoiding images of Africans as helpless victims, this segment places African peoples and Europeans at the same level. Nonetheless, by failing to emphasize the long history of the African continent before the arrival of Europeans on its shores, the exhibition missed the opportunity to challenge dominant white narratives about the African continent. As it stands now, *Slavery and Freedom* reinforces prevalent views according to which the African continent only emerged as an entity after the encounter with European powers.

Following the segment focusing on Africa and Europe, the second section of the exhibition explores "The Middle Passage and the Transatlantic Slave Trade." More interactive than the previous showcases, this segment starts with a video evoking the experience of confinement in slave dungeons, featuring images and sounds of waves and chains. In contrast with the representations of the Middle Passage of the International Slavery Museum, the gallery is darker and narrower and depending on the number of visitors on a given day the sensation of confinement can be largely amplified. Emphasizing that the regularity of the trade in enslaved Africans to the Americas was motivated by the emerging sugar industry, a glass display features an enormous iron sugar pot, utilized "to boil down cane sugar," and also underscores that the "life expectancy for an enslaved worker on early sugar plantations was seven years."

This section makes clear that the Atlantic slave trade was an international enterprise involving three continents, many Western European countries, West Africa and West Central African societies, and regions of the Americas. As visitors move through the exhibition, they can see engraved on the metal clad walls information on four hundred slave voyages, alternated with maps, the well-known representation of the slave ship *Brookes*, and quotes from slave narratives recounting the Middle Passage experience. Enclosed in these walls are glass displays featuring images of slave ships, accompanied by data from *Voyages: The Transatlantic Slave Trade Database*.[53] Using a contentious approach that solely focuses on demographic data (similar to that adopted in the Memorial to the Abolition of Slavery in Nantes examined in Chapter 4), the walls display ship names, as well as the number of enslaved Africans embarked in African ports and disembarked in the Americas by each European nation.

Whereas other parts of this gallery also explore the process of enslaving Africans and the economic dimensions of the trade, the exhibition continues to push the visitor inside the bowels of the slave-trading experience by representing the Middle Passage. Passing a small door and walking along a wood ramp, visitors can tour a dark room that conjures the environment of a slave ship. The chamber tells the story of the Portuguese slave ship *São José Paquete de África* excavated off the coast of South Africa in 2015. The text displayed on one of the room's walls reproduces a primary source: "Left Lisbon on 27 April 1794, destined for Mozambique to fetch a cargo of slaves and then set sail for Morronhas in Brazil." Indeed, the ship carried more than five hundred enslaved Africans from Mozambique to the northern Brazilian state of Maranhão ("Morronhas"), but it sank off the coast of South Africa in 1794, killing almost the half of its human cargo.[54] The horrors of the Middle Passage are highlighted in extracts from slave narratives in English language and accounts by slave ship captains displayed on the walls and conveyed through audio recordings. In addition, a few artifacts are also featured in this room. Enclosed in the walls is one glass display exhibiting two iron shackles as well as a curious artifact that according to the vague descriptive label is said to be a seventeenth-century or eighteenth-century "miniature pair of shackles used as a protective amulet of the Lobi tribe of West Africa in what is now Ghana."[55] Yet the central elements of this room are four iron ballasts (used to counterbalance the weight of the human cargo) and one piece of timber that were recovered from the sunken slave ship identified as *São José Paquete de África*. Currently part of the collections of the Iziko Museums in South Africa and on long-term loan to the National Museum of African American History and Culture, the pieces are affixed to metal pedestals and illuminated as they were works of art. But despite showcasing these artifacts, this section fails to contextualize the history of the Portuguese vessel in the overall dynamics of the Luso-Brazilian slave trade by rather presenting the remains as those of a generic slave ship.

African American historian Lonnie G. Bunch III, the founding director of the National Museum of African American History and Culture, explained that up to this day, the slave ship *São José Paquete de África* is the only known vessel that "sank with enslaved people on it." Despite its point of departure as a museum that did not have an existing collection, Bunch III recognizes that "in building a national museum you needed to find certain artifacts that people had never seen, that would excite them in profound ways" then "finding some relic pieces of a slave ship would be something important for us to do." At the same time, the director refers to the slave ship display as "almost designed as a memorial space," a place for reflection, introspection that attempts to connect the visitors with the experiences of enslaved Africans who died during the Middle Passage.[56] Contrasting with the section providing demographic data on slave voyages, the slave ship combines two different dimensions. On the one hand, for the director and the curators, presenting the actual parts of a sank slave ship mattered. On the other hand, the divers salvaged very few pieces that alone could never provide to large audiences a convincing representation of a slave vessel. Therefore, the choice of placing the recovered artifacts in a memorial of sorts is an effective response to circumvent the problem of scarcity of artifacts. In addition, the display is a smart solution to avoid the trap of previous figurative representations of slave ships that proved to be contentious, such as the one presented in the permanent exhibition *Of the People: The African American Experience* at the Charles H. Wright Museum (Detroit, MI), whose depictions of enslaved Africans were considered inaccurate and therefore were largely criticized.[57]

The subsequent sections of the exhibition are crowded and seek to cover every single relevant period of the history of the United States under slavery. The segment "Colonial North America" examines slavery and indentured servitude in several areas and colonies of what would later become the United States of America. Using very few artifacts, this section comprises several panels and vitrines using images and text to tell the history of the Bacon's Rebellion (an insurrection by white settlers), the Natchez Revolt, as well as individual and collective resistance by enslaved individuals, such as the Samba Bambara Conspiracy, the New York Conspiracy, and the Stono Rebellion. It also highlights the trajectories of some enslaved persons. The segment "American Revolution" examines how black people, either enslaved or free, participated in the revolutionary war that led to the American independence.

After walking through this tight exhibition space, visitors are eventually led to a large hall titled "The Paradox of Liberty and the Founding of America" (examined in Chapter 2). The large space features a great wall displaying the quote of the US Declaration of Independence: "All men are created equal…with certain unalienable Rights…whenever any form of government becomes destructive of these ends it is the right of the people to alter or abolish it." Across from this wall stands a large statue of Thomas Jefferson, surrounded by other sculptures of iconic black social actors, including Toussaint Louverture. Although taking the international context into account by emphasizing the importance of the Saint-Domingue Revolution, this and the next segments seek to highlight the fact that despite the end of colonial rule, slavery persisted and expanded in the United States. This expansion is underscored in the section "Slavery and the Making of a New Nation" showing how slavery fueled the cotton industry. Featuring the words "King Cotton" is a giant rectangular structure of stacked bales in which is enclosed a cotton gin. The textual panels across from this structure explain the expansion of slavery, showing how the cotton industry benefited southern planters as well as northern banks, textile companies, and the activities of shipping merchants in the north of the country.

Following the exhibition path, on the right side of the cotton gin, an entire section is dedicated to the domestic slave trade. At this point, visitors are already overwhelmed by the excessive amount of material conveying human suffering. This saturation along with the great number of visitors, including many African Americans, adults, elders, and children, very often moved by stories that are rarely told in an official museum, create a wave of reactions that make it very hard to rationally comprehend the materials presented through words and images in the various displays. Particularly poignant is the section "The Domestic Slave Trade," where these emotions of sadness and anger are amplified by the cacophony of recorded sounds reproducing the voices of the enslaved men and women. Yet these sentiments are anchored in two artifacts greatly invested with a memory of distress associated with family separation provoked by slave auctions during slavery. The first is a 1600-pound "carved marble Calc-silicate shist stone with a flattened top and bottom, squared back and sides, and a rounded front" used as "slave auction block" in Hargerstown, Maryland (Figure 4.7). Displayed in a vitrine is a plaque that reads "GENERAL ANDREW JACKSON AND HENRY CLAY SPOKE FROM THIS SLAVE BLOCK IN HARGERSTOWN DURING THE YEAR 1830."[58] This powerful artifact, although removed from its original location to the museum's interior, is imprinted with pain as it marks the very place where enslaved bodies were inspected, violated, and sold, and where husbands were separated from their wives, where mothers were torn apart from their children.

In another glass vitrine in the wall just next to the auction block, another object represents a painful and more intimate story from the point of view of enslaved people. The mid-nineteenth-century artifact described as "Ashley's Sack" is a cloth seed or feed sack embroidered with a text telling the story of the sale of Ashley, an enslaved nine-year-old girl who was given a sack as a memento by her mother when she was sold. The embroidered text reads:

FIGURE 4.7 *Auction Block, Permanent exhibition* Slavery and Freedom, *National Museum of African American History and Culture, Washington DC, United States. Photograph by Alex Jamison, 2019. Courtesy: National Museum of African American History and Culture.*

My great grandmother Rose
mother of Ashley gave her this sack when
she was sold at age 9 in South Carolina
it held a tattered dress 3 handfulls [*sic*] of
pecans a braid of Roses hair. Told her
It be filled with my Love always
she never saw her again
Ashley is my grandmother

—Ruth Middleton, 1921

The sack currently on long-term loan to the National Museum of African American History and Culture surfaced in a flea market in Springfield, Tennessee, in 2007, and was acquired by Middleton Place, South Carolina. Despite recognizing the difficulties of retracing the stories of Rose, Ashley, and Ruth, anthropologist Mark Auslander conducted archival research that confirmed the accuracy of the story embroidered on Ashley's sack.[59] Yet today, crystallized in a museum display, this object remains an important example of how collective and individual memories of slavery circulated and were passed down from generation to generation. The artifact also keeps alive the stories of women and men who were often prevented from owning property and constructing written narratives about the times they lived in bondage.

Additional sections of the exhibition explore fights for freedom, the abolitionist movements, slave resistance and daily actions of insurgency, life and work during slavery, as well as the tumultuous period of the Civil War, emancipation, and Reconstruction. Despite the expected flaws, *Slavery and Freedom* is unprecedented in its coverage of the entire history of slavery in the United States. Through text, images, and, to a lesser extent, the display of artifacts, the exhibition is also unique in establishing a few connections with other spaces in the Americas. Examining topics that are hardly addressed to large audiences in a national museum, *Slavery and Freedom* is the largest, the richest, and the most authoritative permanent exhibition surveying the history and memory of the Atlantic slave trade and slavery ever held in a museum in the world.

Official Stories

Starting in the 1990s, slavery and the slave trade eventually entered the museum spaces of Atlantic societies. This achievement resulted from a combination of different dynamics largely fueled by decades of battles of public memory waged by black concerned citizens either individually represented or organized in associations (and in several cases supported by academics and politicians). Although museums are vibrant spaces that change over time, the inclusion of the history of slavery and the Atlantic slave trade in these institutions confirms that these human atrocities are now officially recognized as such. In other words, in one of its missions (that of educating the population) the museum is therefore forced to embrace the violent chapters of a painful history shared by European, American, and African nations.

Still, the inclusion of slavery and the Atlantic slave trade in the museum exposes the nuanced national approaches through which each country engages with its own black and white communities. It also reveals how each state deals with its regional, national, and international pasts. Although France incorporated slavery and the Atlantic slave trade in its national official history and memory through the implementation of commemorative activities, the inclusion of slavery in the museum space has been more problematic. To this day, France has no national slavery museum. Certainly, the country's slave-owning and slave-trading pasts are now included in city history museums such as the Nantes History Museum and the Museum of Aquitaine. But in these two permanent exhibitions, the institution of slavery and the commerce of enslaved Africans are presented as belonging solely to the localized history of the ports of Nantes and Bordeaux. In the accounts presented in these two museums, these atrocities remain dissociated from the French colonial project that existed through and persisted after the end of French slavery and slave trade. Despite the inadequacies of their approaches and their limited financial means, the two French museums conceived dynamic exhibitions that have impacts outside the walls of the institutions. On the one hand, by introducing the works of artists problematizing the objects of its collection, the Nantes History Museum introduces a self-reflective dimension that is usually absent from permanent initiatives intended to be official. On the other hand, the Museum of Aquitaine's permanent exhibition tells the story of Bordeaux's slave-trading activities by mainly relying on historical artworks acquired by one single collector. Yet the museum makes a timid effort to explore the legacies of slavery. However, none of these two French museum establishes any connection between slavery, slave trade, and colonialism and rarely disturb the white supremacist narrative that continues to shed light on white enslaver elites at the detriment of enslaved people. Regardless these shortcomings, the creation of monuments and memorials commemorating slavery in Nantes and Bordeaux suggests that the work initiated by these two institutions is having an impact on bringing the history of slavery to the public space.

In contrast, the International Slavery Museum is not a city museum that aims to incorporate the history of the Atlantic slave trade to the official history of Liverpool. According to the words of its own director, Richard Benjamin, the museum was conceived as "a campaigning museum and an active supporter of social change and social justice."[60] Although with limited resources, the museum examines these atrocities from an international perspective that encompasses the African continent and establishes crucial links between the history of slavery and the slave trade and the legacies of racism and white supremacy. The exhibitions of the International Slavery Museum are not intended to convey an authoritative history of slavery. Provoking its visitors, the museum has embraced the use of art to formulate questions and to problematize the history and memory of slavery and the slave trade. In a similar fashion, the exhibition *Slavery and Freedom* of the National Museum of African American History and Culture provides an international dimension to the history of slavery in the United States. Yet, as a first experiment of this kind, the exhibition attempts to tell every single detail of the complex history of slavery, while at the same time engaging with its collective memory. This pioneering exhibition, saturated by objects, texts, images, films, and audio records, attempts to fill all gaps, leaving the visitor very limited time and space to assimilate this traumatic past. Notwithstanding this saturation, the exhibition is often successful in alternating coherent historical narrative with settings that intend to raise emotions and connect the visitor with the experiences of enslaved men, women, and children. Clearly, *Slavery and Freedom* is the only exhibition in an official national institution in the world to recount the history of slavery from the point of view of the African American community whose ancestors were enslaved. But despite this crucial achievement, in the sections exploring the encounters between Africans and Europeans and the birth of the United States as an independent nation, the ghost of white supremacy insists to haunt the exhibition spaces. This persistence suggests that incorporating the memory of slavery in the confined space of official museums remains a challenging task.

5

Memory and Public History

George Washington's Mount Vernon and Thomas Jefferson's Monticello, the two plantation complexes owned by founding fathers of the United States, are among the oldest and most visible preserved slavery heritage sites in the United States. Since the nineteenth century local, national, and international tourists to the nation's capital have visited these two estates, both situated in the state of Virginia in a distance between twenty and a hundred miles from Washington DC. The institution of slavery was an essential part of the lives of the two presidents and central to the existence of Mount Vernon and Monticello. Over the last years, like many other dozens of former plantations, these two sites have established initiatives interpreting slavery for their thousands of annual visitors.

After the death of Washington and Jefferson and with the abolition of slavery in the United States in 1865, the most visible traces of the inhuman institution were purposefully and gradually erased from Mount Vernon and Monticello. Visits to these properties generally omitted references to slavery and slaves. Over the nineteenth and the twentieth centuries, many thousands of white tourists, and a much smaller number of black guests, visited these two estates. But not surprisingly, the interpretation of these heritage sites remained intended to celebrate the glorious lives of the two founding fathers.

The rise of the Civil Rights Movement and the emergence of a public memory of slavery in the second half of the twentieth century impacted these heritage sites in a range of ways. Domestically and internationally, black citizens demanded governments, public authorities, and private institutions to acknowledge the role of slavery and the contribution of enslaved Africans and their descendants in the public space. Likewise, starting in the 1990s, historians increasingly investigated the controversial ties between the US founding fathers and slavery.[1] Public historians, guides, and heritage site managers were forced to react to the criticism of black social actors and academics. This new context progressively led to the remodeling of entire sections of these plantations. By the turn of the twenty-first century, special exhibitions, slavery tours, printed guides, and websites are among the new tools intended to highlight slavery in these heritage sites. Especially after the election of Barack Obama as president of the United States in 2008, both Mount Vernon and Monticello started to increasingly include the long history of slavery in their public narratives.

Conceiving public history as an approach developed by professional and academic historians that seeks to make the various dimensions of the past accessible to general audiences, this chapter discusses the development of initiatives aimed at telling the history of slavery in Mount Vernon and Monticello to the wider public.[2] How does public history engage with the problem of Atlantic slavery? In contrast with the work of memory, public history endeavors are generally committed to historical accuracy. I argue that the presentation of slavery to large audiences in both Mount Vernon and Monticello draws from the dialogues between collective memory (a notion explored in Chapter 1) carried out by the descendants of Washington and Jefferson, as well as the descendants of the slaves owned by them, and the battles of public memory of slavery (a concept examined in Chapter 3).

Making Slavery Visible in Mount Vernon

Since the seventeenth century, George Washington's paternal family owned land in Virginia. Following the death of his father in 1743, Washington inherited two farms and ten enslaved persons.[3] In 1752, after the demise of his half-brother, Lawrence Washington (1718–1752), he inherited several other bondspeople as well as Mount Vernon, a plantation of 2,100 acres located on the western shore of the Potomac River. In 1759, Washington married the widow Martha Dandridge Custis (1731–1802), a mother of four children, who brought to her new marriage as dower assets consisting of one-third of the properties of her deceased husband, Daniel Parke Custis (1711–1757). These properties, which were not actually owned by the widow or the new husband but continued to belong to the deceased husband's estate (and his heirs), included nearly eighty-four "dower slaves," which the Washingtons could not sell or emancipate.[4] During their lifetimes, these men and women, as well their descendants, remained enslaved in the five farms that composed Mount Vernon: the Mansion House, the Dogue Run, Muddy Hole, Union, and River Farms.

At first, Mount Vernon rotated the cultivation of tobacco, corn, and wheat. In the 1760s, Washington abandoned tobacco cultivation and made wheat the plantation's main cash crop. Mount Vernon's enslaved men, women, and children composed most of its workforce. Bondsmen and bondswomen executed all kinds of activities. They cultivated grains and raised livestock.[5] In addition to work in the fields, enslaved people toiled as overseers, carpenters, masons, gardeners, coopers, bricklayers, and blacksmiths. Most enslaved women worked in the wheat fields. In the Mansion House Farm, bondspeople performed activities such as weaving, spinning, sewing, cooking, washing, and cleaning. Some free wageworkers, including farm managers, overseers, and various artisans, such as gardeners, weavers, tailors, masons, joiners, blacksmiths, and carpenters, also worked in the five farms.[6]

In the next decades, Washington's enslaved property continued growing, either through purchase of new slaves or via reproduction. In 1774, approximately 135 enslaved men, women, and children lived and worked in Mount Vernon.[7] Upon Washington's death in 1799, Mount Vernon was an 8,000-acre estate worked by a total of 317 enslaved men, women, and children. Washington owned a total of 124 slaves: forty men, thirty-seven women, four working boys, three working girls, and forty children.[8] Other forty enslaved workers were hired through a contract with Penelope French (*c.* 1739-1771), from whom since 1786, he leased five hundred acres. Additionally, Martha Washington's 153 "dower slaves also worked in the property."[9]

As far as the official history is concerned, Washington fathered no biological children.[10] On his will of December 14, 1799, he determined that after his wife's death the 124 enslaved persons owned by him should be emancipated. The testament reflected Washington's concerns that emancipation could lead to family separation because several of his bondspeople married his wife's "dower slaves." Moreover, as several of these enslaved individuals were old and ill and additional ones would not be able to support themselves, Washington instructed his executors to provide the newly emancipated men, women, and children with food, clothing, and education.[11] Despite looking generous, these measures were not exceptional. They simply followed Virginia's manumission legislation that prescribed provisions to support freedpeople older than forty-five years, together with freed children.[12] In his will, Washington gave to his nephew Bushrod Washington (1762–1829) Mount Vernon's mansion and other buildings, along with 4,000 acres of its land. The rest of the estate was left to the couple Lawrence Lewis (1767–1839), his nephew, and Eleanor Parke Custis Lewis (1779–1854), Martha's granddaughter. Washington also bequeathed additional land to George Fayette Washington (1790–1867) and Lawrence Augustine Washington (1774–1824).[13]

Washington's will, liberating his human chattel, was not a benevolent act. Under public scrutiny during the period in which he served as president, in the 1780s, he had already stopped selling his bondspeople. Thus, the emancipation decision may have been influenced in part by him not knowing anymore what to do with his slaves.[14] Yet, as historian Erica Dunbar demonstrated, during his lifetime Washington made great efforts to keep his human property intact. In 1790, when the first couple moved to Philadelphia, then the US national capital, they made sure to always bring back their enslaved property to Mount Vernon and avoid Pennsylvania's gradual abolition laws that mandated the emancipation of bondspeople who lived in the state for more than six months. In 1796, just three years before Washington wrote his celebrated generous will, Ona Judge, the daughter of one of Martha Washington's "dower slaves," ran away from bondage. During the many months that followed her escape, the couple persisted in chasing the self-emancipated woman but were never able to bring her back to slavery.[15]

Washington was in debt by the time of his death and despite his instructions, on January 1, 1801, Martha Washington emancipated her husband's 124 enslaved property. Her decision to free Washington's human chattel before her death was not a benevolent act either. She was motivated by two main reasons. First, she felt unsafe in the hands of men and women who knew they would be set free upon her death.[16] Second, she lacked the resources to maintain Mount Vernon's large enslaved population. Following her demise in 1802, as instructed in Washington's will, his nephew, Bushrod Washington, received Mount Vernon's mansion and 4,000 acres of its land, corresponding to the half of the estate. By this time, Bushrod was an established politician and attorney who since 1798 served as Associate Justice of the Supreme Court of the United States.

Upon Martha Washington's death, none of her four children were alive. Hence, her late first husband's 153 "dower slaves" were passed down to her four grandchildren.[17] This inheritance distribution negatively impacted many enslaved families whose members were separated and occasionally sold. Eleanor Parke Custis Lewis (wife of Lawrence Lewis, Washington's nephew) kept her enslaved men, women, and children in one of the five farms of Mount Vernon she also inherited. However, most of the other "dower slaves" were relocated in Washington DC. Elizabeth Parke Custis Law (1776–1831), who inherited thirty-five enslaved persons, may either have brought them to the national capital or sold them away. George Washington Parke Custis (1781–1857) took his newly inherited enslaved property to his estate, the Arlington House and plantation. Located today in the Arlington Cemetery in Arlington County, Virginia, the Arlington House was part of the Alexandria County by then situated within Washington DC's territory. Likewise, his sister Martha Parke Custis Peter (1777–1854) also brought her human chattel to the Tudor Place in the national capital. Despite this dispersion, Mount Vernon's enslaved population continued growing as Bushrod Washington brought to the plantation his own slaves, either inherited from his parents or purchased by himself.[18]

Until the eve of the Civil War, Mount Vernon remained a living site of slavery. In the six decades that followed the passing of George and Martha Washington, slavery continued to exist in Virginia. Indeed, the first US Census of 1790, compiled just one decade before Washington's death, showed that of the 3,893,635 individuals who lived in the United States in 1790, 694,280 were enslaved.[19] By that time, Virginia was already the state with the largest enslaved population, a rank maintained until 1860.[20]

When George Washington was still alive, earlier before the emergence of heritage tourism in the United States, Mount Vernon already attracted local and international visitors. Most tourists reached the plantation by steamboat through the Potomac River and toured the site led by Washington's family members. After Washington's death, although in smaller numbers, white visitors continued to come to Mount Vernon to know more about the founding father and pay homage to him by visiting his tomb. Rapidly, the estate and its mansion were transformed into a site of pilgrimage.[21] By 1850s, Mount Vernon appeared in several travel guides and was described in various travelogues.[22] For the tourists who visited Washington's home, who perhaps were also slave owners, slavery was not an abstraction; it was a living reality that remained visible in the plantation site.

In 1816, Mount Vernon's new owner, Bushrod Washington, became the first president of the American Colonization Society, whose goal was to support black emigration to West Africa. Despite his leadership position in this organization, unlike his uncle, Bushrod made no plans to emancipate his own human property during his lifetime or in his will. By 1821, he owned eighty-three enslaved men, women, and children and was facing financial problems. Convinced that his bondspeople planned to run away, he sold fifty-four enslaved persons to two Louisiana planters, including families who worked in the Mansion house and the Union Farm.[23] In 1822, in order to avoid attracting public attention to Mount Vernon, Bushrod not only prohibited steamboats to dock at the property but also banned visitors from eating, drinking, and dancing.[24]

Upon his death in 1829, Bushrod Washington left to his wife most of Mount Vernon's land and a more than ten enslaved people, including Ann, Luisa and her children; Jessy, Clark and his wife Sylvia, along with their daughter, and future children, as well as Jenny.[25] But because Bushrod's wife died just two days after his own demise, John Augustine Washington II (1789–1832) and his wife, who were also slave owners, finally inherited Mount Vernon's land and mansion. The remaining enslaved men, women, and children were bequeathed to his nephews and niece. These new divisions resulted in the sale of several enslaved people, provoking again family separation.[26]

The new owners of Mount Vernon spent most part of their time at their Blakeley plantation in West Virginia. During their long periods of absence, they left enslaved men and women in charge of the property. Before the rise of public history and heritage tourism, bondspeople took responsibility for carrying out Mount Vernon's preservation. As victims and living witnesses of slavery, they led informal tours of the mansion, outbuildings, and the plantation, telling the visitors stories about its most illustrious owner.[27] Although one can assume that in these early tours bondspeople could not highlight the hardships of slavery, however, as the leading informal guides they did present the property and Washington's stories from their point of view. In the framework of a slave society like

Virginia, enslaved people were visible social actors in the plantation setting and the leading guides of Mount Vernon tours.

With the passing of Washington II, his wife Jane Charlotte Washington (1786–1855) took control of Mount Vernon. She started renting the property to her son, John Augustine Washington III (1821–1861). In 1850, he became its formal owner and continued acquiring new human property, several of whom left their families behind.[28] Facing hardships to maintain the estate, he developed two initiatives to make Mount Vernon a tourist attraction. After more than two decades of prohibition, he again allowed steamboats to transport visitors to dock at the plantation and even ordered the construction of a wharf. He also made investments to construct the Alexandria, Mount Vernon, and Accontik Road to attract tourists traveling by land. Although these efforts impacted positively Mount Vernon's visitation rates, the estate continued to fall into a great state of decay.

Eventually, the successful efforts to preserve Mount Vernon came neither from Virginia nor from the Washington family, but rather from a South Carolina rich woman: Ann Pamela Cunningham (1816–1875). A member of a family of large slaveholders, Cunningham was the daughter of the wealthy planter Robert Cunningham (1786-1859), the slaveholder and owner of Rosemont, a 2,100-acre plantation of indigo, tobacco, and cotton, located in Laurens County, South Carolina. Upon his death in 1859, he owned 155 enslaved men, women, and children. Therefore, two years before the beginning of the Civil War, his daughter inherited part of his assets, including his enslaved property, by also becoming a slaveholder.[29]

During a steamboat trip from Philadelphia to South Carolina through the Potomac River, Cunningham's mother, Louisa Bird Cunningham (1794–1873), observed the increasing degradation of Washington's old home. She then wrote a letter to her infirm daughter, suggesting her to call upon other southern women to recover Mount Vernon. Cunningham accepted the challenge and invited other influential white southern women "to make of Mount Vernon a shrine sacred to the memory of the Father of his Country."[30] In 1853, Ann Pamela Cunningham founded the Mount Vernon Ladies' Association. As its first regent, Cunningham became the leading character in the preservation of Mount Vernon plantation and mansion. In her own words:

> When I started the Mount Vernon movement it was a Southern affair altogether. My appeal was to Southern ladies. The intention was simply to raise $200,000; give it to Virginia, to hold title and to purchase 200 acres of the Mount Vernon property, including the Mansion and Tomb—Virginia to keep it for a public resort. The ladies to have it in charge and adorn it if they could have the means.[31]

In other words, the preservation of Mount Vernon was gendered and conducted by white women who were slaveholders and active bearers of white supremacy in southern slave societies. These women were also instrumental to the preservation of the memory of male slave owners during slavery's final years and after the end of the Civil War, in the several decades marking the rise of the ideology of Lost Cause of the Confederacy.[32]

In the subsequent five years, whereas Cunningham made efforts to convince John Augustine Washington III to sell Mount Vernon to her association, she also led a national campaign to collect the necessary amount to purchase the property.[33] Her project relied on a rudimentary conception of heritage in a period when the very notion of public history did not exist. Evidently, presenting slavery was not the central factor motivating this initiative. The leading women in this initiative came from families of slave owners and were slaveholders themselves. By the time they started campaigning to preserve Mount Vernon, the evil institution remained alive in the South, and like in the previous decades several enslaved men, women, and children continued living and working in Mount Vernon. As in previous attempts to preserve the plantation and the mansion, the main goal of Cunningham and the Mount Vernon Ladies' Association of the Union was protecting and promoting George Washington's legacy.

On February 22, 1859, the Mount Vernon Ladies' Association completed the purchase of the mansion and two hundred acres of Mount Vernon's land. One year later, the organization took possession of the site, opening it to the public, who now paid an admission fee to visit the property. As in any former plantation, the tangible traces of slavery remained everywhere, even though during the five decades that followed Washington's death old built structures such as the eighteenth-century greenhouse and adjacent slave quarters were destroyed. Likewise, although during the Civil War, Mount Vernon was neutral ground, the estate was left abandoned, preventing its development as a heritage site. Despite these obstacles, the Mount Vernon Ladies' Association made efforts to preserve Washington's home to as close to as it was during his lifetime. But with the end of the Civil War and the passing of the Thirteenth Amendment abolishing slavery in 1865, it was untenable to feature the existence of enslaved workers and slave labor in Mount Vernon. As the south lost a war fought to protect the institution of slavery, the supporters of the Lost Cause of the Confederacy certainly did not want to see this sensitive dimension of the nation's past highlighted in a heritage site associated with a founding father and situated a few miles from Washington DC. In accordance with this view, during the 1860s and 1870s several advisors to the board suggested the association take down the plantation buildings that were surviving reminders of slavery.[34] Although this recommendation was never implemented, the tentacles of white supremacy continued to be active through silences. Discursively erased, slavery remained an uncomfortable topic that was constantly avoided in Mount Vernon's heritage interpretation. During the Jim Crow era, Washington's home remained a nostalgic representation of the South that contributed to the promotion of a benevolent image of slavery.[35] Despite promoting this falsified history, as a heritage site intended to be preserved, tangible references to slavery could never be effectively suppressed.

In 1912, the Mount Vernon Ladies' Association published a souvenir book and guide illustrated with photographs describing the various premises of Mount Vernon. Only one instance includes the term "negroes" to refer to enslaved people, who three other times are designated as "servants" in the text. A section presenting the spinning house is described as "where much material was prepared to clothing the servants and where rag carpets and other fabrics were woven for the use of the family. Flax, cotton, wool, and silk were there put through the various processes of spinning and weaving by skilled servants."[36] Here, despite the intentional vagueness, the reader must conclude that enslaved individuals wove rough cloths for themselves and that valuable fabrics such as silk were intended for the use of the Washington family only. Even more interesting is the next page describing the "servants' quarters" located at the "two long, red-roofed buildings" next to the conservatory. The misleading photograph taken from the garden shows the two brick buildings that from a distance look like large comfortable residences. Potentially acknowledging the limited size and the suggested good living conditions evoked by the deceptive photograph, the text adds that these "were the quarters for a limited number of servants needed at the Mansion." Yet the next sentences show a clear effort to promote the idea that slavery in Mount Vernon was a benign institution and that the dozens of enslaved people working from day to night in that estate received some sort of special treatment. According to the text "[c] omfortable cabins to house the rest [meaning here the great majority] of the negroes were located at convenient distances about the plantation."[37]

By 1920, most workers of Mount Vernon were white and traces of slavery in the former plantation were gradually concealed from public view. During the twentieth century, a few initiatives memorialized the presence of enslaved men, women, and children in Washington's plantation. In 1928, during the annual meeting of the Mount Vernon Ladies' Association, the chairman of the Tomb Committee, Frances C. Maxey (1851–1938) from Texas, warned the board that the vestiges of the unmarked graves of Mount Vernon's slave cemetery (where possibly more than a hundred enslaved were buried) were disappearing.[38] Following his recommendation to create a gravestone to mark the slaves' graveyard, Annie B. Jennings (1855–1939), vice-regent for Connecticut, offered to contribute with funds to purchase the memorial stone.[39] The association eventually unveiled the tombstone, in 1929, with the inscription: "In Memory of the Colored Servants of the Washington Family Buried at Mount Vernon from 1760 to 1860 their unidentified graves surround this spot." Despite acknowledging the existence of the burial ground the association obviously avoided using the term "slave." By referring to enslaved people as colored servants, the burial marker suggests that the workers interred in the cemetery were free. Once again, despite preserving the heritage of enslaved workers in Mount Vernon, these early projects contributed not only to obscure the existence of slavery in the plantation but also to promote the paternalistic myth of slavery as a benevolent institution.

In the following decades, reactions against the growing invisibility of Mount Vernon's slavery's past continued to be at stake. The Mount Vernon Ladies' Association put forward plans to reconstruct the plantation's greenhouse, destroyed by a fire in 1835.[40] Completed in 1787, the brick building originally included two one-story wings that were added to each side of its structure in 1792. The barrack-style slave quarters (that appear in the photograph of the illustrated guide published in 1912) may have accommodated sixty individuals, mostly house servants and craftsmen. Eventually, on February 22, 1962, the day of Washington's 230th birthday, the reconstructed greenhouse slave quarters were opened to the public.[41] The initiative was considered "one of the first and most important depictions of slave life ever completed."[42] Its restored version included wooden beds set on brick structures, even though the documentary evidence confirming the quarters contained permanent beds is inconsistent.[43] But despite these new additions, during the 1960s, slavery and the experiences of enslaved workers remained very marginal, if not concealed, elements in Mount Vernon's heritage interpretation. Usually the visitors followed the embellished information made available on printed guides and asked additional questions to the staff working in the site. At the summit of the Civil Rights era, the Mount Vernon Ladies' Association briefly offered visitors recorded tours, wherein the issue of slavery could not be avoided. Unsurprisingly, the script emphasized Washington as the benevolent slave owner, insisting on his uneasiness in face of the evil institution.[44]

Over the two decades after the unveiling of the slave quarters, the presence of enslaved people and slavery were persistently concealed in Mount Vernon. Eventually pressures came from the professional black communities of the Washington DC area. What happened next reveals how the development of public history of slavery at Mount Vernon and other slavery heritage sites is not dissociated from the battles of public memory, fought by community groups to make their perspectives of the slave past prevail in the public space. These public reactions from the black social actors came to the surface in 1983. During the Black History Month, Dorothy Butler Gilliam, an African American journalist, published in the *Washington Post* an article denouncing the slave burial ground's state of abandonment. She emphasized how the interpretation of Mount Vernon simply ignored the existence of the cemetery: "It seems not to matter that these men and women provided the free labor on which the plantation operated."[45]

Soon a group of African Americans mobilized to put political pressure to enforce the preservation of the slave cemetery. After reading Gilliam's article, Fairfax County Supervisor James Scott contacted Frank Matthews, the legal counsel to the Fairfax County National Association for the Advancement of Colored People (NAACP), to let him know about Mount

Vernon Ladies' Association's plans to open two tax-exempt restaurants on Mount Vernon's ground. Backed by an organization representing hundreds of members defending black rights, Matthews attended the Board of Supervisors meeting that would decide on the request. He opposed it by arguing that the association could not get its restaurants the tax-exempt status until memorialization of the slave burial ground was instituted. Rapidly, the association cleared the site and opened it to tourists. Next, a working group of African American leaders met the association to discuss the creation of a memorial.[46]

Eventually, without opening a contest, the project was assigned to a group of students of the School of Architecture of the historically black Howard University. Still, the Mount Vernon Ladies' Association informed the competitors of several requirements. First, images of degradation should be avoided. Second, the memorial should underscore the "courage and strength of a people." Dedicated on September 21, 1983, the memorial, consisting of a three-step circular platform (Figure 5.1), each one respectively engraved with the words "faith," "hope," and "love," finally materialized. A granite column at the center of the third step in the middle of the circle is engraved with the following words: "In Memory of the Afro Americans who served as slaves at Mount Vernon." Contrasting the tombstone unveiled in 1929, which ambiguously referred to "colored servants," the language of the new memorial no longer concealed the legal status of enslaved men and women. But for most Mount Vernon's ordinary visitors the slave memorial continues to pass unnoticed. Although plaques along the site signal the directions to reach the cemetery, most people only stop by at the tomb of George Washington, which is not very far from the location of the slave burial ground.

During the 1980s, although a benevolent view of slavery in Washington's Mount Vernon continued to prevail, a few initiatives started highlighting the existence of the inhumane institution, underscoring various dimensions of the working and living conditions of its enslaved workforce. The *Mount Vernon Official Guidebook* published by the Mount Vernon Ladies' Association gradually addressed the issue of slavery. In 1987, the creation of a Department of Archaeology contributed to the development of research that revealed new dimensions of slave life in Washington's estate and led the installation of several interpretive signs in the outbuildings.

Through the activism of members of the black community of the District of Columbia and Virginia, and the work of public historians, the next two decades marked the implementation of a growing number of projects to make slavery visible in Mount Vernon. Once again black women were those leading these initiatives. In 1990, Sheila Bryant Coates, founder of Black Women United Action, established an annual event held during the fall at the slave cemetery memorial to commemorate the contributions of African Americans to Fairfax County. Likewise, in 1991, the W. K. Kellogg Foundation funded a new initiative recreating the Pioneer Farm, where most workers were enslaved men, women, and children. The site features a

FIGURE 5.1 *Slave Cemetery and Memorial, Mount Vernon, Virginia, United States. Photograph by Ana Lucia Araujo, 2015. Courtesy: George Washington's Mount Vernon.*

sixteen-sided barn, animals such as sheep and horses, along with a variety of living performances in which reenactors hoe the fields, crack corn, plow fields, and winnow wheat.

Despite the attempts of annihilating the role of bondspeople in building Mount Vernon, enslaved men and women and their descendants were the first informal interpreters of slave life in Washington's plantation. Yet, only by 1995, Gladys Quander Tancil (1921–2002) introduced slavery tours at the property. Tancil was not an ordinary reenactor. Hired as Mount Vernon's first African American interpreter in 1973, she belonged to one of the oldest enslaved families of Mount Vernon and was a descendant of Nancy Carter Quander (1788–?), daughter of Suckey Bay, an enslaved woman who lived on River Farm. In contrast to the tours led by docents who are trained to learn about the site's history, her tours were based on the collective memory of slavery transmitted in her family. When touring Mount Vernon, Tancil shared oral histories and traditions, therefore bringing to life the perspective of her enslaved ancestors.[47]

Today, all over Mount Vernon, plaques and other markers reference slave life. But public representations of slavery remain problematic. Although offering visitors a living interpretation of the site, performances reenacting the work performed at the Pioneer Farm are very misleading. Because most reenactors, including children, are white volunteers, visitors are led to believe that free whites composed the majority of the workers in the Pioneer Farm, when indeed the great majority of Mount Vernon's workforce were enslaved. In a public site, this distorted representation becomes a useful vehicle to reinforce white supremacy that here operates through the erasure of black presence and the concealment of the horrible realities of slavery. Still, the absence of black reenactors has been justified by the lack of black individuals willing to play the roles of enslaved people in heritage sites where white visitors (who often distance themselves from slavery), prevail. One of the best examples of these pitfalls is the case of Colonial Williamsburg, the living-history museum that recreates colonial life in Williamsburg, Virginia. At the end of the 1970s, the site hired students of the historically black Hampton University to reenact the roles of enslaved people. But very often African American reenactors faced hostility by white visitors, whereas black visitors were also offended by seeing these reenactors in positions of submission.[48] The emerging tensions eventually led to a major public outrage. In 1994, Christy Coleman Matthews, who is racialized as an African American and who was the head of the Colonial Williamsburg Foundation's Department of African American Interpretation, along with her team, decided to develop the reenactment of an auction of four enslaved persons. Despite the objections manifested by the Virginia National Association for the Advancement of Colored People (NAACP) and the Southern Christian Leadership Conference (SCLC) as to why Colonial Williamsburg would be able to reenact with sensitivity such a dreadful event, the performance was maintained. During the presentation, protestors challenged the black reenactors, whereas other visitors supported the staff decision to develop the program. Yet the reenactment portraying the horrors of slavery was not performed again.[49]

Mount Vernon's historic interpreters faced similar challenges. By failing to understand that African American reenactors were telling the stories of their ancestors, white guests often asked insensitive questions. Obviously, black reenactors could hardly respond to these queries during the tours. Yet Azie Mary Dunguey, an actress, comedian, and writer, who worked as a reenactor in Mount Vernon, developed a powerful humorous instrument to engage with whites' thoughtless questions by creating the web series *Ask a Slave*, a monologue in which she responds, in an amusing way, to questions addressed to her during the tours.[50]

Despite these developments, Mount Vernon is a private entity that relies on the revenues from entrance fees, as well as the profits generated from its restaurant, cafeteria, and gift shop. In this commodified setting, slavery remains a marginal element in Mount Vernon's presentation to tourists. Most visitors to the property are whites, who solely pay a visit to George Washington's tomb and mansion. Offered every five minutes, nearly eighty times a day, the twenty-minute tour of the mansion where enslaved men and women worked could be a central occasion to talk about slavery. Still, the mansion contains no material references to the enslaved people who labored in the building. Moreover, docents rarely discuss the work of bondspeople in the mansion, except when a visitor exceptionally asks a question. Although a short tour could hardly effectively engage visitors in discussing complex issues, in plantations like Mount Vernon the mansion remains a symbol of white supremacy, a sacred space of the Washington family, where allusions to slavery remain avoided.

Outside the mansion, however, visitors can interact with one or two black performers such as Brenda Parker who remain stationed near the Mansion Circle at the front lawn, playing the roles of slaves who lived and worked in Mount Vernon. But to hear about the history of enslaved men, women, and children who worked in the estate, tourists must pay an additional fee to take the one-hour tour "The Enslaved People of Mount Vernon," which by 2019 was offered only twice a day between April and December and once a day between February and March. Like in other plantation heritage sites, the only circuit to specifically discuss the institution of slavery and address the living and work conditions of those who comprised the majority of Mount Vernon's residents is segregated as if this crucial element could be addressed separately from other dimensions of the site's history.[51] Today this segregated circuit that usually covers the greenhouse slave quarters and the slave cemetery is led mostly by white docents, and despite some changes it does not dramatically differ from what it was two decades ago.[52] Although these professionals receive consistent guidance, how they present slavery highly depends on their personal engagement with the topic through additional training and readings. During the visits, these discrepancies are noticeable when docents adapt their narratives depending on the audience, most of whom are white families from all over the United States.

In some instances, interpretation of slavery in Mount Vernon is oriented to raise emotions among its visitors. Particularly in February, during US Black History Month, the slavery tour tends to include a stop at the slave burial ground, where visitors can pay homage to those who labored in Mount Vernon. Yet these attempts to create empathy among white guests toward the enslaved population who lived and worked in Mount Vernon are often mitigated during the period of questions and answers. On several occasions, white men, women, and even children ask about how Washington treated his slaves and whether he allowed his slaves to learn to read and write. In these exchanges, US white visitors are rarely confronted about their acquired beliefs, as it appears clear they hope to hear that slaves were treated well and therefore appease their guilt. Likewise, despite the new visibility of slavery in Mount Vernon, the reconstructed greenhouse slave quarters and the Pioneer Farmer's slave cabin can provide only a very small sample of the large number of Mount Vernon's slave dwellings.[53] Like in other plantations, as Mount Vernon has only one reconstructed slave cabin, visitors are not in a position to accurately grasp the actual large number of slaves who worked in the site. Despite these gaps, when entering the site, visitors are provided with Mount Vernon general map guide that features the slave memorial, even though all other pictures only show Washington, animals, and white individuals performing a variety of activities. Still, starting in 2019, visitors can obtain the brochure "Enslaved People of Mount Vernon," which provides a map locating places and buildings associated with the enslaved population. However, only the kitchen's outbuilding, and not the mansion, appears on the map.

The presentation of Mount Vernon's slavery history is not limited to its actual heritage site. From all over the world, individuals can access through its website a variety of historical data, photographs, maps, graphs, and teaching materials telling the history of slavery in Washington's home. As discussed in Chapter 2, the temporary exhibition *Lives Bound Together: Slavery at George Washington's Mount Vernon*, exploring the various dimensions of the institution of slavery in Washington's home, opened in 2016 at Mount Vernon's Donald W. Reynolds Museum and Education Center. Curated by Susan P. Schoelwer (identified as white), the exhibition is an attempt to tell the history of slavery in Mount Vernon through the lens of nineteen enslaved men and women. But because the center is located far from Washington's mansion and tomb, fewer visitors see the exhibition. Moreover, despite centering its narrative on the lives of bondspeople, all over the various exhibition's displays, George Washington remains an omnipresent figure, whereas enslaved individuals, represented by silhouettes, continue to occupy coadjutant positions. Even though the exhibition is accompanied by a large catalog, ordinary visitors rarely purchase it. Not differing much from what it did one century ago, *Mount Vernon Official Guidebook* rapidly mentions slavery in the sections presenting the greenhouse slave quarters, the slave burial grounds and memorials, and the Pioneer Farm. Even the short section "Slavery at Mount Vernon" highlights Washington's will that instructed his wife Martha to free his slaves after her death, therefore once again reinforcing his image as the benevolent slave owner.[54] As late as February 2020, Mount Vernon's shop was still selling a fridge magnet reproducing the only Washington's denture that survived to this day and that was partially made with teeth of enslaved people. Like other plantation heritage sites, Mount Vernon shows how public memory and collective memory of slavery greatly interfere in the ways that the history of slavery is presented to large audiences.

Making Slavery Visible in Monticello

Like Mount Vernon, the new visibility of slavery at Thomas Jefferson's Monticello was the result of a very long process. Near Charlottesville, but located about two hours from Washington DC, Monticello was built atop a mountain, largely separated from the neighboring communities, and therefore did not become a tourist attraction during Jefferson's lifetime. Like Washington, Jefferson belonged to a wealthy slaveholding family. He was raised in a refined household in Shadwell, Albemarle County, in Virginia. His mother, Jane Randolph Jefferson (1720–1776), was born in Britain and, according to existing sources, did not bring enslaved individuals to her marriage. His father, Peter Jefferson (1708–1757), was a cartographer and surveyor who, during the course of his life, became a wealthy planter and slave owner.[55] In 1749, along with other surveyors and planters, Jefferson's father started the Loyal Land Company. The enterprise, whose purpose was to recruit settlers, was awarded 800,000 acres of land in Virginia, West Virginia, and Kentucky. In the 1750s, Peter Jefferson established a tobacco farm in the mountains of Shadwell.

After the death of his father, Thomas Jefferson inherited nearly half of 5,000 acres of land that his father owned in Albermale County in Virginia, including the estate he subsequently named Monticello, which was composed of four farms, the Monticello home farm, Shadwell, Tufton, and Lego. Jefferson also inherited a few more than thirty enslaved persons. This number increased to fifty-two by 1774, when Jefferson inherited from his father-in-law 135 enslaved men, women, and children. During his lifetime, he owned an average of two hundred slaves, half of whom lived and worked in Monticello.[56]

A student of classic architecture, Jefferson sketched the plans of a mansion following the neoclassical style to be built at the top of where Monticello plantation was located. In 1768, enslaved workers started building the mansion that over the years became the symbol of his tobacco plantation. Like other plantations, the mansion's sophistication contrasted with the living and working conditions of nearly 120 bondspeople who on average labored at Jefferson's Monticello. Enslaved men and women who performed more specialized professions such as cooks, maids, bricklayers, and blacksmiths were lodged not far from the mansion along an alley of cabins called Mulberry Row. The alley stood out far from the units that accommodated field slaves and comprised a dairy, a nailery, stables, smokehouses, a furniture workshop, and a weaving house.

After returning from France, in 1790, Jefferson developed plans of renovation and expansion of Monticello's mansion inspired by French architecture. In 1809, after his two terms as president of the United States, he retired to Monticello, where he resided for the next fifteen years until his death in 1826. Also, in 1809, his daughter Martha Jefferson Randolph along with her husband (from whom she was separated) and her children moved to Monticello. As other tobacco planters of his time, Jefferson died with an enormous debt of more than $100,000. By this time, Monticello was already deteriorating.[57] His will determined that his lands at Poplar Forest would go to his grandson Francis Wayles Eppes VII (1801–1881) and that the remaining properties would pay his debts.[58] As Jefferson's executor, his grandson Thomas Jefferson Randolph was responsible of disposing of any remaining properties. His surviving daughter Martha Jefferson Randolph inherited Monticello and the rest of the assets.[59] However, one decade later, she could no longer afford residing in the estate. On January 19, 1827, the family auctioned Monticello's farm animals, equipment, household furniture, and furnishings. Enslaved men, women, and children were also part of the auction that resulted in family separation. For example, take the case of Joseph Fossett, a blacksmith who was the son of Mary Hemings Bell, the eldest daughter of Elizabeth Hemings, who was among the five enslaved individuals freed by Jefferson. Although he was freed according to Jefferson's will, his wife Edith Hearn Fossett (1787–1854) was sold along with her children in six separate lots, and only a decade later Joseph was able to purchase the freedom of his wife and children.[60] After the death of Jefferson's son-in-law, in 1828, the family decided to sell Monticello's land and mansion, which was already in a great state of decay. Not only were no buyers found but the property was vandalized by individuals looking for souvenirs.[61]

Eventually, on November 1, 1831, a Charlottesville pharmacist, James Turner Barclay (1807–1874), purchased Monticello's mansion. Not particularly interested in Jefferson, the new owner invested little to improve the property that continued to deteriorate. In 1834, apparently tired of the growing number of tourists who wanted to visit Jefferson's home, Barclay sold the mansion and its 218 acres of surrounding land to Uriah Phillips Levy (1792–1862). A Jewish commodore of the US Navy, Levy admired Jefferson's views promoting religious freedom.[62] In 1832, the young Levy may have met Marquis de Lafayette (1757–1834) during a trip to Paris. On that occasion, Lafayette, who visited Monticello two times in 1824 and 1825, inquired about the fate of Jefferson's home. Levy promised him to visit and look at the state of Monticello.[63] These circumstances and Levy's admiration for Jefferson may have led him to purchase the property and preserve it.

Levy resided in Monticello during the summer and like previous residents he owned enslaved people who lived and worked in the estate.[64] Moreover, in 1860, Levy hired as overseer Joel Wheeler (c. 1807–1881), who brought to Monticello several enslaved men, women, and children.[65] Despite the new owner's absence, the residence was open to visitation.[66] By the middle of the nineteenth century, Levy had successfully recovered Monticello's old structure. Following his death in March 1862, during the Civil War, the Confederate government appropriated Monticello "as the property of an enemy alien" and used it as military hospital.[67] Levy's heirs entered a legal battle to contest his will of 1858, which bequeathed Monticello to the people of the United States.[68] Eventually, in November 1863, the New York Supreme Court voided the will.[69] On November 17, 1864, the Confederate government ordered the sale of Monticello and Levy's nineteen enslaved individuals.[70] Lieutenant Colonel Benjamin Franklin Ficklin (1827–1871) from Albermale County purchased the property and several buyers acquired the various enslaved persons. With the end of the war Monticello's ownership returned to Levy's estate.

Since the sale of Levy's enslaved property in 1864, Monticello remained without any maintenance. Photographs of the 1870s show the mansion's great deterioration.[71] During this period, thousands of tourists visited Monticello to see Jefferson's tomb and mansion.[72] In the years that followed emancipation, freedpeople once owned by Levy's overseer remained living in the property. Likewise, Levy's former enslaved may have returned to the estate, whereas other freedpeople came to work in Monticello as sharecroppers.[73] Eventually, in 1879, Jefferson Monroe Levy (1852–1924), one of Levy's nephews, won the judicial battle and became the legal owner of Monticello. Like his uncle, he made Monticello his summer residence. Despite restoring the house, he also altered its original architecture. Whereas at the end of the nineteenth century, Monticello was featured in US travel guides and travelogues, on the eve of the twentieth century, as the use of automobile made the property more accessible, tourism to the site increased to nearly 50,000 visitors per year.[74] Like in the previous decades, until the late nineteenth century, stories about visitors to the estate who left Monticello carrying as mementos pieces of its monuments and buildings were normal occurrence. During his period as Monticello's owner, Levy organized numerous parties whose guests included members of the US Congress, university professors, as well as the elite members of New York and Charlottesville.[75] Yet tourists often complained about Levy's lack of hospitality, leading to a growing number of calls to change Monticello's private property status and to officially transform it into a monument to Jefferson. In 1897, Amos J. Cummings (1836–1902), a former New York congressman, published in the newspaper *The New York Sun* an article with anti-Semitic contours detracting the Levy family for failing to preserve Monticello.[76] Also, William Jennings Bryan (1860–1925), who ran for the Democratic Party in the presidential election of 1896, started campaigning for the federal government's acquisition of Monticello.[77] As these first voices reclaiming Monticello emerged, elite women became the most visible social actors demanding the US government to buy the property and make it a national shrine to the US founding father.

Like the initiative to preserve George Washington's Mount Vernon, the first endeavors to make Monticello a touristic heritage site led by white elite women were not intended to highlight the existence of slavery in the estate but rather to preserve white supremacy structures by paying homage to Jefferson. Maud Elizabeth Wilson Littleton (*c.*1872–1953) was the first leading figure in this movement. Born in Texas, she was married to Martin Wiley Littleton (1872–1934) who served as New York congressman between 1911 and 1913. In 1909, she accompanied her husband who was delivering the Founder's Day speech at the University of Virginia in Charlottesville. On the occasion, the couple visited Monticello and was shocked by the property's state of decay.[78] Following the visit, Maud Elizabeth Wilson Littleton started a campaign to push the US government to purchase Monticello from Levy. In a pamphlet titled *One Wish*, she made her plea by insisting that Levy stated this wish in his will.[79] In 1912, she created the Jefferson-Monticello Memorial Association, a national organization to lobby the US Congress to have the federal government acquiring Monticello and transforming it into a national monument honoring Jefferson.[80]

During Littleton's campaign, the disputes on who should operate Monticello reached the public sphere, especially Virginia newspapers. Like it happened with Mount Vernon, white women descendants of pro-slavery families were once again at the forefront of the public debate. Groups such as the Daughters of the Confederacy opposed Littleton's proposal by arguing that Virginians, and not the federal government, should oversee Jefferson's home. According to one of its representatives, identified in an article as Mrs. Frank Anthony Walke, "Monticello belongs to Virginia in the future, and the government should not own it, because Jefferson Levy has told the Virginia Division of the Daughters of the Confederacy that they shall have the old home of Jefferson in the near future."[81] These debates led by white women show that for groups representing the North and the South, the appropriation of Jefferson's image was a central element of the symbolic struggle to occupy the public space and control the narrative regarding the nation's views on slavery. Neither views challenged the image of Jefferson as a large slaveholder.

Despite Littleton's work and the pressures from the US Congress, Jefferson Levy refused to sell Monticello to the federal government. But the efforts to make Monticello a national monument continued. In 1920, Ruth Read Cunningham (1887–1941) created the Thomas Jefferson Memorial

Association, an organization composed of prominent white women. A native of Richmond, Virginia, Cunningham claimed to be a direct descendant of Ann Pamela Cunningham, the wealthy member of a slaveholder family and creator of Mount Vernon Ladies' Association of the Union that purchased Washington's Mount Vernon in the nineteenth century. Eventually in 1920, Jefferson Levy agreed to sell Monticello if the property was transformed into a national memorial to Jefferson. But in the next three years two other organizations aimed at acquiring Monticello emerged. In 1923, Marietta Minnegerode Andrews (1869–1931), a painter, writer, and socialite, along with Rose de Chine Gouverneur Hoes (1860–1933), the suffragist, activist of the Democratic Party, and great-granddaughter of President James Monroe, created the National Monticello Association, a new nonprofit organization whose mission was raising funds to procure Monticello. Likewise, a group of New York prominent lawyers formed the Thomas Jefferson Foundation, a nonprofit organization incorporating members of the two previous associations.

At the end of 1923, after a period of negotiations and a fundraiser campaign, the newly created Thomas Jefferson Foundation acquired Monticello. In 1924, right before Levy's demise, the foundation got the property title.[82] In the next decades, the organization collected funds to repair and restore Monticello's mansion and the rest of the property. The entity also led campaigns to acquire artifacts that once belonged to Jefferson. After adding more than 1,000 acres to the estate, today the foundation owns 2,060 acres, including Jefferson's farms of Tufton and Shadwell.[83]

Over the years after the property's acquisition, the Thomas Jefferson Foundation restored Monticello to make it as close as possible to what it was when Jefferson completed the mansion's construction.[84] In this process, the memory of Levy's family who owned Monticello longer than Jefferson himself was nearly erased from the site. By then, very few plaques mentioning the Levy family were on view in Monticello. Carrying anti-Semitic contours, the signs quickly referred to Uriah Levy as a Jew who purchased the property and later sold it, omitting his contribution to the estate's preservation. It was not until 1985 that the Thomas Jefferson Foundation publicly recognized the role of the Levy family in saving Monticello.[85]

In the decades that followed the Thomas Jefferson Foundation's acquisition of Monticello, the number of visitors to the site steadily increased. Paying fifty cents admission fee in 1924, 20,000 people visited Monticello, a number that increased to 50,000 in 1927 and to 75,000 in 1929.[86] Although slavery continued to be concealed during the visits of Monticello, from 1923 to 1951, six African American males guided the visit to the mansion. Wearing navy blue uniforms and red waistcoats with brass buttons, contemporary accounts illustrate that the guides entertained the visitors by telling them anecdotes. One of these stories, reproduced in contemporary written sources, stated that during the American Revolutionary War, the British General Bastre Tarleton (1754–1833) "raided Monticello and rode up the marble staircase, through the magnificent hall and out through the salon on his fruitless search for Jefferson," printing a horse's hoof on the wooden floor.[87] But these expressions of African American collective memory that remained alive in the site clashed with the development of white-led public history in Monticello. Fiske Kimball (1888–1955), pioneer in architectural preservation and chairman of the Thomas Jefferson Foundation's restoration committee, and Marie Goebel Kimball (1889–1955), a historian who served as first curator of Monticello, advised the African American guides to better emphasize Jefferson's numerous achievements and to exclude their amusing stories narrated during the tour. Eventually, in 1951 the foundation's board of trustees decided to eliminate African American docents and replace them with white middle-class hostesses in order to improve "quality and accuracy."[88] Admittedly, although led by African Americans, the previous tour was conceived by the white curators and excluded references to enslaved men and women who daily ran the mansion during Jefferson's lifetime. However, the decision to remove African American guides, whose collective memories of Monticello surpassed the period when Jefferson resided in Monticello, contributed to definitively suppress the only occasion when black perspectives were offered during the tour of the property. The new mansion tour led by the white hostesses, who were oriented to provide specific descriptions of each room of the house, remained in place for the next twenty-five years.[89] These guides obviously avoided any references to slavery and to the enslaved men, women, and children who labored in Monticello.

In 1943, the bicentennial of Jefferson's birth drove new interest in Jefferson's life and presidency with the publication of several new studies and biographies. After years of planning, on April 13, 1943, during the Second World War, the Thomas Jefferson Memorial was unveiled in Washington DC. In 1946 alone, 100,000 visitors toured Monticello, whereas in 1951, this number increased to 200,000.[90] During the next three decades, a growing number of guests continued visiting Monticello and new scholarly research provided more information concerning the lives of enslaved people on the site. In the summer of 1957, archaeologists led the first excavations at Mulberry Row, the alley located south of the southern terrace where domestic and skilled enslaved men and women lived and worked, uncovering three structures: the nailery, the joinery, and the storehouse.[91] Gradually Monticello acquired official heritage status. It was listed as a US National Historic Landmark in 1960 and entered the US National Register of Historic Places in 1966. In 1969, it was included in Virginia Landmarks Register. Yet, like in the previous century, most visitors to Monticello were whites who toured the property to know more about Jefferson and not about how slavery operated in the site.

Since the second half of the twentieth century, as discussed in Chapter 1, new studies, biographies, novels, and documentary films on Jefferson emphasized his relationship with the enslaved woman Sally Hemings, leading the Thomas Jefferson Foundation to hire more public historians to finally start addressing the work and lives of enslaved men and women in Monticello. In 1976, the bicentennial of the American Revolution once again renewed the public interest in Monticello. That year 671,486 visitors visited Jefferson's home.[92] Still, the tours of the property continued omitting any references to the bondspeople who worked the site. In an article published in the magazine *The Crisis* in 1975, Thomas A. Greenfield (1934-2017), an instructor at the historically black Virginia Union University, accurately summarized how during the mansion's visit white hostesses deliberately concealed any mentions to the work and the presence of enslaved men and women in Monticello. This disavowal appeared through the use of passive voice to describe the tasks performed by enslaved people, whereas in contrast the hostesses used the active voice to emphasize Jefferson's achievements.[93] In response to the article, Raymond J. Jirran, a professor of history at the Thomas Nelson Community College in Hampton, Virginia, wrote a letter to the editor of *The Crisis* to confirm that during a visit to Monticello taken several years before, the tour guide "feigned ignorance when asked about Sally Hemings."[94] Despite these criticisms, for several decades, the Thomas Jefferson Foundation maintained the same model of the mansion's tour.

Starting in the 1980s visitors were encouraged to explore other sections of Monticello, such as the gardens and mansion surroundings. During these years, the new director of the Thomas Jefferson Foundation, historian Daniel P. Jordan, created the departments of research, restoration, education, visitor services (with the creation of a visitors' center), as well as development and public affairs. Funding from the National Endowment for the Humanities also allowed the development of archaeological research on the site. In 1982, new excavations revealed the slave quarters of Mulberry Row. This work opened a new opportunity to discuss the history of slavery in Monticello. Hence, in the late 1980s, a few plaques were placed along the alley to acknowledge the presence of enslaved workers and their professions. Monticello's public historians also introduced the first self-guided tour of Mulberry Row, including information uncovered during archaeological excavations. Yet, like Mount Vernon, this was a segregated visit, an optional tour that visitors could simply decide to skip. Indeed, by then these timid initiatives were never sufficient to effectively provide an accurate picture of the importance of slavery in Monticello in a context where most docents were whites, like the greatest majority of the tourists who visited the site to know about Thomas Jefferson's glorious life. As historian Louis E. Horton reminds us, much like in Mount Vernon, during the visits of Mulberry Row there were reports of incidents involving black guides and white visitors, including an occasion when "one recently recruited black guide about to conduct his first tour was greeted by a white visitor who declared, 'So you are our slave for today.'"[95]

Monticello resisted in recognizing slavery as a central feature in its interpretation. Yet, as a pivotal national monument in the United States, the site could not escape the international wave that emerged in Europe,

Africa, and the Americas during the 1990s, when black social actors pushed to make slavery and the slave trade visible in the public space. Gradually, based on the work of historians and archaeologists, Thomas Jefferson Foundation made additional efforts to interpret slavery in Monticello. In 1991, the department of education published a teacher's guide on slavery in Monticello comprising a unit titled "Finding Isaac Jefferson: A Monticello Slave."[96] In 1992, a memo instructed the guides who toured the mansion to discuss slavery at least at three or four of the nine stops of the tour. They were also oriented to tell the story and to be open to answer questions regarding Sally Hemings.[97] However, it is very unlikely that docents ever consistently followed these recommendations. Similar to what occurred in Mount Vernon, tourists continued visiting Monticello to spend the day exploring its scenic grounds, enjoying its panoramic mountain views and of course paying homage to the US founding father, by appreciating his mansion's architecture and refined furniture. Despite the efforts made by public historians, their work was not always visible on the grounds, where what continued to prevail was Jefferson's memory with which white audiences were eager to engage. In this context, slavery interpretation continued to clash with the power of white supremacy that haunted heritage sites such as Monticello since the eighteenth century.

In 1993, the 250th birth anniversary of Thomas Jefferson, the number of visitors to Monticello reached 622,137. Parallel to this celebration, the efforts to tell the history of slavery during the tours also increased. In the same year, a team of public historians led by Lucia Stanton started researching the lives of the enslaved men and women slaves who worked at Monticello by collecting documents and interviewing their descendants. This initiative gave birth to the oral history project *Getting Word*, which also allowed the development of the "Plantation Community Tour," presenting slavery in Monticello and discussing Jefferson's relation with the evil institution.[98] Contemporary reports indicate that visitors positively reacted to the tour, encouraging the development of additional programs.

Between 1981 and 2001, at least 500,000 visitors came to Monticello every year.[99] This same period witnessed a growing number of scholarly works, especially the groundbreaking book by historian Annette Gordon-Reed, emphasizing the relations between Jefferson and enslaved Sally Hemings, with whom he had six children.[100] Eventually, results of DNA tests confirmed what Jefferson's contemporaries and historians already suspected. Even if many members of Jefferson's white family resisted to recognize the evidence, the work of black and white scholars as well as of militants, educators, and ordinary citizens put more pressure on the Thomas Jefferson Foundation to include slavery in Monticello's heritage interpretation. In the fall of 2001, the Thomas Jefferson Foundation commemorated the slave burial ground. During the ceremony, the names of known enslaved men and women who worked in Monticello were read aloud. But despite these developments, slavery continued to be a very marginal feature in Monticello's interpretation even though the workforce of bondspeople was the main engine, which made the existence of Jefferson's plantation possible.

In 2008, the election of Barack Obama as president of the United States greatly contributed to accelerate the need of publicly acknowledging the nation's slave past. This emphasis emerged not only from the fact that Obama was the first US black president, but especially because since the presidential campaign, he underscored the slave ancestry of the First Lady Michelle Obama.[101] Not surprisingly, the homes of the founding fathers such as Washington, Jefferson, and also James Madison's Montpelier, all of them near the national capital, were among the first heritage sites to start revising their narratives to include the history of slavery. In February 2012, Monticello opened *Landscape of Slavery: Mulberry Row at Monticello*, a new outdoor exhibit exploring the lives of the enslaved men, women, and children who lived and worked in Mulberry Row (Figure 5.2).

FIGURE 5.2 *Cabin of enslaved master carpenter John Hemmings and his wife Priscilla Hemmings at Mulberry Row, Monticello, Charlottesville, Virginia, United States. Photograph by Ana Lucia Araujo, 2015. Courtesy: Thomas Jefferson Monticello.*

Tourists can visit the exhibition by themselves utilizing the Slavery at Monticello smartphone application. Visitors can also choose to take the tour "Slavery at Monticello" covering Mulberry Row, which is included in the general admission fee. More popular than the Mount Vernon's slavery tour, this visit runs hourly from April to October. However, it remains segregated because it is still the only tour specifically focusing on the issue of slavery. Like in other plantations around the United States, visitors give priority to visit the mansion and can simply decide to not spend one hour at the slavery tour. As in Mount Vernon, most Monticello's docents and visitors are white, and the tours are conceived to address the concerns of white tourists. To explain working and living conditions in Mulberry Row to an audience composed mainly by white visitors, docents use the term "enslaved" and not "slave" to humanize instead of highlighting their legal statuses. Guests, although curious, often feel clearly uncomfortable. As in other plantations owned by founding fathers, white adults and children ask if the enslaved could learn how to read and write and if they were treated well. On these occasions, docents tell stories of fugitive slaves such as James Hubbard (1783–?) who, after escaping slavery two times, was recaptured, severely punished, and then sold. This story clearly suggests that Jefferson was not a benevolent slaveholder.

On January 2012, parallel to featuring slavery in Monticello, the temporary exhibition *Slavery at Jefferson's Monticello: Paradox of Liberty* exploring the lives of Monticello's enslaved men, women, and children was launched in the Smithsonian National Museum of American History in Washington DC. In the next ten months, more than one million people visited the exhibition. As seen in Chapter 2, the opening room showcased Jefferson's life-size statue, whereas in the background a large red mural (see Figure 2.5) contained the names of all enslaved men, women, and children he owned during his life. One of the displays surrounding the statue and the wall of names, titled "This Deplorable Entanglement," indicated that "Jefferson and many other patriots believed slavery should be abolished in the new American nation" but also emphasized that "over of the course of his life Jefferson himself owned 600 people." Despite the prominent presence of Jefferson in the opening room, exhibition that today is traveling around the country emphasizes the lives and working activities of Monticello's bondspeople. One section titled "The Nailery" invites the visitor to experience the work performed by enslaved men in Mulberry Row's nailery. A display shows different kinds of nails and reproduces a quote by Isaac (Granger) Jefferson, one of the enslaved workers who labored in the nailery. Additionally, visitors are encouraged to lift a nail bucket "to feel the weight of ten pounds of nails." Interactivity was also employed in another display titled "Running Way." The panel displays an ad by Thomas Jefferson published in the *Virginia Gazette* on September 14, 1769, in which he searches for "a Mulatto slave called Sandy" who ran away with a white horse, carrying his shoemaker tools, and is described in the ad as "addicted to drink."[102] On the one hand, the display approaches fugitiveness from Jefferson's point of view by failing to explain what did lead Sandy to run away. On the other hand, the interactive part of this same display showcases a section titled "Making Hard Decisions" highlighting compliance by referring to David Hern Jr., a wagoner who drove by himself between Monticello and Washington DC, but who decided to not run away. Visitors are then asked the question "If you were enslaved in Monticello, would you try to run away?" and are invited to answer the question by tapping one of the tablets indicating "yes" or "no." Finally, the exhibition also gave a prominent place to Sally Hemings and her children fathered by Thomas Jefferson and showcased videos from the oral history project *Getting Word*.

During more recent years, the number of visitors to Monticello slightly declined. In 2003, 463,733 individuals toured the site, whereas between 2008 and 2018, nearly 440,000 people visited Monticello annually.[103] It is hard to determine the reason for this small decrease in the number of visitors. The decline may suggest that Jefferson is no longer as popular as he used to be. Yet it may reveal the unwillingness of white visitors to see slavery as part of Monticello's interpretation. Admittedly, Monticello continues to be a space of affirmation of white supremacy, intended for white audiences. However, starting in the second half of the twentieth century, the descendants of the men and women owned by Jefferson along with African American scholars, journalists, and activists were successful in putting pressures to bring slavery to light in Monticello. On June 16, 2018, the foundation unveiled several new exhibitions featuring reconstructed buildings of Mulberry Row. Also, the new exhibition *The Life of Sally Hemings* was opened in Monticello's south wing slave quarters, in a room just next to the kitchen area that probably served as her bedroom.[104] Newspapers and television channels from all over the world covered the exhibition that finally gave Sally Hemings a prominent place in Monticello's interpretation. The exhibition's inauguration was accompanied by a huge ceremony gathering descendants of the enslaved people who once lived and worked in the plantation. Today, Monticello also offers once a day the Hemings Family Tour. Lasting more than three hours, this guided visit is not included in the general admission fee and costs almost the same price as Monticello day pass. In June 2018, Monticello also announced it will be phasing out the mansion's tour that barely mentions slavery, a change that if confirmed will greatly impact the ways other plantations in the United States present slavery.[105]

Slavery as Public History

Following the death of Washington and Jefferson, successive owners transformed Mount Vernon and Monticello heritage sites of slavery by adding other layers to the natural landscapes and buildings. In these two sites, docents are trained to cover certain topics, to emphasize specific points of views, and to tell particular stories. Yet although based on accurate historical information, the narratives conveyed during the plantation tours are also subject to change, depending on the level of education, age, race, gender, and class of docents and visitors. Moreover, because visitors carry with them previous knowledge and experiences, their views, responses, and reactions impact how slavery is interpreted as well. Because of the crucial living dimension of these sites, public historians do not perform their work by relying on bilateral relations, as seen in exhibitions, but rather on multilateral interactions. In other words, the work of public historians addressing the problem of slavery is always in dialogue with different modalities of memory explored in previous chapters.

At one level the collective memory and the public memory that prevailed in Mount Vernon are those of the Washington family and their descendants, even though enslaved men and women and their descendants pioneered the interpretation of slavery at both sites. Despite public knowledge about Jefferson's children with Sally Hemings, the views of his white family are those that predominate in Monticello. In Mount Vernon and Monticello, the narratives by descendants of slave owners were preserved and promoted by white groups, who traditionally represented southern families who fought to maintain slavery during the Civil War. In Mount Vernon, these groups, very often led by white women slaveholders or descendants of slaveholders, have controlled the site's conservation and preservation. Southerners, including female descendants of pro-slavery individuals, also claimed Jefferson's legacy after his death. But their attempts to control Monticello had failed. Whereas the Levys, a Jewish family, owned Monticello much longer than the Jefferson's family, the Thomas Jefferson Foundation was not a southern initiative.

Today, historical accuracy is a central concern that guides the work of public historians and docents leading slavery tours in both Mount Vernon and Monticello. Despite the enormous hindrances to represent slavery in these two sites, the view that evacuates the existence of slavery and ignores the experience of enslaved people has been contested since the beginning of the process that made Washington's and Jefferson's homes heritage sites open to public visitation. After restoring buildings, leading excavations, promoting research, and unveiling exhibitions (initiatives associated with the work of public historians, archaeologists, and heritage site professionals), two goals remain to be achieved. First, creating empathy among white visitors through narratives that emphasize the hardships experienced by enslaved individuals who composed the great majority of the population who lived and worked in these estates. Second, although few black tourists visit Mount Vernon and Monticello every year, public historians also face the problem of successfully conveying the history of slavery to African American audiences, whose lives were, and in many cases, still are, deeply shaped by the trauma of slavery experienced by their ancestors. In both cases, the interplay of memory and history is crucial for successfully conveying the history of slavery in these two heritage sites. Telling the history of slavery to popular audiences in sites that are symbols of white supremacy remains a hard challenge.

6

Art of Memory

Visual arts are a rich framework through which memory of slavery has reached the public space. Embodying different modalities of memory (individual, collective, public, cultural, and official), European, American, and African visual artists have produced works addressing the issue of slavery and the slave trade. Through these artworks, they have exposed its multiple layers, sensitive zones, obscure dimensions, and opposing perspectives. Part of a solo or group, national and international, exhibitions these works have contributed not only to raise questions about human atrocities during the era of slavery but also to problematize the enduring legacies of slavery.

Drawing from the discussion on various dimensions of memory presented in previous chapters, I show how through painting, sculpture, photography, installation, and other media, contemporary artists Cyprien Tokoudagba, Romuald Hazoumè, William-Adjété Wilson, Rosana Paulino, Nona Faustine, and François Piquet have engaged with the slave past by destabilizing binary oppositions between victims and perpetrators while also bringing to light debates on the history and memory of slavery and its present-day legacies. Arguing that their artworks are modeled and affected by the international context in which the past of slavery and the Atlantic slave trade emerges during the 1990s, I also emphasize how their artistic productions are inseparable from specific social frameworks, including family and religion. While underscoring how the works of these artists are shaped by the societies from which they emerge and modeled by the artists' own racial identities, I argue that visual arts carry on as one of the most complex and probably the most comprehensive instrument to engage with the various dimensions of the slave past.

Vodun Gods and the Art of the Slave Trade

Artists based on the African continent as well as Europe and the Americas utilized the cosmologies and symbols of African-based religions such as Vodun to discuss the impacts of slavery and the Atlantic slave trade in their societies. As discussed in Chapter 1, Vodun is a religion practiced in West Africa. It relies on spirit possession, trance, and the existence of multiple deities. Worshippers honor these deities with food, drinks, and dance. Transplanted to the Americas during the era of the Atlantic slave trade, and amalgamated with Catholicism and Native American cosmologies, Vodun is also a space of dialogue between the past and present as well as between life and death; it became a vehicle through which to establish a link between the two shores of the Atlantic Ocean forcefully brought together during the transatlantic slave trade.

Like Christian religions that have their own temples, art, and relics, tangible heritage is also part of African or African-based religions. In the compounds of Vodun temples, worshippers gather to dance, drink, eat, and celebrate *voduns* (deities) and their ancestors. As Marc Augé explains, these deities are also ancestors, and they were people like us: "They call us to order those who forget them, who neglect to make offerings and to make sacrifices that are necessary for all [V]odun gods in order to allow them to survive in one or the other of their appearances."[1] Priests and initiates install these divinities in shrines located in particular sites, where they are honored with offerings of food and drinks. Worshippers decorate these temples with images and words to commemorate these gods.

Vodun arts have been practiced in the Kingdom of Dahomey since its inception, but during the French rule, colonizers repressed public manifestations of African-based religions. After successive military regimes that followed the end of the colonial rule in 1960, Mathieu Kérékou (1933–2015) established a "Marxist-Leninist" dictatorship (1972–1991). To affect a rupture with the colonial past, he renamed the country the Republic of Benin. This authoritarian regime, which ruled the country for nearly two decades, greatly repressed Vodun public ceremonies. When popular protest put an end to the military government, an outcome favored by the conclusion of the Cold War in the late 1980s, and the fall of the Soviet Union in 1991, new prospects for memorializing slavery and the Atlantic slave trade emerged in the Republic of Benin.

As Charles Mills pointed out, the 500th anniversary of the arrival of Columbus in the Americas in 1992 generated vivid debates that "confronted many whites with the uncomfortable fact [...] that we live in a world which has been *foundationally shaped for the past five hundred years by the realities of European domination and the gradual consolidation of global white supremacy*."[2] In the context of these debates, Haiti proposed the development of a program highlighting the impact that Africa and the slave trade had on the expansion of the Americas, urging the Republic of Benin to take the lead in this project. Responding to these proposals, two projects emerged. In 1993, a festival celebrating Vodun arts and cultures transpired with the goal of underscoring social, cultural, and economic exchanges that resulted from the Atlantic slave trade.[3] In 1994, UNESCO launched the Slave Route Project, in the Republic of Benin, an international scientific program with the aim of understanding the causes and mechanisms of slavery in the world. Yet, for the government and local elites, these ventures were mainly an opportunity to promote cultural tourism in a country in great need of economic development. In this context, where a certain form of commodification of the history, memory, and heritage of slavery and the slave trade prevailed, the emphasis was on attracting African American and Caribbean tourists who traveled to West Africa to seek their roots and visit sites of memory of the Atlantic slave trade.

The festival *Ouidah 92: World Festival of Vodun Cultures, Reunion Americas-Africa* was inspired by the FESTAC 77 (Festival of Black and African Arts and Culture), held in Nigeria in 1977, and the Festival Mondial des Arts Nègres (World Black Arts Festival) organized in Senegal in 1968. As part of the Vodun festival, which actually occurred in February 1993, the city of Ouidah built the Slaves' Route, an unpaved three-mile road from the city's downtown area to the beach. The festival's organizers commissioned nearly one hundred statues and memorials to mark the various points along the road. Cyprien Tokoudagba (1939–2012), a self-taught artist from Abomey (the old capital of the Kingdom of Dahomey in the present-day Republic of Benin) created most of the sculptures representing Vodun deities distributed along the Slaves' Route. Other local artists such as Gnonnou Dominique (alias Kouass), Fortuné Bandeira, Théodore Dakpogan, Calixte Dakpogan, and Yves Apollinaire Kpédè (1959–2019) also created some of the artworks placed along the road.

In many ways, the works of these artists addressed issues related to Vodun religion and the Atlantic slave trade. Tokoudagba belonged to a family of artisans very close to the royal family of Dahomey.[4] As his work became known through his wall paintings, local priests commissioned him to paint Vodun temples façades, and Tokoudagba was initiated to the society of Tohossou. A water deity, the *vodun* Tohossou represents deformed royal children who after birth were returned to sacred waters from where it was believed they came.[5]

Tokoudagba's work is in conversation with long-existing figurative art forms that use a variety symbols to tell stories commemorating the rulers of Dahomey. Appliqué cloth for example is an art form that consists of sewing on fabric panel textiles of different colors representing people, animals, and a variety of objects. Like appliqué cloths, bas-reliefs decorating the walls of the royal palaces of Abomey also depict humans, animals, and other objects to narrate stories associated with the Dahomean kings, including military campaigns during which their soldiers captured and killed their opponents who were locally enslaved or sold into slavery to the Atlantic market.[6] Still, as painting provides more resources than appliqué cloths and bas-reliefs, Tokoudagba's murals convey richer and more detailed representations of human figures. In his frescos, he renders Vodun priestesses and other characters through a treatment of light and shade that creates a naturalistic effect of volume absent from Dahomean traditional art forms. Gradually, Tokoudagba started conceiving mud sculptures on similar topics and painted in various colors. He also transposed the motifs of his frescoes to canvas that could be sold abroad. In 1987, the artist was hired to work in the restoration of the Abomey's palaces; at that time, the original bas-reliefs were removed and replaced with replicas that he and other artists helped to recreate.[7]

During the 1980s, Tokoudagba's work acquired an international reputation. His paintings were featured in the exhibition *Les magiciens de la terre* (The Magicians of the World) curated by white art historian and curator Jean-Hubert Martin and held at Center Pompidou in Paris from May 18 to August 14, 1989. This exhibition marked a turning point for European contemporary art shows and for African art, which until recently had only been exhibited in ethnography and natural history museums. In the years that followed his participation in *Les magiciens de la terre*, Tokoudagba showed his work in several collective and individual international exhibitions, including the Brazilian São Paulo Art Biennial of 1989. Consequently, the choice of Tokoudagba to conceive most of the monuments unveiled in Ouidah during the Vodun festival was motivated by his reputation and because Vodun was already at the heart of his work.

Tokoudagba's sculptures, displayed along the Slaves' Route, embody the collective memory of the Atlantic slave trade in the ancient Kingdom of Dahomey by featuring the experiences of the enslavers and the enslaved. His cement statues, painted in different colors, portray enslaved men and women. Yet several works also depict amazons, women warriors who were part of a regiment of the Dahomean army and who, during the wars against neighboring kingdoms, captured prisoners who were sold into slavery. Other statues are renderings of Vodun deities whose mythologies are linked to the slave trade and to specific Dahomean kings.

Some monuments conceived by Tokoudagba represent different kinds of vodun *Dan* (snake), a deity closely related to the history of the Kingdom of Dahomey whose own name ("in the womb of *Dan*") is derived from it. Since at least the eighteenth century, Dahomean visual representations feature the mythical snake, still worshiped today in the Republic of Benin. The vodun *Dan Ayido Houedo* (Rainbow Serpent) is portrayed in one of the bas-reliefs decorating the walls of his palace in Abomey. As discussed in Chapter 1, the infamous slave trader Francisco Félix de Souza also had several voduns *Dan*. A temple to one of these deities (the *Dagoun*) stands in Ouidah, and locals still associate his great wealth with the cult of this deity. Likewise,

Ouidah's downtown features the Temple of Pythons dedicated to the popular serpent deity. Every year, thousands of tourists visit the large shrine to interact with dozens of snakes. At the temple's façade, a Tokoudagba's statue portrays a Dahomean female figure whose torso is wrapped by a python. In another statue (Figure 6.1), situated along the Slaves' Route in Ouidah, Tokoudagba represents the rainbow serpent, a vodun whose symbol

FIGURE 6.1 *Cyprien Tokoudagba,* Dan Ayido Houedo, *Ouidah, the Republic of Benin. Photograph by Ana Lucia Araujo, 2005.*

is associated with King Guezo (who reigned between 1818 and 1858) and the Atlantic slave trade. Tokoudagba's serpent biting its own tale carries the colors of the rainbow. This representation, conjuring the idea of timeless power and universality, fertility, and death, is also related to *akori* beads.[8] Used as currency in commercial exchanges with Europeans on the West African coasts, since the sixteenth century these beads carried great symbolic value. Oral tradition states that *akori* beads are derived from the snake's excrements. Ultimately, *Dan Ayido Houedo* and its variations represent the wealth generated by the Atlantic slave trade. Therefore, when Tokoudagba conceived a sculpture representing this *vodun* he was not highlighting the victims of the Atlantic slave trade but rather how Dahomean kings, slave merchants, and various intermediaries obtained profits from such inhuman commerce. Tokoudagba's frescoes and sculptures representing royal deities and amazon warriors were modeled by Vodun religion. At the same time, his artworks also adhered to the point of view of Dahomean rulers. However, Tokoudagba's statues are not static and allow for other interpretations. From time to time, the cement sculptures are repainted in different colors. Moreover, although Ouidah's modest population did not have any decision power regarding the choice of artists and monuments, the city's residents leave offerings of food and drinks at the bottom of the statues, transforming them into actual shrines.[9]

The Engines of the Atlantic Slave Trade

The path, opened in the 1990s, brought to the international stage other Beninese artists who explore the theme of the Atlantic slave trade. As discussed in Chapter 3, at the turn of the twenty-first century, the work of these artists was part of a dynamic international context marked by pressures and actions led by organized black groups who instigated the process that gave more visibility to slavery in the public space. In 2001, France passed the Taubira Law recognizing slavery as a crime against humanity. In Europe, Britain was the first country to explicitly acknowledge its deep involvement in the slave trade in the Atlantic. Although its first initiatives to memorialize the slave trade began in the mid-1990s, at the turn of the new millennium British institutions launched numerous projects with the intention of preparing the 2007 activities to commemorate the bicentennial of the abolition of the slave trade.

The year 2007 was marked by a veritable avalanche of exhibitions and the emergence of new works by artists that addressed the Atlantic slave trade and slavery as a central issue. Romuald Hazoumè is one of these artists whose work gained greater visibility during this period. Hazoumè was born in Porto-Novo, today's capital of the Republic of Benin. Much younger than Tokoudagba, his family has roots among Yoruba groups living today within the country's frontiers. The works of both Hazoumè and

Tokoudagba illuminate how collective memories of the Atlantic slave trade are multiple and shaped by religion and family frameworks. In contrast with Tokoudagba, Hazoumè's origins place him in a different position because during the eighteenth and nineteenth centuries, the Dahomean army carried military campaigns against Yoruba towns to subsequently sell the prisoners into slavery to the Americas. Thus, partly because of his family ties, Hazoumè's work engages with Dahomey's slaving past by underscoring the perspective of the victims of the Atlantic slave trade and its present-day legacies.

The history of the Kingdom of Dahomey and the Republic of Benin shaped Hazoumè's work. Although the artist witnessed a dictatorship during his youth, in his early adulthood he also experienced the effervescence of the redemocratization period. Hazoumé is a self-taught artist. In the 1980s, he became the assistant of the French artist Jacques Yves Bruel (1948–2010), who conceived ready-mades with gasoline containers found in Central African Republic and the Republic of Benin. Like Bruel, Hazoumè incorporated gas cans into his work, transforming them into masks, which are largely utilized in Yoruba ceremonies to honor ancestors and various deities. In 1992, his masks were included in *Out of Africa*. The exhibition, held at Saatchi Gallery in London, presented contemporary African art as a "continuous development of traditional means of conception and production."[10] In dialogue with Vodun religion, Hazoumè's artistic production also carries a political dimension. The artist critiqued a society of mass consumption by creating collages with pieces of televisions, computers, and components such as plastic, steel, and oil and incorporating them to his masks.

In the fifteen years that followed Hazoumè's participation in *Out of Africa*, he showed his work in individual and group exhibitions in the United States, the Netherlands, Russia, UK, Australia, Belgium, France, and Finland. In 2007, the British Museum acquired Hazoumè's installation *La bouche du roi* (The King's Mouth).[11] In the making since 1997, the work had already been presented at the French Institute in Cotonou, the Republic of Benin, in 1999; the Menil Collection, in Houston, Texas, in 2005; and at Musée du Quai Branly, in Paris, France, in 2006. Exhibited at the British Museum from March 22, 2007, to May 13, 2007, *La bouche du roi* reproduces the image of the famous *Brookes*, the eighteenth-century Liverpool slave ship, whose representation was widely used by the British abolitionist movement. The installation's title evokes a slave trade site on the coast of the Republic of Benin. *La bouche du roi* marks the point where Ouidah's lagoon ends, and the place from where enslaved Africans embarked into slave ships. But the installation's title also suggests other meanings. The reference to the king's mouth also implies that trade in enslaved Africans nurtured not only European and American nations such as France, England, Portugal, Spain, Brazil, and the United States but also West African states such as the Kingdom of Dahomey. The installation, subsequently exhibited in Hull,

Liverpool, Bristol, and Newcastle, functioned almost as a memorial in a period when Britain had not yet unveiled any memorials to the victims of the Atlantic slave trade.

La bouche du roi consists of 304 masks made of gasoline plastic containers, each with an open mouth, eyes, and nose to represent the slaves transported on board of slave vessels. Hazoumè reworked the gallons by heating them with fire to the breaking point, transforming the discarded containers into a powerful metaphor of the lives lost in the Atlantic slave trade. The installation was not a static setting. The containers emanated sounds and smells calling to mind the tragic experience of being confined in a slave ship. Like in previous works, to build the rest of the installation, Hazoumè also used a variety of discarded objects such as empty bottles, cowry shells, spices, and mirrors representing examples of goods brought to Africa to purchase enslaved men, women, and children.

La bouche du roi also included a film giving details on why the choice of gas cans, used to build the installation, was not fortuitous. In addition to their formal elements suggesting the image of masks, the containers also allude to the huge black market of gasoline between Benin and Nigeria. Motorcyclists transport gasoline between the two countries to be sold by sellers along the roads between Benin and Nigeria. Therefore, Hazoumè's installation sheds light on the connections between the Atlantic slave trade and the present-day traffic of gasoline in the region, in a period when oil is as valued a commodity and in demand as human flesh was at the time of the slave trade. *La Bouche du roi* also establishes a direct link between the Atlantic slave trade, European colonialism in Africa, and their enduring legacies. Emphasizing how life and work in the region remain extremely precarious, the installation is also a powerful allegory of modern forms of social and economic oppression.

Also, as part of the commemoration of the bicentennial of the British abolition of the slave trade, the Victoria and Albert Museum commissioned another artwork from Hazoumè. *Dan Ayido Houedo* was featured in the Madejski Garden as part of the group exhibition *Uncomfortable Truths: The Shadow of Slave Trading on Contemporary Art and Design*. Curated by Zoe Whitley, the show included the works of ten other artists from Europe, Africa, and the Americas.[12] Like the installation *La bouche du roi*, Hazoumè constructed his work with painted gasoline containers to engage not only with the theme of the Atlantic slave trade but also with Vodun cosmology. At first sight, the giant ring of jerry cans seems to be an abstract structure. Very similar to Tokoudagba's work, Hazoumè depicts the vodun *Dan Ayido Houedo*, the sacred rainbow serpent that bites its own tail. The sculpture is a clear statement evoking the bodies of enslaved Africans that here compose the giant vodun snake that has been historically associated with the wealth generated by the Atlantic slave trade. According to Hazoumè, the serpent's body "has been made with dozens of masks representing all the slaves of the world in all their diverse forms."[13] Conveying the idea of continuity, the sculpture symbolizes the legacies of the Atlantic slave trade and serves as a "warning against all forms of modern slavery."[14] After being displayed in the group exhibition *African Cosmos: Stellar Arts* held from June 20 to December 9, 2012, the National Museum of African Art in Washington DC acquired Hazoumè's sculpture, which was later displayed in the exhibition *Visionary: Viewpoints on Africa's Art* that opened in the same museum on November 4, 2017.

French artist William-Adjété Wilson also engages the history and memory of slavery and the Atlantic slave trade. In the twentieth-first century, he developed the series *The Black Ocean*. Its title infers the term "Black Atlantic," which since the publication of Paul Gilroy's book *The Black Atlantic: Modernity and Double-Consciousness* in the 1990s has become popular among scholars.[15] The series covers the exchanges among Europe, Africa, and the Americas during the Atlantic slave trade and colonialism by also exploring how these tragic events led the creation of a common black culture. Translated into Portuguese as *Oceano Negro* and in French as *Océan Noir*, the series also embodies Wilson's position as an artist working and residing in different countries of the African diaspora.

A self-taught artist like Tokoudagba and Hazoumè, Wilson's series *The Black Ocean* is marked by his own family origins. The son of a French mother, the family of Wilson's father had roots in the region of present-day Togo and the Republic of Benin. When he was eighteen years old, he visited his father's homeland for the first time and started investigating his family history. Among others, he learned that his West African ancestors had roots among the Luso-Brazilian community established in the region since the eighteenth century and played the role of intermediaries between the local population and the slave merchants during the Atlantic slave trade. Exploring a variety of techniques, including drawing and painting, Wilson started presenting his work in exhibitions in Europe and the United States since the 1980s.

Despite this knowledge of his family history, Wilson's *The Black Ocean* series took shape much later in 2007, during a period when debates on the Atlantic slave trade past have been increasingly present in the public sphere of Europe, Africa, and the Americas. Between 2007 and 2009, Wilson sojourned four times in Abomey, the capital of the old Kingdom of Dahomey, in the present-day Republic of Benin. In Abomey, Wilson worked with the Beninese artist Yves Apollinaire Kpédè, a textile artist who also conceived some of the sculptures displayed along the Slaves' Route in Ouidah. Utilizing his recognized repertoire of colorful schematic and fantastic figures, Wilson designed eighteen tableaux narrating the history of the Atlantic slave trade and the African diaspora. To conceive these works, Wilson chose the ancient appliqué cloth technique. Since the eighteenth century, Abomey artisans of the royal court combined pieces of cloth in various colors to create forms and figures telling the history and the glories of the Kingdom of Dahomey. Like the bas-reliefs displayed on the walls of Abomey royal palaces, the traditional appliqué cloths praise the reigns of Dahomean rulers and their *vodun*s by also depicting the wars waged against the neighboring kingdoms and the prisoners captured and killed during these military campaigns, which greatly intensified during the eighteenth century to produce captives for the Atlantic slave trade.

The various figures represented in Wilson's appliqué hangings refer to multiple times. They represent both tradition and modernity. In his explanation of one appliqué hanging portraying the kings of Dahomey, Wilson reminds the viewer that oral narratives collected among the families of artisans in Abomey indicate that the appliqué cloth was introduced in the royal court during the reign of King Agaja (r. 1708–1732). During Agaja's rule, Dahomey conquered the kingdoms of Allada and Hueda, thus obtaining access to the Atlantic Ocean. Therefore, the correlation between the emergence of this artistic practice and the growing contacts of Dahomey with European traders suggests that development of appliqué cloth technique is closely associated with the rise of the Atlantic slave trade.

Starting in the middle of the eighteenth century, the Atlantic slave trade became Dahomey's main source of revenue. Especially under the rules of Agonglo, Adandozan, and Guezo, the port of Ouidah (controlled by Dahomey) exported thousands of men, women, and children to Brazil. By that time, the slave trade in the South Atlantic region, covered by Brazil and the Bight of Benin, did not follow the traditional model of triangular voyages. Instead, it followed a bilateral path. Without passing through Lisbon, Luso-Brazilian slave merchants settled on both sides of the Atlantic Ocean, often trafficking directly between the Bight of Benin and Brazil. In Ouidah and other ports of the region, they traded tobacco produced in Bahia for slaves captured by Dahomey during the wars waged against neighboring states and peoples, who they subsequently sold in Bahia.

Wilson's *The Black Ocean* is organized in chronological order; the panels construct a coherent narrative corresponding to the various stages of the Atlantic slave trade, European colonization, fighting for liberation, and present-day connections among the members of the African diaspora. Dahomean kings, slave merchants, and enslaved individuals dominate the universe of the first appliqué cloths presented in the series. Focusing on one theme, each panel contains a symbol infused with a specific meaning and is also accompanied by a citation by philosopher, psychiatrist, writer, and anti-colonial activist Frantz Fanon (1925–1961).

The exhibition's opening cloth presents its title in English (*The Black Ocean*), French (*L'Océan Noir*), and Portuguese (*O Oceano Negro*). Although Wilson's work borrows from the Dahomean art form of appliqué cloths, Fante peoples of the Gold Coast (present-day Ghana) also produced flags utilizing similar techniques. The first banner of the series also displays a Sankofa (Akan pictogram discussed in Chapter 2), represented by a bird, that means "go back to fetch it," or in other words, to "learn from the past."[16] In this same vein, the second and third appliqué cloths portray the first European

FIGURE 6.2 *William-Adjété Wilson,* Slave Traders, *appliqué cloth, 2008–2009. Courtesy: William-Adjété Wilson.*

travelers along the African coasts and the encounter between European and Africans that led to the rise of the Atlantic slave trade. The fourth appliqué represents the twelve kings of Dahomey, reproducing traditional cloths still sold today in Abomey. But the fifth and sixth tapestries engage the most with the history of the Atlantic slave trade and slavery. The fifth cloth entitled *Slave Traders* (Figure 6.2) features two European figures. On the tableau's left side, a European man portrayed wearing eighteenth-century apparel (shoes, pants, a jacket, and a tricorne hat) is holding a huge pan in flames. Sitting inside the pan is a burning black man whose mouth is gagged and hands tied together. On the right side, another white character wearing boots, pants, jacket, and a huge hat is holding a rifle pointed toward a bare-chested black man representing the king of Dahomey. The most prominent character in the composition, the Dahomean ruler is wearing a traditional loincloth and a silver dust cover over his nose, a device that starting in 1894 (after the French conquest) was typically worn by the king.[17] Sitting in a royal stool, the sovereign is presented as the central figure in this narrative. This character is manipulating a wheel inside which only the silhouettes of black men are visible, portraying the captives captured during wars that fed the massive engine of the Atlantic slave trade. But in the sixth cloth, Dahomean kings and European traders disappear. Whereas the left side of the appliqué is dominated by a large building representing European castles along the West African coasts that served as slave depots (and are typically found in present-day Ghana), the right upper side features a slave ship. The bottom of the left side of the cloth displays a line of seven captives in chains, represented with identical physical features and in various shades of brown.

By portraying a range of social actors who participated in the inhuman trade including West African rulers and intermediaries, *The Black Ocean*'s appliqué cloths engage with multiple dimensions of the Atlantic slave trade and slavery, which otherwise would be difficult to convey. Wilson appropriates West African oral narratives, in his memorialization of the slave trade, by evoking the various spaces where African captives were confined such as slave depots and slave ships. The panels representing the stages that followed the end of the slave trade until the period of European colonization, the end of colonial rule, and anti-colonial fight also emphasize resilience and how the violence that resulted from the encounters between Europeans and Africans produced new forms of cultural, spiritual, and economic exchanges. The trauma and forgetting are deeply embedded in the experiences of those who were captured, sold, and separated from their families, to then be confined in slave ships. Nonetheless, the artist stresses the various ways the memory of African societies and ancestors remained alive among enslaved men, women, and children. Unlike many present-day initiatives memorializing the Atlantic slave trade in monuments, memorials, and museums that usually appropriate written and visual accounts from travelogues and slave narratives of the eighteenth and nineteenth centuries, Wilson takes an original approach. *The Black Ocean* relies on a variety of popular narratives, circulating today in West Africa, which have inspired projects memorializing the Atlantic slave trade such as the Slaves' Route in Ouidah. These narratives, although sometimes contested, are not limited to the opposition between victims and perpetrators, blacks and whites, and Europeans and Africans, but also include a wide range of social actors who participated in the dreadful trade at various levels.

Utilizing a traditional royal technique, Wilson's tableaux forms a continuous linkage between the Atlantic slave trade and the European colonization of Africa that can also be found in the works of contemporary Congolese artists such as Chéri Samba and Sammy Baloji. For example, the tenth appliqué hanging depicting the West African coastal bourgeoisie portrays the local elites of the Bight of Benin, who during the Atlantic slave trade developed commercial ties with the European traders and later during the colonial rule continued collaborating with European colonizers. According to Wilson, the thirteenth appliqué cloth pays homage to the African diaspora of the United States because of its great capacity of resistance against oppression, although social and economic achievements are also important features that make African Americans a distinctive group. Whereas in the fifteenth tableau titled *Africa Unite*, Wilson honors the resilience of African populations by including the name of male African leaders and intellectuals like Patrice Lumumba (1925–1961), Nelson Mandela (1918–2013), and Valentin Mundimbe, the sixteenth cloth calls attention to the struggle of Africans who every year attempt to leave the continent to migrate to Europe. Ultimately, through an editing process combining various times and spaces, the series *The Black Ocean* constitutes a rich example of how history, art, and memory come together to interrogate and complicate our understanding of the slave past. In days when the legacies of slavery are constantly the object of debate in former slave societies, Wilson's work provocatively engages the debate on the history of the Atlantic slave trade and the work of memory that stems from it.

Politicized Enslaved Bodies

Other artists who place the tangible bodies of black individuals at the heart of their works have embraced a bolder political stance when engaging with slavery and the Atlantic slave trade. The work of Afro-Brazilian artist Rosana Paulino became visible in Brazil during the middle of the 1990s, the same period that Tokoudagba and Hazoumè gained renown. But unlike these artists, Paulino received academic training. She obtained two college degrees in printmaking and a PhD in Visual Arts from the University of São Paulo in Brazil. Over the last decade, she participated in several group and individual international exhibitions and is among the growing number of Afro-Brazilian artists whose works have received international attention from curators, scholars, and critics. Addressing Brazilian colonial past and its long history of exclusion of populations of African descent, Paulino's work explores the experience of black women in Brazilian society as resulting from the long history of slavery and racism.[18] Working on a variety of techniques, she conceives installations, sculptures, engravings, and drawings in which she discusses the long-standing invisibility of black women in Brazilian society and how their bodies have been appropriated in scientific narratives.

The bodies of black women are central elements in Paulino's works. Her drawing *Seios com Leite e Sangue* (Breasts with Milk and Blood) (2005), part of the series *Ama de Leite* (Wet Nurses), is almost an abstract representation. Whereas several bloody breasts are rendered through combined layers of varying tones of red stain, entangled lines drain the breasts from their substance. This work is a commentary on the role of black women in breastfeeding the children of slave owners during the era of slavery in Brazil.[19] Other works engage with nineteenth-century photographs featuring naked bodies of black women and men, including the controversial racist pictures taken during the Thayer Expedition led by Swiss naturalist Louis Agassiz (1807–1873) in Brazil.[20]

In the exhibition *Atlântico Vermelho* (Red Atlantic) presented in Lisbon from October 14 to December 30, 2017, Paulino addressed the history and legacies of the Atlantic slave trade.[21] *Atlântico Vermelho* includes a variety of mixed-media works. Much like Wilson's cloths, the various works combine digital print on rectangular fabric panels sewed together. As art historian Kimberly C. Cleveland observes, "she sews both to honor something from her own childhood and to pay homage to society's often-marginalized women, like her mother."[22] By incorporating sewing into her work, Paulino adds to her personal experience, as this activity was part of her universe as a child in a modest black family.

Each section of these works features reproductions of nineteenth-century black-and-white photographs manipulated by the artist. One work (Figure 6.3) includes pictures of a vessel symbolizing a slave ship. It also presents portraits and full-body pictures of working black women transporting barrels on their heads or carrying bundles of sugar cane. Defaced, these pictures of faceless enslaved women illustrate their persistent anonymity in Brazilian society. The upper left side of this composition features a full-body profile photograph of a naked black man commissioned by Agassiz to French photographer Augusto Stahl (1828–1877), who since 1853 settled in Brazil.[23] The central axis of the panel contains a sequence of four frames. Discussing Luso-Brazilian colonial heritage, the first, second, and fourth rectangles display Portuguese colonial blue tiles, whereas the third section features the black-and-white image of a femur. Ultimately, slavery through the workforce provided by black bodies fueled the construction of Brazil as a Portuguese colony and later as a nation that continued to practice slavery until 1888. In contrast with the rest of the artwork, all in black and white, this central section of the composition features the blue color of the tiles and displays the title of the series, *Atlântico vermelho* (Red Atlantic), written in red capital letters. The red color is also visible in the rectangle at the bottom of the central section, where sewn red yarn falls from the tile's image, mimicking dripping blood. Here the ocean that staged the development of the Atlantic slave trade is no longer a zone of economic and cultural exchanges, as it appears in Wilson's work, but rather a bloody space of dismemberment and violence against black bodies.

Like Paulino and the other artists considered in this chapter, African American artist Nona Faustine also addresses the history of slavery and the Atlantic slave trade. The artist was born and raised in Brooklyn, New York City, where she still resides today. Academically trained, she obtained a bachelor's degree from the School of Visual Arts and a Masters of Fine Arts from the International Center of Photography at Bard College in New York. Reminiscent of Wilson and Paulino, family identity is a powerful framework that shapes Faustine's production. However, Faustine's own body is the object of her work as a photographer.

White Shoes, Faustine's first solo exhibition, was presented at the Smack Mellon Gallery, Brooklyn, New York City, from January 9 to February 21, 2016. The exhibition consisted of photographic self-portraits in visual dialogue with the history of slavery and the Atlantic slave trade in the United States. Earlier, before conceiving *White Shoes,* Faustine had already developed an interest in the African Burial Ground uncovered

FIGURE 6.3 *Rosana Paulino,* Atlântico vermelho *(Red Atlantic), mixed media, 2017. Courtesy: Rosana Paulino.*

in 1991 (see Chapter 2) and started researching more about the history of New York City.[24] In this context, the exhibition is not dissociated from the growing number of scholarly works that have reached the public sphere in the last two decades not only revealing that slavery existed in northern states, such as New York, Rhode Island, Vermont, Massachusetts, and Connecticut, but also highlighting that the capital generated by the southern cotton production largely financed the industrialization in the North. Indeed, northern banks and insurance companies greatly benefited from slavery, and even the wealth of prestigious institutions such as Harvard University and Brown University was built on the work of enslaved individuals.[25]

In *White Shoes*, Faustine brings the slave past to life, transforming her own body into a vehicle connecting the urban landscape of New York City and its history of slavery, whose tangible traces remain largely unnoticeable today. The artist recalls her "challenge was how to put this history that's largely invisible together with the celebration of this fat, black body who had recently given birth to a baby I was so proud of."[26] Just wearing a pair of high-heeled white shoes, the artist produced self-portraits in which she poses nude in various heritage sites and sites of memory of slavery and the Atlantic slave trade.

In the self-portrait *From Her Body Sprang Their Greatest Wealth* (2013), Faustine stands on the intersection of Wall Street and Pearl Street, where the former slave market operated in New York City between 1711 and 1762.[27] This photograph features the artist's sculpture-like, voluminous, and vulnerable naked body at an empty crossroad in Lower Manhattan.[28] Naked, with iron shackles around her wrists, she is wearing a pair of white pumps. As an imposing central element of the composition, her body evokes all black bodies that were captured, sold, and violated to build the wealth of the United States, here represented by Wall Street, a symbol of American capitalism.

Conceived in the same year as the emergence of the Black Lives Matter movement formed to respond to and denounce the demise of black lives as the result of police violence, Faustine's self-portraits highlighting sites of memory of slavery in Manhattan and Brooklyn are not dissociated from the battles of public memory in New York City, where since the 1990s black social actors have taken action to make the slave past visible. On February 4, 2014, nearly twenty members of the city council, including African American Councilman Jumaane Williams, introduced a bill requiring the creation of a marker to be placed at the site of the New York City's slave market.[29] On June 27, 2015, the city of New York unveiled a plaque at the market's location in Lower Manhattan. On that occasion, Mayor Bill de Blasio also established a connection between history and commemoration, as well as between past and the present, by stating: "Today, we recall that history; we commemorate the lives of all who passed here. The plaque we gather to dedicate is another way to signal something—to say something out loud that was true three centuries ago, even though it was never acknowledged. It was true then; it is true today; it will be true tomorrow. Black lives matter."[30]

The series *White Shoes* also includes self-portraits staged at Brooklyn slavery heritage sites. In the photographic installation *Of My Body I Will Make Monuments in Your Honor* (2014), Faustine pays homage to an elder enslaved man, an enslaved woman and an enslaved girl buried at the Flatbush Reformed Dutch Church Cemetery in Brooklyn.[31] The photograph transforms the image of the artist's own naked body into three defaced sculptures (profile, back, and frontal) set in the middle of the cemetery's existing tombstones.[32] Echoing Paulino's mixed-media works featuring faceless nineteenth-century representations of black women bodies, Faustine discusses the historical invisibility of enslaved people and their descendants, as here her naked black body cannot be invisible. Literally embodying these forgotten social actors, by removing her face from the images, Faustine underscores the complicated task of memorializing enslaved men and women about whom very little information is available.

French artist François Piquet has also explored the connections between black bodies and the profits generated by the slavery institution. Categorized as white, Piquet comes from a working-class family. Unlike Paulino and Faustine, he acquired a degree in engineering and a diploma in industrial design and later developed an interest in graphic arts and multimedia. When he moved from the Paris region to Guadeloupe in 2000, the artist started closely facing the legacies of French colonial history. In 2005, he exhibited for the first time his paintings and sculptures in Guadeloupe and later in other Caribbean countries. In his work, the artist interrogates the respective colonial and postcolonial histories and identities of France and Guadeloupe.

In 2016, Piquet presented the exhibition *Réparations* (Reparations) at the Fonds d'Art Contemporain at the Habitation Beausoleil, Saint-Claude, in Guadeloupe, which at that time housed the collections of Museum Victor Schoelcher (Musée Victor Schoelcher), under renovation. Piquet discusses reparations as a legal term as it relates to slavery and the Atlantic slave trade. According to him, his project is propelled by "the overwhelming responsibility of one who does not want to act as if he were not there." Reminding the viewer that very often the one who repairs is not the one who did the breaking, he takes care of the world "that comes by doing my share from where I am to repair today's world, sick from yesterday."[33] In this exhibition, Piquet emphasizes that his goal is not to demand reparations for slavery but to engage in the act of repair: "It is a question of carrying out repairs, that is to say, restoring or put back in function broken or deficient objects, concepts, representations, relations, or simple residues."[34] In other words, by investigating the slave past and addressing the moral dimensions of the work of memory and repair, in this work Piquet brings to light the debate on symbolic reparations.

The works comprising the exhibition *Réparations* started with an unusual finding. In 2014, while walking along the beach Raisins Clairs in Saint-François, in Guadeloupe, near an old slave cemetery, the artist's daughter found a human skull near a palm tree. Piquet decided to take the skull (part of which was missing) with him. Although it was not determined to whom the bone structure belonged to, he chose to conceive it as being that of an unknown slave.

This experience and the ongoing debates on reparations for slavery in the French Caribbean led the artist to recreate the skull's missing face with charcoal drawings on canvas. Engaging with the commemoration of enslaved individuals, the artist sheds light on the abandonment of Guadeloupe burial grounds and calls for their preservation. Here, Piquet embraces a central dimension of cultural memory of slavery, as discussed in Chapter 2, by recomposing the skull of the nameless individual and bringing to light the humanity of enslaved bodies that were historically dehumanized.[35] The still-life depictions of the bodiless and faceless skulls problematize the ways black bodies were forgotten or appropriated during the colonial and postcolonial periods. In one canvas, the cranium is just a shadow over a dinner plate conjuring the consumption of enslaved bodies and those who were fed thanks to them. In another canvas, the skull is attached to a huge metal u-padlock, whereas another drawing depicts a minstrel blackface mask covering the faceless skull.

The exhibition *Réparations* also includes *La Fabrique du Noir* (The Black's Factory), a set of eleven wooden carved sculptures. These sculptures, which interact with existing pieces displayed in the collection of the Museum Victor Schoelcher, question the construction of race and the representation of black individuals. Using three assorted kinds of wood, the artist carves each piece, representing the face, the torso, and sometimes the entire body of a human figure, then burns each sculpture. The exhibition also includes a film showing the production process of these sculptures, in which the artist interacts with the enslaved bodies he creates. Split, aged, devoured, and eventually rendered black by the fire, each figure is soaked in varnish to solidify its blackness. Eventually, Piquet inserts white teeth in the wooden sculptures' wide-open mouths and throats, an addition that enhances the dramatic effect of these works.

Following the exhibition, Piquet's work received international attention. One of his sculptures (Figure 6.4) was included in the show *Ink and Blood: Stories of Abolition*, held from August 21, 2017, to September 2, 2018, at the International Slavery Museum in Liverpool, UK, to mark the institution's tenth anniversary. Curated by Jean-François Maniçom, the exhibition showcasing historical documents, artifacts, and artworks focused on the history of slavery and abolition in different regions of the Atlantic world. Piquet's sculpture titled *Timalle* (2017), a French term (*petit mâle*) meaning small male, is in dialogue with the series *Réparations* and with a previous series titled *Mounpapyé* (Paper People). *Timalle* is a human figure made of crumbled paper, shaped with tape, and covered with resin. The work is presented in a glass display titled *Art of Abolition* that includes the sculpture *Timalle* and a video documenting its production. In the same glass display

FIGURE 6.4 *François Piquet,* Timalle, *sculpture (paper and resin) exhibition* Ink and Blood, *International Slavery Museum, Liverpool, UK. Photograph by Ana Lucia Araujo. 2017. Courtesy: International Slavery Museum.*

are three eighteenth-century written documents related to slavery as well as a short video *Whip It Good* (2014) of a performance by Copenhagen-based artist of Danish and Trinidadian descent Jeannette Ehlers that also explores the legacies of slavery, the Atlantic slave trade, and colonialism.

Timalle differs from previous paper sculptures produced by Piquet. The work is not made of ordinary papers but of a "Slavery Crimes Victims Reparations Application Form" created and designed by the artist. In his own words, the sculpture symbolizes "a skinned human body that I bonded and shackled with old rum barrel hoops ... and is also the filmed process of a white man transforming Timal—which means small male, in creole—into Timalle—which means suitcase ... a re-enactment, through sculpture and performance, of the enslavement process."[36] Whereas the sculpture is static, the video shows the artist's physical work to put together the paper figure. The video, revealing the lengthy process of production of the sculpture representing the enslaved man, provokes anxiety feelings and makes exhibition visitors uncomfortable. Through Piquet's choice of materials (the iron strips are historical artifacts whereas the fictional reparations forms are his own conception), the *Timalle* sculpture and video connect the slave past and the present-day demands of redress, an approach that continues to influence the artist's current work.

In 2019, Piquet was among the three artists featured in the Biennale of Venice's Guadeloupe Islands pavilion. His work *Colonial Equation* (2019) is an installation combining a monumental sculpture titled *You and Me*, made of braided iron rods representing "two Siamese bodies struggling to separate one from each other," and the video *Pré-requis à la discussion décoloniale* (Pre-Requisites for the Decolonial Discussion). In this video, Piquet no longer documents the sculpture's production but rather features black and white individuals addressing the camera with short statements wherein they position themselves in relation to the legacies of slavery. One section presents the men and women racialized as black who address their white counterparts, whereas in another section individuals categorized as white respond to each of these statements. As he already has done in his previous work, both the video and the sculpture interrogate ideas of guilt, resentment, and race, showing how the debate over the slave past remains alive along racial lines in the present.

Multidimensional Memory

Visual arts engage the past of slavery and the Atlantic slave trade in multiple ways. Through images and words, the works of artists such as Cyprien Tokoudagba, Romuald Hazoumè, William-Adjété Wilson, Rosana Paulino, Nona Faustine, and François Piquet create a new multidimensional mode of memory that simultaneously embraces collective memory, cultural memory, public memory, official memory, and historical memory. Their artworks did not emerge in isolation. They are rather part of an international context in which black citizens, scholars, and institutions started calling the attention to the need of addressing in the public sphere and the public space not only the atrocities committed during the period of slavery but also its persisting legacies. Although carrying specific characteristics associated with the national contexts where they emerge, the works of these artists (racialized as blacks or categorized as whites) discussed in this chapter embody common elements that reflect the shared heritage of slavery in Europe, Africa, and the Americas. Their works highlight the role of African rulers and intermediaries in the Atlantic slave trade, the violence inflicted on black bodies, and how regions such as New York fully profited from the institution of slavery, dimensions that often remain invisible in public initiatives. As Achille Mbembe underscores, "[f]or communities whose history has long been one of debasement and humiliation, religious and artistic creation has often represented the final defense against the forces of dehumanization and death."[37] Escaping the binary positions between evil and good, victims and perpetrators, black and white, that are usually conveyed in initiatives such as monuments, memorials, and museum exhibitions, the artworks discussed in this chapter suggest that art offers a rich, complex, and nuanced alternative to the typical ways of memorializing slavery and the Atlantic slave trade.

Epilogue: The Persistence of the Past

For more than a decade, I sought to understand the growing interest in slavery that emerged in many former slave societies and why several social actors engaged themselves in fights to make the slave past visible in the public landscapes of societies that participated in the Atlantic slave trade and where slavery existed. My research on different projects has shown that individuals, groups, and institutions involved in these ventures were not necessarily attempting to teach the public about the historical past as it is debated by academic historians or discussed in scholarly books. They were rather pursuing a larger enterprise intended to denounce present social and economic exclusion of black populations across Europe, Africa, and the Americas. Exposing white supremacy as a structure that, since the rise of the Atlantic slave trade, made racialization a main trend of modern societies by consistently marginalizing nonwhite populations, individuals and groups connecting these legacies to the long history of slavery and the Atlantic slave trade have occupied the public sphere to denounce racism and racial inequalities.

As explored throughout the various cases examined in the chapters of this book, memory activates the past in the present. In its range of modalities (collective, cultural, public, and official), memory sheds light on different dimensions of the past of slavery and the Atlantic slave trade. Yet these varied forms of memory often overlap. Collective memory entails transmission and operates through many layers. Whereas collective memory embodies the ways a nation engages the past of slavery and the slave trade, this mode of engagement can change over time. Collective memory of slavery is racialized and gendered and varies depending on whether the group is composed of slave traders, slave owners, or enslaved individuals, and whether these men and women relate to each other. Still, the collective memory of slave traders and slaveholders in places as distant as West Africa and the United States carries some degree of stability. The collective memory of the Atlantic slave trade among the family members of a slave merchant such as Francisco Félix de Souza relied not only on his large progeny and great number of individuals who depended on him but also on solid religious frameworks such as Catholic and Vodun religions. Supported by these structures, such groups could transmit their experiences and their assets to future generations who preserved the memory of their ancestors.

In contrast, enslaved individuals lacked that same kind of stability. Family unities among enslaved people, when they existed, were frequently fragile. Sales separating enslaved mothers from their enslaved children and enslaved women from their enslaved husbands, along with sexual violence and high death rates, were just a few of the numerous obstacles to the transmission of experiences among bondspeople. Very often prevented from acquiring and accumulating property, the largest majority of enslaved men's and women's collective memory of slavery is marked by interruptions and gaps. But there is also another factor that adds to this instability. There were groups such as former slaves who settled in the West African Kingdom of Dahomey who became slave merchants. Therefore, their collective memory of slavery includes not only the tragic deportation from Africa and captivity in the Americas but also the involvement in the commerce of human beings. Still, as shown in the first chapter, collective memory of enslaved individuals kept in bondage by prominent slaveholders such as Thomas Jefferson tended to be more stable than that of slaves owned by ordinary whites. Jefferson and his black descendants constitute a rich example to study these nuances. Although constructed through racial lines, Jefferson has a central place in the collective memory of Monticello's enslaved population and their descendants. Still, Jefferson occupies an even more prominent position in the collective memory of the Hemingses, his own enslaved descendants. In other words, collective memory of slavery and the Atlantic slave trade is multidimensional and marked by ruptures, varying among different groups and even among the members of a same group.

Race, religion, gender, and family are central frameworks for the construction of a collective memory of slavery and the Atlantic slave trade. Carried by a variety of groups, collective memory of slavery has been confined to family circles in the domestic sphere. But during the twentieth century, many individuals and groups identifying themselves as descendants of slaves started leading efforts to memorialize the atrocities of slavery and the Atlantic slave trade in the public space. Carrying a collective memory of their forebears or reconstructing the collective memory of their ancestors, these men and women engrossed in commemorating their ancestors through monuments and memorials. Conceived as cultural memory, a mode of memory based on rites and material traces, these initiatives constituted a twofold process. On the one hand, men and women racialized as black grapple with the slave past by exposing existing heritage sites that were either preserved or erased from the public landscapes of cities and rural areas. Embracing their slave ancestry, these activists and ordinary citizens uncover common graveyards and marked tombstones to pay homage to their ancestors in a process that brings to light the subterranean tentacles of white supremacy as a system that dehumanized enslaved individuals racialized as black preventing them from having a marked burial ground and condemning them to oblivion. On the other hand, these initiatives impact existing slavery sites such as historic mansions and plantations, where stakeholders identified as whites recover historical records to create "walls of names" to honor enslaved individuals. Although sometimes successful, as I show in Chapter 2, some of these initiatives, undertaken in the United States, continued to reinforce racialization and white supremacy as the main forces behind commemoration of slavery. In other cases, however, like in France, black citizens identifying themselves as descendants of enslaved people embraced the use of wall of names as the best instrument to humanize and honor their ancestors.

Public memory of slavery emerges through racial lines as well. When public memory is at stake, the battles between groups racialized as blacks and who identify themselves as descendants of slaves and the individuals who are categorized as whites reach the public sphere and the public space. Public memory emerges where the past of slavery and the Atlantic slave trade was once silenced. First and foremost, claims of public memory of slavery are a response to white supremacy, a system shared by societies that participated in the Atlantic slave trade and where slavery once existed, whose engines continue perpetuating racial exclusion and promoting racism and racial inequalities. In this context, black men and women, at times supported by other allies, occupy the public space to demand the official recognition of slavery and the slave trade as human atrocities, the removal of markers honoring slave merchants and pro-slavery individuals, and the creation of tangible structures celebrating the victims of slavery and the slave trade. Examining the contexts of England, France, and the United States and by looking closer at the social and political contexts of cities such as Bristol, Liverpool, Charleston, and Boston, I show that public memory of slavery has been always ignited by conflicts developed over racial lines. Therefore, white supremacy and the persistence of racism keep fueling the fights for public memory of slavery.

There have been opportune times when battles of public memory reach a settlement, and memory of slavery achieves an official status through the establishment of official commemorative dates, the creation of plaques, the construction of memorials, and its inclusion in museums. This recognition through a new official position gives slavery and the Atlantic slave trade a permanent place in spaces from where these atrocities were once deliberately erased. Yet, as the cases discussed in Chapter 4 suggest, this new permanent status is always provisional and unstable. Museums are colonial institutions, not spaces of black protest. Created on the premises of white supremacy, white audiences still prevail in museum spaces that are conceived for them. Therefore, the inclusion of slavery and the Atlantic slave trade in the museum is marked by resistance made evident by the organization of exhibition spaces, the choice of words, the selection of objects, and by persisting silences. Still, institutions such as the Nantes History Museum and the Museum of Aquitaine in France, the International Slavery Museum in England, and the National Museum of African American History and Culture in the United States have attempted, though more or less successfully, to tackle this problem by at least exposing their limitations.

Presenting slavery to wider audiences also remains problematic in historical plantations owned by the founders of the United States. The need of addressing slavery in these sites seems to be much more obvious than it is to make slavery apparent in urban areas of European slave ports. Yet, after the end of slavery, plantations such as Mount Vernon and Monticello gradually made slavery invisible to glorify the lives of the founding fathers and their families. But like in other places associated with slavery, black social actors fought to make slavery visible in these heritage sites of white supremacy that exploited to death the work provided by bondspeople. These spaces preserve elements associated with the collective memory of enslaved individuals, as examined in Chapter 1, and with the cultural memory of slavery, through the presence of slave cemeteries, as explored in Chapter 2. But as places where slavery existed and about which there are copious documentary sources, one would expect that either Mount Vernon or Monticello show their visitors the history of slavery, underscoring how slave labor sustained these properties as well as showing the living and working conditions of these men, women, and children. The reality is that until very recently these places made considerable efforts not to exhibit slavery, but rather to conceal the existence of slavery and erase the presence of enslaved individuals. Although accurately exhibiting this history to general audiences is a mission of public historians, the work of these professionals is always in dialogue with the views of other social actors who make efforts either to conceal or at least to shape and control how slavery is represented to visitors. In this book, I also highlight that, despite its ambitions of objectivity, the efforts of public history to present slavery to large audiences are inseparable from the work of collective, cultural, public, and official memory, and therefore not exempt from the forces of racialization and white supremacy. In other words, public history is also biased. Perhaps artists such as Cyprien Tokoudagba, Romuald Hazoumè, William Wilson, Rosana Paulino, Nona Faustine, and François Piquet, whose artworks addressing the issue of slavery are discussed in Chapter 6, can seize, better than scholars, the complex dialogues among history, memory, past, present, racism, and white supremacy. At least they assure us that the work of memory of slavery and the Atlantic slave trade is always in progress and will persist for as long as the legacies of these past atrocities remain alive.

NOTES

Introduction

1 Neely Tucker and Peter Holley, "Dylann Roof's Eerie Tour of American Slavery at Its Beginning, Middle, and End," *Washington Post*, July 1, 2015.
2 William Faulkner, *Requiem for a Nun* (New York: Vintage Books, 2011), 74.
3 Ethan J. Kytle and Blain Roberts, *Denmark Vesey's Garden: Slavery and Memory in the Cradle of the Confederacy* (New York: The New Press, 2018), 98–9.
4 See Benjamin Forest and Juliet Johnson, "Unraveling the Threads of History: Soviet-Era Monuments and Post-Soviet National Identity in Moscow," *Annals of the Association of American Geographers* 92, no. 3 (2002): 524–47.
5 Eric Foner, "The South's Hidden Heritage," *New York Times*, February 22, 1997.
6 For a recent appraisal of "Rhodes Must Fall," see Richard Drayton, "Rhodes Must Not Fall? Statues, Postcolonial 'Heritage' and Temporality," *Third Text*, 33 (2019): 1–16.
7 The concept was coined by Jurgen Habermas, *The Structural Transformation of the Public Sphere: An Inquiry into a Category of Bourgeois Society* (Cambridge: Massachusetts Institute of Technology Press, 1989). See also Nancy Fraser, "Rethinking the Public Sphere: A Contribution to the Critique of Actually Existing Democracy," *Social Text*, no. 25/26 (1990): 57 and Christopher Balme, "Public Sphere," in *Performance Studies: Key Words, Concepts and Theories*, ed. Bryan Reynolds (New York: Palgrave Macmillan, 2015), 16–17.
8 Letter by the Sons of Confederate Veterans, August 14, 2017.
9 For a quick overview of these debates, see Catherine Clinton, ed. *Confederate Statues and Memorialization* (Athens: University of Georgia Press, 2019).
10 For example, Jacques Le Goff, *Histoire et mémoire* (Paris: Gallimard, 1988); Pierre Nora, "Between Memory and History: Les Lieux de Mémoire," *Representations*, no. 26 (1989): 7–29; and George Cubitt, *History and Memory* (Manchester: University of Manchester Press, 2007).
11 Marc Bloch, *Apologie pour l'histoire ou Métier d'historien* (Paris: Armand Colin, 2013), 73.
12 Michel-Rolph Trouillot, *Silencing the Past: Power and the Production of History* (Boston: Beacon Press, 2015), 4.
13 Tzvetan Todorov, *Les abus de la mémoire* (Paris: Arléas, 1995), 51.
14 David Lowenthal, *The Heritage Crusade and the Spoils of History* (Cambridge: Cambridge University Press, 1998), 118.

15 David Lowenthal, *The Past Is a Foreign Country: Revisited* (Cambridge: Cambridge University Press, 2015), 341.

16 As in the English translation, see Paul Ricoeur, *Memory, History, Forgetting* (Chicago: Chicago University Press, 2006), 87. For the original in French, see Paul Ricoeur, *La mémoire, l'histoire, l'oubli* (Paris: Seuil, 2000), 106.

17 See Jeffrey Andrew Barash, *Collective Memory and the Historical Past* (Chicago: University of Chicago Press, 2016), 52.

18 Barash explores the example of Dr. Martin Luther King Jr.'s speech "I Have a Dream," by explaining how different members of the same community may have watched the speech "in flesh" or on television. See Barash, *Collective Memory and the Historical Past*, 53. The same approach could be applied to the terrorist attacks of September 11, 2001. Whereas thousands of individuals literally lived the tragedy, millions of people experienced it through other mediated forms.

19 Maurice Halbwachs, *Les cadres sociaux de la mémoire* (Paris: Albin Michel, 1994), VII. See also Maurice Halbwachs, *On Collective Memory* (Chicago: University of Chicago Press, 1992), 40.

20 Halbwachs, *Les cadres sociaux de la mémoire,* 221; Halbwachs, *On Collective Memory,* 219. On "fragmented" collective memory, as the "different and even contradictory ways in which the same symbolically embodied memories may be interpreted," and a modality of memory that "constantly undergoes re-elaboration," see Barash, *Collective Memory and the Historical Past*, 59, 110.

21 Jan Assmann, *Cultural Memory and Early Civilization: Writing, Remembrance, and Political Imagination* (Cambridge: Cambridge University Press, 2011), 7.

22 Astril Erll, *Memory in Culture* (New York: Palgrave Macmillan, 2011), 28, and Cubitt, *History and Memory*, 14.

23 Benedict Anderson, *Imagined Communities: Reflections on the Origin and Spread of Nationalism* (London and New York: Verso, 2006), 6.

24 On official memory of slavery, see Johann Michel, *Devenir descendant d'esclave: Enquête sur les régimes mémorielles* (Rennes: Presses Universitaires de Rennes, 2015), 11.

25 These scholars who looked at the significance of slavery and the Atlantic slave trade in the African diaspora formation beyond the context of the United States are Charles Mills, *The Racial Contract* (Ithaca: Cornell University Press, 1997); Jemima Pierre, *The Predicament of Blackness: Postcolonial Ghana and the Politics of Race* (Chicago: University of Chicago Press, 2012); Achille Mbembe and Laurent Dubois, *Critique of Black Reason* (Durham: Duke University Press, 2017); and Crystal Fleming, *Resurrecting Slavery: Racial Legacies and White Supremacy in France* (Philadelphia: Temple University Press, 2017).

26 Mills, *The Racial Contract*, 27. Italics in the original.

27 Pierre, *The Predicament of Blackness*, 8.

28 Mbembe and Dubois, *Critique of Black Reason*, 55.

29 Mills, *The Racial Contract*, 7; Mbembe and Dubois, 55.

30 Mills, *The Racial Contract*, 3.

31 Eduardo Bonilla-Silva, *White Supremacy and Racism in the Post-Civil Rights Era* (Boulder: Lynne Rienner Publishers, 2001), 23.

32 As argued by Pierre, "Africa could not represent a more racialized location." See Pierre, *The Predicament of Blackness*, xii. On racialization in Latin America, see Edward Telles, "The Project on Ethnicity and Race in Latin America (PERLA):

Hard Data and What Is at Stake," in *Pigmentocracies: Ethnicity, Race, and Color in Latin America*, ed. Edward Telles (Chapel Hill: University of North Carolina Press, 2014), 29.

33 For one example from Brazil, see João José Reis, "De Escravo a Rico Liberto: A Trajetória do Africano Manoel Joaquim Ricardo na Bahia Oitocentista," *Revista de História*, no. 174 (2016): 15–68. A shorter version of the same article is published in English as João José Reis, "From Slave to Wealthy African Freedman: The Story of Manoel Joaquim Ricardo," in *Black Atlantic Biography*, ed. Lisa Lindsay and John Wood Sweet (Philadelphia: University of Pennsylvania Press, 2013), 131–45.

34 See, for example, Keri Leigh Merritt, *Masterless Men: Poor Whites and Slavery in the Antebellum South* (New York: Cambridge University Press, 2017).

35 Charles T. Davis and Henry Louis Gates Jr., *The Slave's Narratives* (New York: Oxford University Press, 1985), xxii.

36 Catherine A. Stewart, *Long Past Slavery: Representing Race in the Federal Writers' Project* (Chapel Hill: University of North Carolina Press, 2016), 4.

37 Margaret Mitchell, *Gone with the Wind* (New York: Macmillan, 1936), and *Gone with the Wind*, 1939, directed by Victor Fleming, United States, Selznick International Pictures.

38 Ana Lucia Araujo, *Shadows of the Slave Past: Memory, Heritage, and Slavery* (New York: Routledge, 2014), 180.

39 Alex Haley, *Roots: The Saga of an American Family* (New York: Doubleday, 1976).

40 See Ana Lucia Araujo, *Public Memory of Slavery: Victims and Perpetrators in the South Atlantic* (Amherst: Cambria Press, 2010); Araujo, *Shadows of the Slave Past*, 2014.

41 Catherine Reinhardt, *Claims to Memory: Beyond Slavery and Emancipation in the French Caribbean* (New York: Berghahn, 2008); Araujo, *Shadows of the Slave Past*, 2014.

42 Ira Berlin, *Many Thousands Gone: The First Two Centuries of Slavery in North America* (Cambridge, MA: Harvard University Press, 1998); Ira Berlin, Marc Favreau, and Steven F. Miller, *Remembering Slavery: African Americans Talk about Their Personal Experiences of Slavery and Emancipation* (New York: New Press, 1998).

43 Dalia Ofer, "The Strength of Remembrance: Commemorating the Holocaust during the First Decade of Israel," *Jewish Social Studies* 6, no. 2 (2000): 30; Araujo, *Shadows of the Slave Past*, 184–5.

44 David L. Butler, "Whitewashing Plantations: The Commodification of a Slave-Free Antebellum South," *International Journal of Hospitality and Tourism Administration* 2 (2001): 163–75; Matthew R. Cook, "Counter-Narratives of Slavery in the Deep South: The Politics of Empathy along and beyond River Road," *Journal of Heritage Tourism* 11, no. 3 (2015): 4.

45 Jennifer L. Eichstedt and Stephen Small, *Representations of Slavery: Race and Ideology in Southern Plantation Museums* (Washington DC: Smithsonian Books, 2002), 106–7.

46 Cook, "Counter-Narratives of Slavery in the Deep South," 2; E. Arnold Modlin, Stephen P. Hanna, Perry L. Carter, Amy E. Potter, Candace Forbes Bright, and Derek H. Alderman, "Can Plantation Museums Do Full Justice

to the Story of the Enslaved? A Discussion of Problems, Possibilities, and the Place of Memory," *GeoHumanities* (2018): 3–4.

47 Desiree H. Melton, "Monticello's Whitewashed Version of History," *Washington Post*, August 14, 2015; Talitha Leflouria, "When Slavery Is Erased from Plantations," *The Atlantic*, September 2, 2018.

48 Modlin et al., "Can Plantation Museums Do Full Justice to the Story of the Enslaved?," 21–2.

49 See John R. Oldfield, *Chords of Freedom: Commemoration, Ritual and British Transatlantic Slavery* (Manchester: Manchester University Press, 2007) and Jeffrey R. Kerr-Ritchie, *Rites of August First: Emancipation Day in the Black Atlantic World* (Baton Rouge: Louisiana State University Press, 2007).

Chapter 1

1 See Barash, *Collective Memory and the Historical Past*, 110.

2 Lowenthal, *The Heritage Crusade and the Spoils of History*, 118.

3 Robin Law, *The Slave Coast of West Africa, 1550–1750: The Impact of the Atlantic Slave Trade on an African Society* (Oxford: Clarendon Press, 1991), 269.

4 Zora Neale Hurston, Debora G. Plant, and Alice Walker, *Barracoon: The Story of the Last "Black Cargo"* (New York: Amistad, 2018), 47–9.

5 Robin Law, *Ouidah: The Social History of a West African Slaving "Port," 1727–1892* (Athens: Ohio University Press, 2004), 2. Dahomey controlled the port of Ouidah after conquering the Kingdom of Hueda in 1727.

6 The Malê rebellion of 1835. See João José Reis, *Slave Rebellion in Brazil: The Muslim Uprising of 1835 in Bahia* (Baltimore: Johns Hopkins University Press, 1997).

7 See "Enclosure: Mr Thomas Hutton to Mr Hutton, Cape Coast, August 7, 1850," in *King Gezo of Dahomey, 1850–52: The Abolition of Slave Trade on the West Coast of Africa*, ed. Tim Coates (London: The Stationary Office, Uncovered Editions, 2001), 96; Alberto da Costa e Silva, *Francisco Félix de Souza: mercador de escravos* (Rio de Janeiro: Nova Fronteira, 2004), 12; Robin Law, "A carreira de Francisco Félix de Souza na África Ocidental (1800–1849)," *Topoi* 2, no. 2 (2001): 5; and Araujo, *Public Memory of Slavery*, 281.

8 See Law, "A carreira de Francisco Félix de Souza na África Ocidental (1800–1849)," 13–14; Law, *Ouidah*, 165; Costa e Silva, *Francisco Félix de Souza*, 12, and Araujo, *Public Memory of Slavery*, 282. In exchanged correspondence, the Dahomean ruler referred to him as a clerk. See Araujo, *Public Memory of Slavery*, 284.

9 See Bruce Chatwin, *The Viceroy of Ouidah* (London: Jonathan Cape: 1980) and Werner Herzog's film adaptation, Werner Herzog, *Cobra Verde* (West Germany: Werner Herzog Filmproduktion, ZDF, and the Ghana Film Industry Corporation, 2002 [1987]), DVD video.

10 Suzanne Preston Blier, *African Vodun: Art, Psychology, and Power* (Chicago: University of Chicago Press, 1995), 4.

11 Araujo, *Public Memory of Slavery*, 317.

12 Ana Lucia Araujo, "Dahomey, Portugal, and Bahia: King Adandozan and the Atlantic Slave Trade." *Slavery and Abolition* 3, no. 1 (2012): 7.
13 Herzog, *Cobra Verde*.
14 On this story, see Ana Lucia Araujo, "History, Memory and Imagination: Na Agontimé, a Dahomean Queen in Brazil." In *Beyond Tradition: African Women and Their Cultural Spaces*, ed. Toyin Falola and Sati U. Fwatshak (Trenton, NJ: Africa World Press, 2011), 45–68.
15 John Duncan, *Travels in Western Africa in 1845 & 1846: Comprising a Journey from Whydah, through the Kingdom of Dahomey to Adfoodia in the Interior* (London: Cass, 1968), vol. 1, 114.
16 Frederick Edwyn Forbes, *Dahomey and the Dahomans: Being the Journals of Two Missions to the King of Dahomey and Residence at His Capital in the Years 1849 and 1850* (London: Cass, 1966), vol. 1, 106–8.
17 Araujo, *Public Memory of Slavery*, 323. Praise-names are slogans chanted during commemoration activities paying homage to a family member that are usually passed down along generations.
18 Émile-Désiré Ologoudou, "Tours et détours des mémoires familiales à Ouidah: La place de l'esclavage en question," *Gradhiva* 8 (2008): 84.
19 Araujo, *Public Memory of Slavery*, 321, and Law, *Ouidah,* 215.
20 See Araujo, *Public Memory of Slavery*, 294.
21 Pierre, *The Predicament of Blackness*, 74–5.
22 Interview by the author with Émile-Désiré Ologoudou, Ouidah, July 24, 2005. See also Araujo, *Public Memory of Slavery*, 322.
23 Reis, *Slave Rebellion in Brazil*, 96–7, 127; Araujo, *Public Memory of Slavery*, 104–5.
24 Lisa Earl Castillo, "Mapping the Nineteenth-Century Brazilian Returnee Movement: Demographics, Life Stories, and the Question of Slavery," *Atlantic Studies: Global Currents* 13, no. 1 (2016): 27, and Luciana da Cruz Brito, *Temores da África: Segurança, legislação e população africana na Bahia oitocentista* (Salvador: Editora da Universidade Federal da Bahia, 2016), 183.
25 Alcione Meira Amos, *Os que voltaram: A história dos retornados afro-brasileiros na África Ocidental no século XIX* (Belo Horizonte: Tradição Planalto, 2007), 31.
26 Castillo, "Mapping the Nineteenth-Century Brazilian Returnee Movement," 28.
27 See Araujo, "History, Memory and Imagination," 45–68.
28 Annette Gordon-Reed, *The Hemingses of Monticello: An American Family* (New York: W. W. Norton, 2009), 23.
29 Thomas A. Foster, *Sex and the Founding Fathers: The American Quest for a Relatable Past* (Philadelphia: Temple University Press, 2016), 46.
30 Among the most recent works that promote this view is Annette Gordon-Reed and Peter S. Onuf, "*Most Blessed of the Patriarchs*": *Thomas Jefferson and the Empire of Imagination* (New York: Liveright, 2016), 12.
31 Foster, *Sex and the Founding Fathers*, 75.
32 Madison Hemings, "Life among the Lowly, no. 1," *Pike County Republican*, March 13, 1873.
33 Madison Hemings, "Life among the Lowly, no. 1." On Jefferson's white grandchildren recollections, see Gordon-Reed and Onuf, "*Most Blessed of the Patriarchs*," 21.

34 Hemings, "Life among the Lowly, no. 1."
35 Gordon-Reed, *The Hemingses of Monticello*, 55.
36 Isaac Jefferson, *Memoirs of a Monticello Slave: As Dictated to Charles Campbell in the 1840's by Isaac, One of Thomas Jefferson's Slaves* (Charlottesville: University of Virginia Press, 1951), 10.
37 Gordon-Reed and Onuf, "*Most Blessed of the Patriarchs*," 67–8.
38 Gordon-Reed and Onuf, "*Most Blessed of the Patriarchs*," 63.
39 In the 1940s, Graham believed she had found two Harriet's granddaughters. Conclusions are featured in her correspondence and one article published in 1961. See Moorland Spingarn Research Center (MSRC), Manuscript Division, Thomas Jefferson Genealogical Collection, 117–1, Box 1, folder 3, "Letter by Pearl M. Graham to Dorothy Porter," February 2, 1949, 2, "Letter by Pearl M. Graham to Dorothy Porter," June 6, 1949, and Pearl M. Graham, "Thomas Jefferson and Sally Hemings," *The Journal of Negro History* 46, no. 2 (1961): 89–103. Historian Fawn M. Brodie examined the letters exchanged by these descendants with Graham, but her book did not corroborate the hypothesis that the interviewees were Harriet's descendants, see Fawn M. Brodie, *Thomas Jefferson: An Intimate History* (New York: W. W. Norton, 1974), 554n47.
40 Catherine Kerrison, *Jefferson's Daughters: Three Sisters, White and Black, in a Young America* (New York: Ballantine Books, 2019), Chapter 11.
41 Jan Ellen Lewis, "The White Jeffersons," in *Sally Hemings and Thomas Jefferson: History, Memory, and Civic Culture*, ed. Jan Ellen Lewis and Peter S. Onuf (Charlottesville: University of Virginia, 1999), 132.
42 Lewis, "The White Jeffersons," 150.
43 See Lucia Stanton and Dianne Swann-Wright, "Bonds of Memory: Identity and the Hemings Family," in *Sally Hemings and Thomas Jefferson: History, Memory, and Civic Culture*, ed. Jan Ellen Lewis and Peter S. Onuf (Charlottesville: University of Virginia, 1999), 176, and Gordon-Reed, *The Hemingses of Monticello*, 715n35.
44 Lewis, "The White Jeffersons," 136–7.
45 Letter by Thomas Jefferson to Robert Smith, July 5, 1805, in Brodie, *Thomas Jefferson*, 73–9.
46 Foster, *Sex and the Founding Fathers*, 47.
47 Lewis, "The White Jeffersons," 138.
48 Foster, *Sex and the Founding Fathers*, 57–8.
49 William Wells Brown, *Clotel; or the President's Daughter: A Narrative of Slave Life in the United States* (London: Partridge & Oakey, Paternoster Row, 1853). On Brown and Clotel, see Jill Lepore, *The Story of America: Essays on Origins* (Princeton: Princeton University Press, 2012), 199–200.
50 "U.S. President Had 5 Colored Children. He Acknowledged and Many More He Didn't Because That Was the Custom of His Day," *The Afro-American*, April 20, 1940.
51 Brodie, *Thomas Jefferson*, 497.
52 See Graham, "Thomas Jefferson and Sally Hemings," 89–103.
53 Moorland Spingarn Research Center (MSRC), Manuscript Division, Thomas Jefferson Genealogical Collection, 117–1, Box 1, folder 3, Letter by Charles H. Bullock to Pearl M. Graham, October 10, 1949, 3.

54 These are interviews of Pearl M. Graham with Anna Ezell, Lucy Williams, Minnie Arbuckle, and Charles Bullock, cited by Lucia Stanton, "The Other End of the Telescope: Jefferson through the Eyes of His Slaves," *The William and Mary Quarterly* 57, no. 1 (2000): 145.
55 See "Hemings Family Tree" indicating which slaves were freed, sold, or given as gifts as reproduced in Henry Wiencek, *Master of the Mountain: Thomas Jefferson and His Slaves* (New York: Farrar, Straus and Giroux, 2012), x.
56 Stanton, "The Other End of the Telescope," 145.
57 University of Massachusetts Special Collections and University Archives, W. E. B. Du Bois Papers, 1803–1999, "Letter from Pearl M. Graham to W. E. B. Du Bois," February 13, 1961, 1.
58 Stanton and Swann-Wright, "Bonds of Memory," 170.
59 Stanton and Swann-Wright, "Bonds of Memory," 177.
60 Stanton, "The Other End of the Telescope," 139.
61 Edward Ball, *Slaves in the Family* (New York: Farrar, Straus and Giroux, 2014), 48.
62 Ball, *Slaves in the Family*, 55.
63 Ball, *Slaves in the Family*, 56.
64 Christy Clark-Pujara, *Dark Work: The Business of Slavery in Rhode Island* (New York: New York University Press, 2016), 82; Jay Coughtry, *The Notorious Triangle: Rhode Island and the African Slave Trade, 1700–1807* (Philadelphia: Temple University Press, 1981), 235.
65 Clark-Pujara, *Dark Work*, 90.
66 Michelle Obama, *Becoming* (New York: Crown, 2018), 175.
67 *Traces of the Trade: A Story from the Deep North*, directed by Katrina Browne (San Francisco: California Newsreel, 2008).
68 Mills, *The Racial Contract*, 18.
69 The rhyme is reproduced in Geo Howe, *Mount Hope: A New England Chronicle* (New York: Viking, 1959), 128, Thomas Norman DeWolf, *Inheriting the Trade: A Northern Family Confronts Its Legacy as the Largest Slave-Trading Dynasty in U.S. History* (Boston: Beacon Press, 2008), 50, as well as in a sequence of *Traces of the Trade*, which shows Adjua's graveyard.
70 Pauledore D'Wolf's grave is unmarked. In addition to *Traces of the Trade*, see Glenn A. Knoblock, *African American Historic Burial Grounds and Gravesites of New England* (Jefferson: McFarland & Company, 2016), 189.
71 See *Traces of the Trade* and Knoblock, *African American Historic Burial Grounds*, 190.
72 Tom DeWolf [Thomas Norman DeWolf] in *Traces of the Trade.*
73 Dain Perry in *Traces of the Trade.*
74 See Ledlie Laughlin in *Traces of the Trade.* His acknowledgement of the family slave's past appears in DeWolf, *Inheriting the Trade*, 17.
75 The DeWolf abbreviated family tree is reproduced in DeWolf, *Inheriting the Trade*, VIII.
76 See DeWolf, *Inheriting the Trade*, 4.
77 DeWolf, *Inheriting the Trade*, 17.
78 James DeWolf Perry VI in *Traces of the Trade.*
79 Halbwachs, *Les cadres sociaux de la mémoire*, VII. See also Halbwachs, *On Collective Memory*, 40.

Chapter 2

1 Michael Rothberg, *Multidirectional Memory: Remembering the Holocaust in the Age of Decolonization* (Stanford: Stanford University Press, 2009), 35–6.

2 Ana Lucia Araujo, *Reparations for Slavery and the Slave Trade: A Transnational and Comparative History* (London and New York: Bloomsbury Academic, 2017), 2.

3 See Berlin, *Many Thousands Gone*; and Berlin, Favreau, and Miller, *Remembering Slavery*.

4 Ofer, "The Strength of Remembrance," 30 and Araujo, *Shadows of the Slave Past*, 184–5.

5 Butler, "Whitewashing Plantations", 163–75.

6 Cook, "Counter-Narratives of Slavery in the Deep South, 291; Modlin et al., "Can Plantation Museums Do Full Justice to the Story of the Enslaved?," 337–8.

7 Melton, "Monticello's Whitewashed Version of History," and Leflouria, "When Slavery Is Erased from Plantations."

8 Thomas A. Lacqueur, *The Work of the Dead: A Cultural History of Human Remains* (Princeton: Princeton University Press, 2015), 93. See Michel Lawers and Aurélie Zemour, "Introduction: des morts, de la sépulture et des sciences sociales," in *Qu'est-ce qu'une sépulture ?: Humanités et systèmes funéraires de la Pré-histoire à nos jours. XXXVIe Rencontres internationales d'archéologie et d'histoire d'Antibes*, ed. Michael Lawers et Aurélie Zemour (Antibes: Éditions de l'Association pour la diffusion et la connaissance de l'archéologie, 2016), 11–20.

9 Joel Noret, *Deuil et funérailles dans le Bénin méridional: Enterrer à tout prix* (Brussels: Éditions de l'Université de Bruxelles, 2010), 87; Michael Jindra and Joël Noret, "African Funerals and Sociocultural Change: A Review of Momentous Transformations across a Continent," in *Funerals in Africa: Explorations of a Social Phenomenon*, ed. Michael Jindra and Joël Noret (New York: Berghahn, 2013), 18.

10 Mariza de Carvalho Soares, *Devotos da cor: Identidade étnica, religiosidade e escravidão no Rio de Janeiro, século XVIII* (Rio de Janeiro: Civilização Brasileira, 2000), 144–5; Elizabeth W. Kiddy, "Who Is the King of Congo? A New Look at African and Afro-Brazilian Kings in Brazil," in *Central Africans and Cultural Transformations in the American Diaspora*, ed. Linda M. Heywood (New York: Cambridge University Press, 2002), 157.

11 Craig Steven Wilder, *Ebony and Ivy: Race, Slavery, and the Troubled History of America's Universities* (New York: Bloomsbury, 2013), 200; Daina R. Berry, *The Price for Their Pound of Flesh: The Value of the Enslaved, from Womb to Grave, in the Building of a Nation* (New York: Beacon Press, 2017), 159–60.

12 Araujo, *Shadows of the Slave Past*, 93, Andrea E. Frohne, *The African Burial Ground in New York City: Memory, Spirituality, and Space* (Syracuse: Syracuse University Press, 2015).

13 See Michael L. Blakey and Lesley M. Rankin-Hill, *The Skeletal Biology of the New York African Burial Ground* (Washington DC: Howard University Press, 2009), vol. 1; Warren R. Perry, Jean Howson, and Barbara A. Bianco, *The Archaeology of the New York African Burial Ground* (Washington DC:

Howard University Press, 2009), vol. 2; and Edna G. Medford, *Historical Perspectives of the African Burial Ground: New York Blacks and the Diaspora* (Washington DC: Howard University Press, 2009), vol. 3.

14 Frohne, *The African Burial Ground in New York City*, 1.

15 "Mayor Announces Acceleration of Construction Schedule of City's Third Water Tunnel," *New York Voice*, March 14, 1992.

16 As put by Johann Michel, in this context, social actors also "become descendants of slaves." See Michel, *Devenir descendant d'esclave*, 10.

17 Myiti Sengstacke, "Masses Honor Slave Remains," *Chicago Defender*, October 6, 2003.

18 Sengstacke, "Masses Honor Slave Remains."

19 See "Establishment of the African Burial Ground National Monument: A Proclamation by the President of the United States of America," February 27, 2006, http://georgewbush-whitehouse.archives.gov/news/releases/2006/02/20060227-6.html.

20 Cyril Josh Barker, "Respect Due: African Burial Ground Memorial Opened," *New York Amsterdam News*, October 11, 2007.

21 Erik S. Seeman, "Sources and Interpretations: Reassessing the '*Sankofa* Symbol' in New York's African Burial Ground," *William and Mary Quarterly* 67, no. 1 (2010): 109.

22 Seeman, "Sources and Interpretations," 109.

23 Seeman, "Sources and Interpretations," 112.

24 See African Burial Ground, National Monument, New York, http://www.nps.gov/afbg/index.htm. See also Johanna C. Kardux, "Slavery, Memory, and Citizenship in Transatlantic Perspective," in *American Multiculturalism After 9/11: Transatlantic Perspectives*, ed. Derek Rubin and Jaap Verheul (Amsterdam: Amsterdam University Press, 2009), 165–80.

25 On the exhibition, see Kathleen Hulser, "Exhibiting Slavery at the New York Historical Society," in *Politics of Memory: Making Slavery Visible in the Public Space*, ed. Ana Lucia Araujo (New York: Routledge, 2012), 232–51.

26 Araujo, *Shadows of the Slave Past*, 98.

27 Júlio César Medeiros da Silva, *À flor da terra: O cemitério dos pretos novos no Rio de Janeiro* (Rio de Janeiro: Garamond, 2007), 11.

28 On the cemetery of Pretos Novos, see Portal Arqueológico dos Pretos Novos, http://www.pretosnovos.com.br/. See also Silva, *À flor da terra*, 100.

29 See André Cicalo, "From Public Amnesia to Public Memory: Rediscovering Slavery Heritage in Rio de Janeiro," in *African Heritage and Memories of Slavery in Brazil and the South Atlantic*, ed. Ana Lucia Araujo (Amherst: Cambria Press, 2015), 177; Francine Saillant and Pedro Simonard, "Afro-Brazilian Heritage and Slavery in Rio de Janeiro Community Museums," in *Politics of Memory: Making Slavery Visible in the Public Space*, ed. Ana Lucia Araujo (New York: Routledge, 2012), 223.

30 On the archaeological findings at the site of Valongo Wharf, see Tania Andrade Lima, Glaucia Malerba Sene, and Marcos André Torres de Souza, "Em busca do Cais do Valongo, Rio de Janeiro, século XIX," *Anais do Museu Paulista* 24, no. 1 (2016): 299–391, and Tania Andrade Lima, Marcos André Torres de Souza, and Glaucia Malerba Sene, "Weaving the Second Skin: Protection Against Evil among the Valongo Slaves in Nineteenth-Century Rio de Janeiro,"

Journal of African Diaspora Archaeology and Heritage 3, no. 2 (2014): 103–36. On the political debates associated with the preservation of the Valongo Wharf, see Araujo, *Shadows of the Slave Past*, 99.

31 See UNESCO, World Heritage List, Valongo Wharf Archaeological Site, https://whc.unesco.org/en/list/1548/.

32 Carlos Eugênio Líbano Soares, "Valongo, Cais dos Escravos: Memória da diáspora e modernização portuária na cidade do Rio de Janeiro, 1668–1911" (Postdoctoral report, Universidade Federal do Rio de Janeiro, 2013), 21.

33 Flávia Oliveira, "História desenterrada," *O Globo*, June 29, 2017.

34 Lacqueur, *The Work of the Dead*, 372.

35 Lacqueur, *The Work of the Dead*, 377.

36 Ofer, "The Strength of Remembrance," 26.

37 Ofer, "The Strength of Remembrance," 32.

38 See Yad Vashem, https://www.yadvashem.org/.

39 Marita Sturken, "The Wall, the Screen, and the Image: The Vietnam Veterans Memorial," *Representations* 35 (1991): 119.On the exclusion of names, see Kirk Savage, *Monument Wars: Washington, D.C., the National Mall, and the Transformation of the Memorial Landscape* (Los Angeles: University of California, 2011), 280.

40 Sturken, "The Wall, the Screen, and the Image," 120; Erica Doss, *Memorial Mania: Public Feeling in America* (Chicago: Chicago University Press, 2010), 129.

41 Annie E. Coombes, *History after Apartheid Visual Culture and Public Memory in a Democratic South Africa* (Durham: Duke University Press, 2005), 91.

42 See Stolpersteine, http://www.stolpersteine.eu.

43 Kirsten Harjes, "Stumbling Stones: Holocaust Memorials, National Identity, and Democratic Inclusion in Berlin," *German Politics and Society* 23, no. 74 (2005): 138–51.

44 Matthew Cook and Micheline van Riemsdijk, "Agents of Memorialization: Gunter Demnig's Stolpersteine and the Individual (Re-)creation of a Holocaust Landscape in Berlin," *Journal of Historical Geography* 43 (2014): 139.

45 See Coombes, *History after Apartheid.*

46 See Robyn Autry, *Desegregating the Past: The Public Life of Memory in the United States and South Africa* (New York: Columbia University Press, 2017), 150.

47 In 2006, the Wall of the Righteous was unveiled along the France's Righteous Alley, a walkway alongside the memorial. The wall bears the names of 3,900 men and women who helped in saving Jews in France during the Second World War.

48 Steffi de Jong, *The Witness as Object: Video Testimonies in Memorial Museums* (New York: Berghahn, 2018), 9.

49 The virtual Room of Names can be accessed through the website of the Berlin's Memorial to the Murdered Jews of Europe, https://www.holocaust-denkmal-berlin.de/rundgang/main2.html.

50 Antonius C. G. M. Robben, *Argentina Betrayed: Memory, Mourning, and Accountability* (Philadelphia: Pennsylvania University Press, 2018), 78.

51 James Edward Young, *The Stages of Memory: Reflections on Memorial Art, Loss, and the Spaces Between* (Amherst: University of Massachusetts Press, 2018), 64.

52 Rothberg, *Multidirectional Memory*, 113. On other cases that emphasize how the Holocaust shapes the memorialization of slavery, see Araujo, *Shadows of the Slave Past*, especially chapters 2, 4, and 6.
53 Doss, *Memorial Mania*, 150–1.
54 On Sambo, see Alan Rice, *Creating Memorials, Building Identities: The Politics of Memory in the Black Atlantic* (Liverpool: Liverpool University Press, 2012), 34–6.
55 See Caitlin Galante-DeAngelis Hopkins, "The Beautiful, Forgotten, and Moving Graves of New England's Slaves," *Atlas Obscura*, October 26, 2016, https://www.atlasobscura.com/articles/the-beautiful-and-forgotten-gravesites-of-new-englands-slaves. See also Caitlin Galante-DeAngelis Hopkins, "Pompe Setevens, Enslaved Artisan," *Common-Place* 13, no. 3 (2013), http://www.common-place-archives.org/vol-13/no-03/lessons/index2.shtml.
56 Assmann, *Cultural Memory and Early Civilization*, 38.
57 Sue Giles, "The Great Circuit: Making the Connection between Bristol's Slaving History and the African-Caribbean Community," *Journal of Museum Ethnography*, no. 13 (2001): 16, and Christine Chivallon, "Bristol and Eruption of Memory: Making the Slave-Trading Past Visible," *Social and Cultural Geography* 2, no. 3 (2001): 353.
58 Charles Forsdick, "The Panthéon's Empty Plinth: Commemorating Slavery in Contemporary France," *Atlantic Studies* 9, no. 3 (2012): 280.
59 Araujo, *Reparations for Slavery and the Slave Trade*, 49–50.
60 Coombes, *History after Apartheid*, 202–3.
61 For early scholarship on slavery in South Africa, see Nigel Worden, *Trials of Slavery: Selected Documents Concerning Slaves from the Criminal Records of the Council of Justice at the Cape of Good Hope, 1704–1794* (Cape Town: Van Riebeeck Society for the Publication of South African Historical Documents, 2005); Nigel Worden, Ruth Versfeld, Dorothy Dyer, and Claudia Bickford-Smith, *The Chains That Bind Us: A History of Slavery at the Cape* (Kenwyn, South Africa: Juta, 1996); and Samuel North, "Museums as Tools for Understanding Slavery and Its Legacies in South Africa," *South African Historical Journal* 69, no. 1 (2017): 87.
62 Iziko Slave Lodge Museum, exhibition *Remembering Slavery*, panel "Column of Memory/On being re-named."
63 Ibrahima Seck, *Bouki Fait Gombo: A History of the Slave Community of Habitation Haydel (Whitney Plantation) Louisiana, 1750–1860* (New Orleans: University of New Orleans Press, 2014), 153.
64 Michelle D., Commander, "Plantation Counternarratives: Disrupting Master Accounts in Contemporary Cultural Production," *The Journal of American Culture* 41, no. 1 (2018): 34.
65 David Amsdem, "Building the First Slavery Museum in America," *The New York Times Magazine*, March 1, 2015.
66 Derek H. Alderman, Candace Forbes Bright, David Butler, Perry Labron Carter, Stephen P. Hanna, Arnold Modlin, and Amy E. Potter, "Whitney Plantation Exit Survey Results, National Science Foundation [Grant Number 1359780]," unpublished report, 2015.
67 Assmann, *Cultural Memory and Early Civilization*, 39.
68 Commander, "Plantation Counternarratives," 36.

69 United States Holocaust Memorial Museum, behind Every Name a Story, https://www.ushmm.org/remember/holocaust-reflections-testimonies/behind-every-name-a-story.
70 See Rothberg, *Multidirectional Memory.*
71 Amsdem, "Building the First Slavery Museum in America."
72 Commander, "Plantation Counternarratives," 37.
73 Stephen Small, "Still Back of the Big House: Slave Cabins and Slavery in Southern Heritage Tourism," *Tourism Geographies: An International Journal of Tourism Space, Place and Environment* 15, no. 3 (2013): 418.
74 Shelvin Sebastian, "Sue Williamson and the Slave Trade Narrative," *The New Indian Express*, January 2, 2019, http://www.newindianexpress.com/cities/kochi/2019/jan/02/sue-williamson-and-the-slave-trade-narrative-1919335.html.
75 Witness Stones, "What Is the Witness Stones Project," https://witnessstones.org/what-is-the-witness-stones-project.
76 See Édouard Glissant, *Mémoires des esclavages* (Paris: Gallimard, 2007).
77 On this essay-report, see Charles Forsdick, "Monuments, Memorials, Museums: Slavery Commemoration and the Search for Alternative Spaces," *Francosphères* 3, no. 1 (2014): 92.
78 Fleming, *Resurrecting Slavery*, 78. On the genealogical work conducted by the group and the existing names database, see Les noms de familes guadeloupéennes et martiniquaises, http://www.anchoukaj.org/.
79 Thibault Camus, "Esclavage: une Fondation pour la mémoire à l'hôtel de la Marine," *Radio France Internationale*, April 28, 2018, http://www.rfi.fr/france/20180428-esclavage-traite-fondation-memoire-hotel-marine-macron-pantheon.
80 Brown University, *Slavery and Justice: Report of the Brown University Steering Committee on Slavery and Justice* (Providence: Brown University, 2007), 83–7.
81 See Wilder, *Ebony and Ivy*.
82 For an overview, see Leslie M. Harris, James T. Campbell, and Alfred L. Brophy, eds. *Slavery and the University: Histories and Legacies* (Athens: University of Georgia Press, 2019).
83 Ruth Serven Smith, "UVA Begins Project to Identify, Contact Descendants of Slaves," *Richmond Times-Dispatch*, July 19, 2019. More information on the memorial is available at Memorial to Enslaved Laborers at the University of Virginia, https://www2.virginia.edu/slaverymemorial.
84 The Lemon Project: A Journey of Reconciliation, https://www.wm.edu/sites/lemonproject/.
85 Susan Svrluga, "College of William & Mary to Explore the Legacies of Slavery and Racism," *Washington Post*, July 31, 2019.

Chapter 3

1 David Olusoga, *Black and British: A Forgotten History* (London: Pan Books, 2017), 30.
2 See Olusoga, *Black and British*, 57. For various biographies of black men and women living in Tudor England, see Miranda Kaufmann, *Black Tudors: The Untold Story* (London: One World, 2017).

3 See Katie Donington, Ryan Hanley, and Jessica Moody, eds. *Britain's History and Memory of Transatlantic Slavery: Local Nuances of a "National Sin"* (Liverpool: Liverpool University Press, 2016). Also, of crucial importance is the project retracing the indemnities paid to former slave owners after the abolition of slavery in the British empire; see Legacies of British Slave-Ownership, https://www.ucl.ac.uk/lbs/.

4 Among the works focusing on Bristol's slave trade, see David Richardson, *Bristol, Africa and the Eighteenth-Century Slave Trade to America: The Years of Expansion 1698–1729* (Bristol: The Bristol Record Society, 1986); David Richardson, *Bristol, Africa and the Eighteenth-Century Slave Trade to America: The Years of Ascendancy 1730–1745* (Bristol: The Bristol Record Society, 1987); David Richardson, *Bristol, Africa and the Eighteenth-Century Slave Trade to America: The Years of Decline 1746–1769* (Bristol: The Bristol Record Society, 1991); David Richardson, *Bristol, Africa and the Eighteenth-Century Slave Trade to America: The Final Years 1770–1807* (Bristol: The Bristol Record Society, 1996); Kenneth Morgan, *Bristol and the Atlantic Trade in the Eighteenth Century* (Cambridge: Cambridge University Press, 1993); and Madge Dresser, *Slavery Obscured: The Social History of the Slave Trade in an English Provincial Port* (London: Continuum, 2001). Therefore, I use the recent edition: Madge Dresser, *Slavery Obscured: The Social History of the Slave Trade in an English Provincial Port* (London: Bloomsbury, 2018).

5 *Voyages: The Transatlantic Slave Trade Database*, http://www.slavevoyages.org.

6 See Christine Chivallon, "Bristol and the Eruption of Memory: Making Slave-Trading Past Visible," *Social and Cultural Geography* 2, no. 3 (2001): 351.

7 Vagrancy Act 1824, https://www.legislation.gov.uk/ukpga/Geo4/5/83/section/4.

8 Paul Gilroy, *There Ain't No Black in the Union Jack: The Cultural Politics of Race and Nation* (New York: Routledge, 1992), 125.

9 West of England Partnership, Office for National Statistics, 1991 Census of population, Ethnic Groups by Unitary Authority, http://www.westofengland.org/research–statistics/census-/1991-census.

10 Jane Mills, "Equality Profile: Black Africans Living in Bristol" (Bristol: Performance, Information, and Intelligence, Bristol City Council, October 2014); Jane Mills, *Equalities Profile: African Caribbeans Living in Bristol* (Bristol: Performance, Information, and Intelligence, Bristol City Council, October 2014).

11 Madge Dresser, "Remembering Slavery and Abolition in Bristol," *Slavery and Abolition* 30, no. 3 (2009): 229; Olivette Otele, "Bristol, Slavery, and the Politics of Representation: The Slave Trade Gallery in the Bristol Museum," *Social Semiotics* 22, no. 2 (2012): 156.

12 Otele, "Bristol, Slavery, and the Politics of Representation," 161.

13 See Chivallon, "Bristol and the Eruption of Memory," 355. However, this was not the first novel exploring Bristol's slave-trading activities. Madge Dresser reminds that in 1941, Liverpool-born Margaret Sean published the novel *The Sun Is My Undoing*. The book, exploring the life of a Bristolian family that participated in the Atlantic slave trade, was so successful that it had several editions. See Margaret Sean, *The Sun Is My Undoing* (London: Collins, 1941) and Dresser, "Remembering Slavery and Abolition in Bristol," 227.

14 Philippa Gregory, *A Respectable Trade* (Toronto: HarperCollins, 1995).
15 Giles, "The Great Circuit," 16; Chivallon, "Bristol and the Eruption of Memory," 352; and Otele, "Bristol, Slavery, and the Politics of Representation," 171n1.
16 Giles, "The Great Circuit," 16. See also Rebecca Casbeard, "Slavery Heritage in Bristol: History, Memory, Forgetting," *Annals of Leisure Research* 12, no. 1–2 (2011): 143–66.
17 Madge Dresser, Caletta Jordan, and Doreen Taylor, *Slave Trade Trail around Central Bristol* (Bristol: Bristol Museums and Art Gallery, 1998).
18 Otele, "Bristol, Slavery, and the Politics of Representation," 159.
19 Chivallon, "Bristol and the Eruption of Memory," 358.
20 Otele, "Bristol, Slavery, and the Politics of Representation," 159.
21 Dresser, "Remembering Slavery and Abolition in Bristol," 230.
22 Richard Benjamin, "Museums and Sensitive Histories: The International Slavery Museum," in *Politics of Memory: Making Slavery Visible in the Public Space*, ed. Ana Lucia Araujo (New York: Routledge, 2012), 180.
23 Kenneth Morgan, *Edward Colston and Bristol* (Bristol: Bristol Branch of the Historical Association, 1999), 4.
24 Morgan, *Edward Colston and Bristol*, 3.
25 Dresser, *Slavery Obscured*, 3.
26 James Williams Arrowsmith, *How to See Bristol: A Complete, Up-to-Date, and Profusely Illustrated Guide* (Bristol: J. W. Arrowsmith, 1906), 26.
27 Dresser, "Remembering Slavery and Abolition in Bristol," 227. The oil painting is housed at the Bristol Museum and Art Gallery.
28 The permanent gallery *Bristol and Transatlantic Slavery* at the then Industrial Museum exhibited the painting in the late 1990s; see Otele, "Bristol, Slavery, and the Politics of Representation," 161. See also Dresser, *Slavery Obscured*, 3.
29 See H. J. Wilkins, *Edward Colston: A Chronological Account of His Life and Work* (Bristol: J. W. Arrowsmith, 1920), and Dresser, "Remembering Slavery and Abolition in Bristol," 227.
30 Peter Webb, *Exploring the Networked Worlds of Popular Music: Milieux Cultures* (New York, London: Routledge, 2007), 45–6.
31 Chivallon, "Bristol and the Eruption of Memory," 355.
32 Chivallon, "Bristol and the Eruption of Memory," 355.
33 Chivallon, "Bristol and the Eruption of Memory," 356.
34 Alan Rice, "The History of the Transatlantic Slave Trade and Heritage from Below in Action: Guerrilla Memorialisation in the Era of Bicentennial Commemoration," In *Heritage from Below*, ed. Iain J. M. Robertson (New York and London: Routledge, 2016), 210.
35 Olivette Otele, "Colston: What Can Britain Learn from France," in *Rhodes Must Fall: The Struggle to Decolonise the Racist Heart of Empire*, ed. Roseanne Chantiluke, Brian Kwoba, and Athniangamso (London: Zed Books, 2018), 176. See also Drayton, "Rhodes Must Not Fall?," in which he connects the movement to remove Rhodes's statues and other similar movements in Britain, South Africa, and the West Indies.
36 See Dresser, "Remembering Slavery and Abolition in Bristol," 237.
37 See Countering Colston: Campaign to Decolonise Bristol, https://counteringcolston.wordpress.com/colston-statue/.

38 Michael Yong, "Ball and Chain Attached to Edward Colston's Statue in Bristol City Centre," *BristoLive*, May 6, 2018, https://www.bristolpost.co.uk/news/bristol-news/ball-chain-attached-edward-colstons-1539315.
39 Tristan Cork, "100 Human Figures Placed in Front of Colston Statue in City Centre," *BristoLive*, October 18, 2018, https://www.bristolpost.co.uk/news/bristol-news/100-human-figures-placed-front-2122990.
40 Different from the position of Mayor of the city, the post of Lord Mayor is occupied by a different councilor each year. The Lord Mayor is the city's first citizen. His or her role is to promote the city, the city council, and Bristol's organizations.
41 Steven Morris, "Slave Trader's Portrait Removed from Bristol Lord Mayor's Office," *The Guardian*, June 19, 2018, https://www.theguardian.com/uk-news/2018/jun/19/slave-traders-portrait-removed-from-bristol-lord-mayors-office.
42 Kenneth Morgan, "Liverpool's Dominance in the British Slave Trade, 1740–1807," in *Liverpool and Transatlantic Slavery*, ed. David Richardson, Suzanne Schwarz, and Anthony Tibbles (Liverpool: Liverpool University Press, 2007), 15. See *Voyages: The Transatlantic Slave Trade Database*, http://www.slavevoyages.org.
43 Jessica Moody, "The Memory of Slavery in Liverpool in Public Discourse from the Nineteenth Century to the Present Day," (PhD dissertation, University of York, 2014), 51–2.
44 Sven Beckert, *Empire of Cotton: A Global History* (New York: Alfred A. Knopf, 2014), 202.
45 Beckert, *Empire of Cotton*, 260. See also Moody, "The Memory of Slavery in Liverpool," 54.
46 Abercromby Square is named after Ralph Abercromby (1734–1801), a Scottish politician and soldier whose trajectory is deeply connected to British colonial history. Among others, he became a lieutenant-general in the British Army and Governor of Trinidad. He was also a commander of the British Army in Egypt, where he was killed during the Battle of Alexandria.
47 Check the online exhibition *Liverpool's Abercromby Square and the Confederacy during the U.S. Civil War*, curated by Christopher Williams, Jim Powell, and Joseph Kelly, University of Liverpool, 2005, http://ldhi.library.cofc.edu/exhibits/show/liverpools-abercromby-square.
48 Moody, "The Memory of Slavery in Liverpool," 57.
49 Moody, "The Memory of Slavery in Liverpool," 199.
50 Mark Christian, "An African-Centered Approach to the Black British Experience: With Special Reference to Liverpool," *Journal of Black Studies* 28, no. 3 (1998): 294.
51 Christian, "An African-Centered Approach to the Black British Experience," 295–6.
52 Hourcade, *Les ports négriers face à leur histoire*, 62.
53 Araujo, *Shadows of the Slave Past*, 3.
54 See among others Averil M. Grieve, *The Last Years of the English Slave Trade: Liverpool 1750–1807* (London: Frank Cass, 1968); Roger Anstey and P. E. H. Hair, *Liverpool, the African Slave Trade, and Abolition: Essays to Illustrate Current Knowledge and Research* (Liverpool: Historic Society of Lancashire

and Cheshire, 1989); Gomer Williams and David Eltis, *History of the Liverpool Privateers and Letters of Marque with an Account of the Liverpool Slave Trade, 1744–1812* (Montreal: McGill-Queen's University Press, 2004); Suzanne Schwarz, *Slave Captain: The Career of James Irving in the Liverpool Slave Trade* (Liverpool: Liverpool University Press, 2008); David Richardson, Suzanne Schwarz, and Anthony Tibbles, eds. *Liverpool and Transatlantic Slavery* (Liverpool: Liverpool University Press, 2010); Anthony Tibbles, *Liverpool and the Slave Trade* (Liverpool: Liverpool University Press, 2018).

55 Jacqueline Nassy Brown, *Dropping Anchor, Setting Sail: Geographies of Race in Black Liverpool* (Princeton: Princeton University Press, 2005), 65; Jump Ship Rat, "Getting Away With It," in *Cultural Hijack: Rethinking Intervention*, ed. Ben Perry, Myriam Tahir, and Sally Medlyn (Liverpool: Liverpool University Press, 2011), 302.

56 See Tony Gifford, Wally Brown, and Ruth Bundey, *Loosen the Shackles: First Report of the Liverpool 8 Into Race Relations in Liverpool* (London: Karia Press, 1989).

57 To emphasize this ancient presence, Small uses the term "indigenous." See Stephen Small, "Racialised Relations in Liverpool: A Contemporary Anomaly," *Journal of Ethnic and Migration Studies* 17, no. 4 (1991): 514.

58 Brown, *Dropping Anchor, Setting Sail*, 71.

59 Brown, *Dropping Anchor, Setting Sail*, 164.

60 "Transcript of Speech Given by Eric Lynch in 1980," in Gifford, Brown, and Bundey, *Loosen the Shackles*, 247.

61 For detailed descriptions of this early tours, see Brown, *Dropping Anchor, Setting Sail*, especially Chapter 1. Renaud Hourcade also interviewed two other citizens who joined memory of slavery activism in the middle of the 1990s; see Hourcade, *Les ports négriers face à leur histoire*, 168.

62 The permanent exhibition became known as *Transatlantic Slavery Gallery: Against Human Dignity*; see Elizabeth Kowaleski Wallace, *The British Slave Trade and Public Memory* (New York: Columbia University Press, 2006); Moody, "The Memory of Slavery in Liverpool," 310–26; and Jessica Moody, "Liverpool's Local Tints: Drowning Memory and 'Maritimising' Slavery in a Seaport City," in *Britain's History and Memory of Transatlantic Slavery: Local Nuances of a "National Sin,"* ed. Katie Donington, Ryan Hanley, and Jessica Moody (Liverpool: Liverpool University Press, 2016), 157–8.

63 See Stephen Small, "Slavery, Colonialism and Museums Representations in Great Britain: Old and New Circuits of Migration," *Human Architecture: Journal of the Sociology of Self-Knowledge* 9, no. 4 (2011): 117–28.

64 Celeste-Marie Bernier, "Transatlantic Slavery: Against Human Dignity;" "A Respectable Trade?: Bristol and Transatlantic Slavery;" "Pero and Pinney Exhibit," *The Journal of American History* 88, no. 3 (2001): 1007.

65 Hourcade, *Les ports négriers face à leur histoire*, 286.

66 This omnipresence of slavery in the city's landscape is underscored by Caryl Philips, *The Atlantic Sound* (London: Faber and Faber, 2000), 90, and Wallace, *The British Slave Trade and Public Memory*, 31.

67 Moody, "The Memory of Slavery in Liverpool," 48. For the names of all twenty-five mayors with interests in the slave trade, see Peter Fryer,

Staying Power: The History of Black People in Britain (London: Pluto Press, 2010), 485–6 n31.

68 Simon Gikandi, *Slavery and the Culture of Taste* (Princeton, NJ: Princeton University Press, 2014), 112.

69 James Walvin, *The Zong: A Massacre, the Law and the End of Slavery* (New Haven: Yale University Press, 2011).

70 Walvin, *The Zong*, 161.

71 Tours of Liverpool's Old Dock, http://www.liverpoolmuseums.org.uk/maritime/visit/old_dock_tours.aspx.

72 A full description of the digital work is available here at Layers of the Old Dock, https://layers-of.net/olddock/about.html.

73 Moody, "The Memory of Slavery in Liverpool," 270.

74 See Hourcade, *Les ports négriers face à leur histoire*, 90, and Olivette Otele, "History of Slavery, Sites of Memory, and Identity Politics in Contemporary Britain," in *A Stain on Our Past: Slavery and Memory*, ed. Abdoulaye Gueye and Johann Michel (Trenton: Africa World Press, 2017), 195.

75 On the memorialization of slavery and the slave trade in London, see Madge Dresser, "Set in Stone? Statues and Slavery in London," *History Workshop Journal* 64 (2007): 163–99. On the permanent gallery *London, Sugar, and Slavery*, see David Spence, "Making the London, Sugar and Slavery Gallery at the Museum of London Docklands," in *Representing Enslavement and Abolition in Museums: Ambiguous Engagements*, ed. Laurajane Smith, Geoffrey Cubitt, Ross Wilson, and Kalliopi Fouseki (New York: Routledge, 2011), 149–63. I also discuss the exhibition in a previous book; see Araujo, *Shadows of the Slave Past*, 26–7.

76 UNESCO, World Heritage Convention, Liverpool Maritime Mercantile City, https://whc.unesco.org/en/list/1150.

77 Larry Neild, "Slavery Streets May Be Wiped from the Map," *Daily Post*, July 7, 2006, 10.

78 Lee Glendinning, "Renaming Row Darkens Penny Lanes's Blue Suburban Skies," *The Guardian*, July 10, 2006.

79 Laurent Westgaph, *Read the Signs: Street Names with a Connection to the Transatlantic Slave Trade and Abolition in Liverpool* (Liverpool: Liverpool City Council, 2007).

80 Kytle and Roberts extensively examined these debates about the construction of a monument honoring Vesey, and explored the perceptions of white residents, see Kytle and Roberts, *Denmark Vesey's Garden*, 284.

81 Ta-Nehisi Coates, "Killing Dylann Roof," *The Atlantic*, May 26, 2016.

82 Tucker and Holley, "Dylann Roof's Eerie Tour of American Slavery."

83 Peter Holley and DeNeen L. Brown, "Woman Takes Down Confederate Flag in Front of South Carolina Statehouse," *Washington Post*, June 27, 2015.

84 Kytle and Roberts, *Denmark Vesey's Garden*, 98–9.

85 Karen L. Cox, *Dixie's Daughters: The United Daughters of the Confederacy and the Preservation of Confederate Culture* (Gainesville: University Press of Florida, 2003), 159.

86 See Kevin M. Levin, *Searching for Black Confederates: The Civil War's Most Persistent Myth* (Chapel Hill: University of North Carolina Press, 2019), 123–5.

87 See Cox, *Dixie's Daughters*, 50.
88 Maggie Astor, "Protester in Durham Topple a Confederate Monument," *New York Times*, August 14, 2017.
89 Kali Holloway, "Confederate Monuments: Where Are They Now?," *Salon*, August 18, 2019, https://www.salon.com/2019/08/18/confederate-monuments-where-are-they-now_partner/.
90 Nigel Roberts, "New Confederate Monuments Going Up Despite Uproar," *The Jacksonville Free Press* 30, no. 47 (2017): 2.
91 Rachel L. Swarns, "Yale College Dean Torn by Racial Protests," *New York Times*, November 15, 2015.
92 Andrew Buncombe, "Yale University Keeps College Named after White Supremacist despite Protests," *Independent*, April 26, 2015; Isaac Stanley Becker, "Yale Keeps the Calhoun Name Despite Racial Controversy but Ditches the 'Master Title'," *Washington Post*, April 27, 2016.
93 Yale University, Office of the President, Decision on the Name of Calhoun College, https://president.yale.edu/decision-name-calhoun-college.
94 Abram English Brown, *Faneuil Hall and Faneuil Hall Market or Peter Faneuil and His Gift* (Boston: Lee and Shepard, 1900), 98.
95 Jared Ross Hardesty, "'The Negro at the Gate': Enslaved Labor in Eighteenth-Century Boston," *The New England Quarterly* 87, no. 1 (2014): 73.
96 Brown, *Faneuil Hall*, 12.
97 According to *Voyages: The Transatlantic Slave Trade Database,* voyage ID 25185, https://www.slavevoyages.org. See also Brown, *Faneuil Hall*, 45.
98 Caleb Hopkins Snow, *A History of Boston: The Metropolis of Massachusetts from Its Origin to the Present Period with Some Account of the Environs* (Boston: Abel Bowen, 1825), 233–4.
99 Snow, *A History of Boston*, 234.
100 Brown, *Faneuil Hall*, 135.
101 Marcelo Philip, "Should Boston Rename Meeting Hall with Slave Ties?" *Philadelphia Tribune*, August, 25, 2017, 4B.
102 United States Census Bureau, Boston, Massachusetts, https://www.census.gov/quickfacts/bostoncitymassachusetts.
103 Jule Pattison-Gordon, "Bostonians Mark City's History with Slavery," *The Boston Banner*, August 27, 2015.
104 Mark Pratt, "Should Liberty Icon Faneuil Hall's Slave Ties Mean Renaming," *Philadelphia Tribune*, June 18, 2018.
105 Sarah Betancourt, "Boycott Looms for Landmark Named after Slave Owner," *Philadelphia Tribune*, August 3, 2018.
106 Adrian Walker, "The Nearly Erased Artist behind the Hidden Face of the Proposed Faneuil Hall Memorial," *Boston Globe*, August 21, 2018.
107 Felicia Gans, "Protestors Reenact Slave Auction to Demand Change for Faneuil Hall," *Boston Globe*, November 10, 2018.
108 Kellen Browning, "Artist Pulls Out of Faneuil Hall Slave Memory Project after NAACP Announces Opposition," *Boston Globe*, July 12, 2019.
109 Steven Locke, "Why I Withdrew My Proposed Slave Memorial at Faneuil Hall," *Boston Globe*, August 4, 2019.

Chapter 4

1 Nelly Schmidt, "Teaching and Commemorating Slavery and Abolition in France: From Organized Forgetfulness to Historical Debates," in *Politics of Memory: Making Slavery Visible in the Public Space*, ed. Ana Lucia Araujo (New York: Routledge, 2012), 113–14.

2 See Aimé Césaire, "Discours prononcé par M. Aimé Césaire," in *Commémoration du centenaire de l'abolition de l'esclavage: Discours prononcés à la Sorbonne le 27 avril 1948*, ed. Gaston Monnerville, Léopold Sédar Senghor, and Aimé Césaire (Paris: Presses Universitaires de France, 1948), 21–33. For an analysis of these speeches, see Michel, *Devenir descendant d'esclave*, 26–8.

3 Gert Oostindie, "Public Memories of the Atlantic Slave Trade and Slavery in Contemporary Europe," *European Review* 17, no. 3 and 4 (2009): 616; Renaud Hourcade, "Commemorating a Guilty Past: The Politics of Memory in the French Former Slave Trade Cities," in *Politics of Memory: Making Slavery Visible in the Public Space*, ed. Ana Lucia Araujo (New York: Routledge: 2012), 131.

4 André Videau, "Les Anneaux de la Mémoire à Nantes jusqu'au 4 février 1994 au château des ducs de Bretagne," *Hommes et migrations*, no. 1170 (1993): 63.

5 For a quick overview of the exhibition, see Institut National de l'Audiovisuel, "Les Anneaux de la mémoire," France 3, December 5, 1992, https://fresques.ina.fr/auran/fiche-media/Auran00105/les-anneaux-de-la-memoire.html.

6 Hourcade, "Commemorating a Guilty Past," 128.

7 See the comment by Jean-Pierre Chesne (Director of the Sea International Center) in Institut National de l'Audiovisuel, "Les Anneaux de la mémoire."

8 Hourcade, *Les ports négriers face à leur histoire*, 202.

9 Hourcade, "Commemorating a Guilty Past," 128–9.

10 Christine Chivallon, "Resurgence of the Memory of Slavery in France: Issues and Significations of a Public and Academic Debate," in *Living History: Encountering the Memory of the Heirs of Slavery*, ed. Ana Lucia Araujo (Newcastle: Cambridge Scholars Publishing, 2009), 87.

11 See Chivallon, "Resurgence of the Memory of Slavery in France," 89. For a "typology" of these different groups, see Fleming, *Resurrecting Slavery*, 73, 81, and Abdoulaye Gueye, "The Past Is a Contentious Field: The Memory of the Atlantic Slave Trade in the Black Organizational Debate," in *A Stain on Our Past: Slavery and Memory*, ed. Abdoulaye Gueye and Johann Michel (Trenton: Africa World Press, 2018), 100, and Forsdick, "Monuments, Memorials, Museums," 94.

12 Comité pour la mémoire de l'esclavage, "Mémoires de la traite négrière, de l'esclavage et de leurs abolitions," April 12, 2005, 2.

13 See Glissant, *Mémoires des esclavages*.

14 Comité pour la mémoire de l'esclavage, "Mémoires de la traite négrière," 21.

15 *Le Voyage à Nantes: Dossier de presse, Bilan de fréquentation du voyage à Nantes 2017*, August 31, 2017.

16 This and other exhibition labels were translated from French into English by the author.
17 Hourcade, "Commemorating a Guilty Past," 136.
18 Forsdick, "Monuments, Memorials, Museums," 97. On the ephemeral sculpture, see also Sophia Khadraoui-Fortune, "The Abolition of Slavery," in *Postcolonial Realms of Memory: Sites and Symbols in Modern France*, ed. Etienne Achille, Charles Forsdick, and Lydie Moudileno (Liverpool: Liverpool University Press, 2020), 195–203.
19 The first discussions started in 1998; see Hourcade, *Les ports négriers face à leur histoire*, 387–9.
20 On the creation of the memorial, see Emmanuelle Chérel, *Le memorial de l'abolition de l'esclavage de Nantes: enjeux et controversies* (Rennes: Presses universitaires de Rennes, 2012).
21 Forsdick, "Monuments, Memorials, Museums," 97.
22 These debates are explored in Nicola Frith, "The Art of Reconciliation: The Memorial to the Abolition of Slavery in Nantes," in *At the Limits of Memory: Legacies of Slavery in the Francophone World*, ed. Nicola Frith and Kate Hodgson (Liverpool: Liverpool University Press, 2015), 68–86.
23 Hourcade, *Les ports négriers face à leur histoire*, 436–7; Christine Chivallon, "L'émergence récente de la mémoire de l'esclavage dans l'espace public: Enjeux et significations," *Revue d'histoire moderne et contemporaine*, no. 52–54 (2005): 74.
24 See Éric Saugera, *Bordeaux port négrier: Chronologie, économie, idéologie, XVIIe–XIXe siècles* (Biarritz: J & D, 1995). On the impact of Saugera's book see Hourcade, *Les ports négriers face à leur histoire*, 241–2.
25 Musée d'Aquitaine, *Regards sur les Antilles: Collection Marcel Châtillon* (Bordeaux and Paris: Musée d'Aquitaine and Réunion des musées nationaux, 1999), exhibition catalog. See also Hourcade, *Les ports négriers face à leur histoire*, 448.
26 Hourcade, *Les ports négriers face à leur histoire*, 449.
27 The association started its activities in 1998. Hourcade, *Les ports négriers face à leur histoire*, 450.
28 *Bordeaux, le commerce atlantique et l'esclavage: Nouvel espace permanent au Musée d'Aquitaine à Bordeaux, ouverture le 10 mai 2009* (Bordeaux: Musée d'Aquitaine, 2009), press pack, 5.
29 Fleming, *Resurrecting Slavery*, 37.
30 The objects of the Museum of Aquitaine's permanent exhibition on slavery and the slave trade are featured in Musée d'Aquitaine, *Bordeaux au XVIIIe siècle: Le commerce atlantique et l'esclavage* (Bordeaux: Le Festin and Musée d'Aquitaine, 2018), exhibition catalog.
31 See Blier, *African Vodun*, 239, and Rosalind Shaw, *Memories of the Slave Trade: Ritual and the Historical Imagination in Sierra Leone* (Chicago: University of Chicago Press, 2002), 14.
32 See Hourcade, *Les ports négriers face à leur histoire*, 455.
33 Musée d'Aquitaine, *Bordeaux au XVIIIe siècle*, 88, 90, 103.
34 A delegation from Bordeaux including the museum director and the mayor visited the International Slavery Museum in 2007 and at various occasions made clear that the British museum influenced the approach developed in

the Museum of Aquitaine's slave trade and slavery permanent exhibition. See Hourcade, *Les ports négriers face à leur histoire*, 450–1.

35 *Tourisme en Gironde: Les chiffres clés 2018*, Bordeaux: Gironde Tourisme, 2018, pamphlet.

36 "Le Musée d'Aquitaine affiche un cartel aux relents révisionnistes sur la traite négrière," *Le Monde*, May 21, 2009.

37 "Le Musée d'Aquitaine est un musée d'histoire, locale, régionale et mondiale," *Le Monde*, June 13, 2019.

38 The commission was created in 2016. It was composed by the adjunct to the mayor Marik Fetouh and supported by the mayor of Bordeaux, Alain Juppé. Its other members were Carole Lemée, anthropologist affiliated to the University of Bordeaux, research director at the French National Center for Scientific Research (CNRS) and Sciences Po Bordeaux, and President of the Institut Afrique; François Hubert, anthropologist, former director of the Museum of Aquitaine; Myriam Cottias, research director at the CNRS; and Yoann Lopez, PhD in sociology, in charge of Memory and Diversity Cultural Affairs and Citizenship, rapporteur of the committee. On the report, see Commission de réflexion sur la traite négrière et l'esclavage, "La mémoire de l'esclavage et de la traite négrière à Bordeaux: Visibilité, pédagogie, cohésion," Rapport final, May 3, 2018, 38.

39 "À Bordeaux, une sculpture pour rappeler le passé négrier de la ville," *Le Monde*, December 3, 2019.

40 Mémoire de l'esclavage et de la traite négrière, https://www.memoire-esclavage-bordeaux.fr/histoire.

41 Benjamin, "Museums and Sensitive Histories," 182.

42 Mary O'Hara, "Museums Show Up Past and Present," *The Guardian*, July 25, 2007.

43 Benjamin, "Museums and Sensitive Histories," 183.

44 *Voyages: The Transatlantic Slave Trade Database*, www.slavevoyages.org, and Araujo *Shadows of the Slave Past*, 9.

45 Richard Benjamin, the museum's director, confirmed this strategy in an interview to Hourcade, *Les ports négriers face à leur histoire*, 425.

46 Benjamin, "Museums and Sensitive Histories," 188.

47 Association of Leading Visitors Attractions, 2018 visitor figures, http://www.alva.org.uk/details.cfm?p=609.

48 Benjamin, "Museums and Sensitive Histories," 185.

49 National Museums Liverpool, Museum of Liverpool, *Liverpool Black Community Trail*, Liverpool, 2020, pamphlet.

50 For an overall discussion on these first initiatives, see Araujo, *Shadows of the Slave Past*, 3–6; 97–8.

51 Smithsonian National Museum of African American History and Culture, The Collection, https://nmaahc.si.edu/explore/collection.

52 Ira Berlin, "From Creole to African: Atlantic Creoles and the Origins of African- American Society in Mainland North America," *The William and Mary Quarterly* 53, no. 2 (1996): 251–88.

53 *Voyages: Transatlantic Slave Trade Database,* http:www.slavevoyage.org.

54 Paul Gardullo, "Meditation," in *From No Return: The 221-Year Journey of the Slave Ship São José, 1794*, ed. Jaco Jacques Boshoff, Lonnie G. Bunch III, Paul

Gardullo, and Stephen Lubkemann (Washington DC: Smithsonian National Museum of African American History and Culture, 2016), 1.

55 The object (number 2013.46.1) is described as "Amulet in the form of miniature shackles," entered the museum's collection in 2013, but the provenance is unclear. Its full description can be found in the museum's collection database at https://nmaahc.si.edu/explore/collection.

56 Roger Catlin, "Smithsonian to Receive Artifacts from Sunken 18th-Century Slave Ship," *Smithsonian Magazine*, May 31, 2015, https://www.smithsonianmag.com/smithsonian-institution/sunken-18th-century-slave-ship-found-south-africa-180955458/.

57 See Araujo, *Shadows of the Slave Past*, 79–80.

58 The auction block (object number 2015.213) is described in the museum's collection database at https://nmaahc.si.edu/explore/collection.

59 Mark Auslander, "Slavery's Traces: In Search of Ashley's Sack," *Southern Spaces*, November 29, 2016, https://southernspaces.org/2016/slaverys-traces-search-ashleys-sack.

60 Benjamin, "Museums and Sensitive Histories," 179.

Chapter 5

1 Numerous books have focused on founding fathers and slavery but the two monographs by Anette Gordon-Reed on Thomas Jefferson and the Hemingses were crucial not only to deepen the scholarly debate on founding fathers and slave ownership but also to make this debate available to larger audiences. Annette Gordon-Reed, *Thomas Jefferson and Sally Hemings: An American Controversy* (Charlottesville: University of Virginia Press, 1997), and Gordon-Reed, *The Hemingses of Monticello: An American Family*.

2 David Dean, "Introduction," in *A Companion to Public History*, ed. David Dean (Malden: Wiley Blackwell, 2018), 2.

3 Lorena S. Walsh, "Slavery and Agriculture at Mount Vernon," in *Slavery at the Home of George Washington*, ed. Philip J. Schwarz (Mount Vernon: Mount Vernon's Ladies' Association, 2001), 50.

4 Mary V. Thompson, "*The Only Unavoidable Subject of Regret": George Washington, Slavery, and the Enslaved Community of Mount Vernon* (Charlottesville: University of Virginia Press, 2019), 13.

5 Walsh, "Slavery and Agriculture at Mount Vernon," 49.

6 Philip J. Schwarz, "Introduction," in *Slavery at the Home of George Washington*, ed. Philip J. Schwarz (Mount Vernon: Mount Vernon's Ladies' Association, 2001), 27. See also Gwendolyn K. White, "Commerce and Community: Plantation Life at George Washington's Mount Vernon, 1754 to 1799" (PhD dissertation, George Mason University, 2016).

7 Fritz Hirschfeld, *George Washington and Slavery: A Documentary Portrayal* (Columbia: University of Missouri Press, 1998), 12; Schwarz, "Introduction," 17.

8 Hirschfeld, *George Washington and Slavery*, 212.

9 Edna G. Medford, "Beyond Mount Vernon: George Washington's Emancipated Laborers and Their Descendants," in *Slavery at the Home of George*

Washington, ed. Philip J. Schwarz (Mount Vernon: Mount Vernon's Ladies' Association, 2001), 138.

10 Foster, *Sex and the Founding Fathers*, 16.

11 In the eighteenth-century Virginia, it was neither uncommon nor illegal for enslaved people to learn to read and write. See Mary V. Thompson, "'They Appear to Live Comfortable Together': Private Lives of the Mount Vernon Slaves," in Slavery at the Home of George Washington, ed. Philip J. Schwarz (Mount Vernon: Mount Vernon's Ladies' Association, 2001), 89.

12 May 1782, 6th of Commonwealth, Chapter XXI, *An Act to Authorize the Manumission of Slaves* stated: "That all slaves so set free, not being in the judgement of the court, of sound mind and body, or being above the age of forty-five years, or being males under the age of twenty-one, or females under the age of eighteen years, shall respectively be supported and maintained by the person so liberating them, or by his or her state," see William Waller Hening, ed. *The Statutes at Large; being a Collection of All the Laws of Virginia from the First Session of the Legislature, in the Year 1619* (Richmond: J. & G. Cochran, 1821), vol. 11, 39.

13 "General George Washington's Will," in *The Pedigree and History of the Washington Family: Derived from Odin, The Founder of Scandinavia, B. C. 70, Involving a Period of Eighteen Centuries and Including Fifty-Five Generations, Down to General George Washington, First President of the United States*, ed. Albert Welles (New York: Society Library, 1879), 147.

14 Schwarz, "Introduction," 38.

15 See Erica Dunbar, *Never Caught: The Washingtons' Relentless Pursuit of Their Runaway Slave, Ona Judge* (New York: Atria/37 INK, 2017). See also Thompson, "*The Only Unavoidable Subject of Regret*," 40; 287.

16 Scott E. Casper, *Sarah Johnson's Mount Vernon: The Forgotten History of an American Shrine* (New York: Hill and Wang, 2008), 5.

17 Hirschfeld, *George Washington and Slavery*, 222.

18 Casper, *Sarah Johnson's Mount Vernon*, 6.

19 United States, *Return of the Whole Number of Persons within the Several Districts of the United States, According to "An Act Providing for the Enumeration of the Inhabitants of the United States*," Passed March the First, One Thousand Seven Hundred and Ninety-One [I.E. 1790] (Philadelphia: Childs and Swaine, 1791), 4.

20 Charles Manfred Thompson, *History of the United States: Political, Industrial, Social* (Chicago: Benj. H. Sanborn & Co, 1917), 293.

21 Casper, *Sarah Johnson's Mount Vernon*, 5; 12.

22 Lydia Mattice Brandt, *First in the Homes of His Countrymen: George Washington's Mount Vernon in the American Imagination* (Charlottesville: University of Virginia Press, 2016), 26. Among these guides are J. H. Colton, *Colton's Traveler and Tourist's Guide-Book through the United States of America and the Canadas: Containing the Routes and Distances on the Great Lines of Travel, by Railroads, Canals, Stage-Roads, and Steamboats; Together with Descriptions of the Several States, and of the Principal Cities, Towns, and Villages in Each* (New York: J. H. Colton, 1850), 93; Benson J. Lossing, *Mount Vernon and Its Associations, Historical, Biographical, and Pictorial* (New York: W. A. Towsend & Company, 1859).

23 Casper, *Sarah Johnson's Mount Vernon*, 20.
24 Casper, *Sarah Johnson's Mount Vernon*, 18.
25 "Will of Bushrod Washington (page 183), of Mount Vernon, Virginia, Dated 19 July 1828," in Welles, *The Pedigree and History of the Washington Family*, 321.
26 Casper, *Sarah Johnson's Mount Vernon*, 9–10; 28.
27 Casper, *Sarah Johnson's Mount Vernon*, 29–31; Brandt, *First in the Homes of His Countrymen*, 27.
28 Casper, *Sarah Johnson's Mount Vernon*, 60–1.
29 Rosemont Plantation National Register of Historic Places Registration Form, April 28, 1993, OMB No. 110024–0018, 2.
30 Mount Vernon Ladies' Association of the Union, *Historical Sketch of Ann Pamela Cunningham, "The Southern Matron," Founder of "The Mount Vernon Ladies' Association"* (Jamaica, NY: Printed for the Association at the Marion Press, 1988), 5–6.
31 Mount Vernon Ladies' Association of the Union, *Historical Sketch of Ann Pamela Cunningham*, 7.
32 On women slaveholders in the United States, see Thavolia Glymph, *Out of the House of Bondage: The Transformation of the Plantation Household* (New York: Cambridge University Press, 2003), and Stephanie E. Jones-Rogers, *They Were Her Property: White Women as Slave Owners in the American South* (New Haven: Yale University Press, 2019). On white women as bearers of public memory of pro-slavery white men, see Cox, *Dixie's Daughters*.
33 Barbara J. Howe, "Women in Historic Preservation: The Legacy of Ann Pamela Cunningham," *The Public Historian* 12, no. 1 (1990): 33.
34 James C. Rees, "Looking Back, Moving Forward: The Changing Interpretations of Slave Life on the Mount Vernon Estate," in *Slavery at the Home of George Washington*, ed. Philip J. Schwarz (Mount Vernon: Mount Vernon's Ladies' Association, 2001), 159.
35 Brandt, *First in the Homes of His Countrymen*, 93–4.
36 Mount Vernon Ladies' Association of the Union, *Illustrated Handbook of Mount Vernon, the Home of George Washington* (Washington DC: Lee Brothers, 1912), 46.
37 Mount Vernon Ladies' Association of the Union, *Illustrated Handbook of Mount Vernon*, 48–9.
38 Minutes of the Council of Mount Vernon Ladies' Association of the Union, 1928, Mount Vernon, Virginia, 75 cited by Rees, "Looking Back, Moving Forward," 163. On the slave cemetery, see Thompson, *"The Only Unavoidable Subject of Regret,"* 216–17.
39 Rees, "Looking Back, Moving Forward," 63.
40 Dennis J. Pogue, "The Domestic Architecture of Slavery at George Washington's Mount Vernon," *Winterthur Portfolio: A Journal of American Material Culture* 37, no. 1 (2002): 8.
41 See Mount Vernon Ladies' Association of the Union, *Illustrated Handbook of Mount Vernon*, 49.
42 "The West Quarter," Annual Report of the Mount Vernon Ladies' Association (1962), 24, cited by Rees, "Looking Back, Moving Forward," 165. See also Brandt, *First in the Homes of His Countrymen*, 169.

43 Pogue, "The Domestic Architecture of Slavery at George Washington's Mount Vernon," 10. See also Thompson, *"The Only Unavoidable Subject of Regret,"* 164–6.
44 Brandt, *First in the Homes of His Countrymen*, 171.
45 Dorothy Gilliam, "Remembrance," *Washington Post*, February 6, 1982.
46 Dorothy Gilliam, "Memorial," *Washington Post*, February 28, 1983.
47 Susan P. Schoelwer, ed. *Lives Bound Together: Slavery at George Washington Mount Vernon* (Mount Vernon: Mount Vernon Ladies' Association, 2016), exhibition catalog, 107.
48 W. Fitzhugh Brundage, *The Southern Past: A Clash of Race and Memory* (Cambridge, MA: Belknap, 2005), 298, and Jack Jacobs, "Former Historical Interpreters Reflect on Early Days of African American Programming at Colonial Williamsburg," *The Virginia Gazette*, May 14, 2019.
49 See Cary Carson, "Colonial Williamsburg and the Practice of Interpretive Planning in American History Museums," *The Public Historian* 20, no. 3 (1998): 11–51, and Erin Krutko, "Colonial Williamsburg's Slave Auction Re-enactment: Controversy, African American History and Public Memory," (MA thesis, College of William and Mary, 2003).
50 *Ask a Slave: A Web Series*, http://www.askaslave.com/home.html.
51 On segregated plantation tours, see Eichstedt and Small, *Representations of Slavery*, Chapter 6.
52 The visit essentially covers the same grounds covered at the end of the 1990s, when Eichstedt and Small took this tour. See Eichstedt and Small, *Representations of Slavery*, 174–9.
53 Pogue, "The Domestic Architecture of Slavery at George Washington's Mount Vernon," 4–5.
54 *George Washington's Mount Vernon: Official Guidebook* (Mount Vernon: Mount Vernon's Ladies' Association, 2017), 193–197.
55 Susan Kern, "The Material World of the Jeffersons at Shadwell," *The William and Mary Quarterly* 62, no. 2 (2005): 217.
56 The rest of the men, women, and children owned by him lived in a property in Bedford County, where he also cultivated tobacco. John B. Boule, *Jefferson: Architect of American Liberty* (New York: Basic Books, 2017), 461.
57 Marc Leepson, *Saving Monticello: The Levy Family's Epic Quest to Rescue the House That Jefferson Built* (New York: Free Press, 2001), 3.
58 See "Thomas Jefferson: Will and Codicil, 16–17 Mar. 1826, 16 March 1826," *Founders Online*, National Archives, last modified June 13, 2018, http://founders.archives.gov/documents/Jefferson/98-01-02-5963, and Boule, *Jefferson: Architect of American Liberty*, 513–14.
59 Francis D. Cogliano, *Thomas Jefferson: Reputation and Legacy* (Edinburgh: Edinburgh University Press, 2006), 109.
60 See Wiencek, *Master of the Mountain* and Boule, *Jefferson: Architect of American Liberty*, 517.
61 Cogliano, *Thomas Jefferson*, 110.
62 Boule, *Jefferson: Architect of American Liberty*, 518 and Charles Miller, and Peter Miller, *Monticello: The Official Guide to Thomas Jefferson's World* (Washington DC: National Geographic, 2016), 25.
63 Leepson, *Saving Monticello*, 66–7.

64 Uriah P. Levy Collection, American Jewish Historical Society, Center for Jewish History, Sam Towler, "Residents of Monticello 1853–1883," undated document, Box 2, folder 3, 1. See also Leepson, *Saving Monticello*, 83.
65 Uriah P. Levy Collection, American Jewish Historical Society, Center for Jewish History, Sam Towler, "Residents of Monticello 1853–1883," undated document, Box 2, folder 3, 2.
66 Leepson, *Saving Monticello*, 72.
67 Cogliano, *Thomas Jefferson*, 110.
68 Leepson, *Saving Monticello*, 91–2.
69 Charles B. Hosmer Jr., "The Levys and the Restoration of Monticello," *American Jewish Historical Quarterly* 53, no. 3 (1964): 223.
70 Uriah P. Levy Collection, American Jewish Historical Society, Center for Jewish History, Sam Towler, "Residents of Monticello 1853–1883," undated document, Box 2, folder 3, 2.
71 See Melvin I. Urofsky, *The Levy Family and Monticello, 1834–1923: Saving Thomas Jefferson's House* (Charlottesville: Thomas Jefferson Foundation, 2001), 133.
72 Cogliano, *Thomas Jefferson*, 111.
73 Uriah P. Levy Collection, American Jewish Historical Society, Center for Jewish History, Sam Towler, "Residents of Monticello 1853–1883," undated document, Box 2, folder 3, 4.
74 For guides and travel accounts featuring Monticello, see *The Englishman's Illustrated Guide Book to the United States and Canada* (London: Longmans, Green Reader, and Dyer, 1880), 174, and Jefferson Club of St. Louis, MO, *The Pilgrimage to Monticello: The Home and Tomb of Thomas Jefferson* (St. Louis: Con. P. Curran Printing Company, 1908).
75 Leepson, *Saving Monticello*, 129.
76 Amos J. Cummings, "A National Humiliation," *New York Sun*, August 24, 1902.
77 Leepson, *Saving Monticello*, 133.
78 Leepson, *Saving Monticello*, 144.
79 Mrs. Martin W. Littleton, *One Wish* (Washington, 1912), 14–15.
80 Leepson, *Saving Monticello*, 148.
81 "Mrs. Littleton vs. Mrs. Walke," *Times-Dispatch*, November 18, 1912, 1.
82 Hosmer, "The Levys and the Restoration of Monticello," 251–2.
83 Leepson, *Saving Monticello*, 238; 242.
84 Cogliano, *Thomas Jefferson*, 116.
85 Leepson, *Saving Monticello*, 246.
86 Leepson, *Saving Monticello*, 242.
87 *Nineteenth Annual Report, 1914, of the American Scenic and Historic Preservation Society to the Legislature of the State of New York, Transmitted to the Legislature March 24, 1914* (Albany: J. B. Lyon Company, Printers, 1914), 532.
88 Cogliano, *Thomas Jefferson*, 121.
89 Cogliano, *Thomas Jefferson*, 121.
90 Cogliano, *Thomas Jefferson*, 117.
91 Jonathan Scholnick, Derek Wheeler, and Fraser Neiman, "Mulberry Row Reassessment: The Building l Site" (Charlottesville: Monticello Department of Archaeology Technical Report Series, no. 3, 2001), 3–4.

92 See Scot A. French and Edward L. Ayers, "The Strange Career of Thomas Jefferson: Race and Slavery in American Memory, 1943–1993," in *Jeffersonian Legacies*, ed. Peter S. Onuf (Charlottesville: University of Virginia Press, 1993), 434, and Cogliano, *Thomas Jefferson*, 117.

93 Thomas A. Greenfield, "Race and Passive Voice at Monticello," *The Crisis*, April 1975, 146–7.

94 Raymon J. Jirran, "To the Editor," *The Crisis* 82, no. 9 (November 1975): 370.

95 Lois E. Horton, "Avoiding History: Thomas Jefferson, Sally Hemings, and the Uncomfortable Public Conversation on Slavery," in *Slavery and Public History: The Tough Stuff of American Memory* (Chapel Hill: University of North Carolina Press, 2006), 138.

96 Linda M. Lisanti, Thomas Jefferson Memorial Foundation, "Finding Isaac Jefferson: A Monticello Slave," Charlottesville: Monticello Education Department, 1991.

97 Cogliano, *Thomas Jefferson*, 123.

98 See *Getting Word*, https://www.monticello.org/getting-word. See also Horton, "Avoiding History," 140.

99 "Monticello Passes 25 Million Plateau," *Monticello Newsletter* 15, no. 2, 2004, 1–2.

100 Gordon-Reed, *The Hemingses of Monticello*.

101 Araujo, *Shadows of the Slave Past*, 5.

102 The full text of the ad can be found at the National Archives, Founders Online, https://founders.archives.gov/documents/Jefferson/01-01-02-0021.

103 See Cogliano, *Thomas Jefferson*, 119, and Samantha Baars, "With a Tough Year for Tourism in our Rearview, The Road Ahead Looks Bright," *C-ville*, June 15, 2018, http://www.c-ville.com/tough-year-tourism-rearview-road-ahead-looks-bright/.

104 *The Life of Sally Hemings*, https://www.monticello.org/sallyhemings/.

105 Farah Stockman, "Monticello Is Done Avoiding Jefferson's Relationship with Sally Hemings," *New York Times*, June 16, 2018, https://www.nytimes.com/2018/06/16/us/sally-hemings-exhibit-monticello.html.

Chapter 6

1 Marc Augé, *Oblivion* (Minneapolis: University of Minnesota Press, 2004), 16.

2 Mills, *The Racial Contract*, 20. Italics in the original.

3 Many works have addressed the debates that led to the organization of the Vodun festival Ouidah 92 and the launching of the UNESCO Slave Route Project in 1994. See Emmanuelle Kadya Tall "De la démocratie et des cultes voduns au Bénin," *Cahiers d'Études Africaines* 137 (1995): 195–208; Nassirou Bako-Arifari, "La mémoire de la traite négrière dans le débat politique au Bénin dans les années 1990," *Journal des Africanistes* 70, no. 1–2 (2000): 221–31; Robin Law, "Commemoration of the Atlantic Slave Trade in Ouidah." *Gradhiva*, no. 8 (2008): 11–27; Araujo, *Public Memory of Slavery*, Chapter 4; Dana Rush, *Vodun in Coastal Benin: Unfinished, Open-Ended, Global* (Nashville: Vanderbilt University Press, 2013); and Gaetano Ciarcia,

Le revers de l'oubli. Mémoires et commémorations de l'esclavage au Bénin (Paris: Karthala, 2016).

4 Araujo, *Public Memory of Slavery*, 156.

5 Edna G. Bay, "Cyprien Tokoudagba of Abomey," *African Arts* 8, no. 4 (1975): 25.

6 See Gaëlle Beaujean, *L'art de la cour d'Abomey: Le sens des objets* (Paris: Presses du réel, 2019), 93–5.

7 Francesca Piqué and Leslie H. Rainer, *Palace Sculptures of Abomey: History Told in Walls* (Los Angeles: The Getty Conservation Institute and the J. Paul Getty Museum, 1999), 45.

8 There is no consensus on the origin of *akori* (also called "aggrey" or "aggry") beads. Described as having several colors, especially blue, its composition (coral, stone, or glass) is still debated. On Western African beads, see Claire C. Davison, Robert D. Giauque and J. Desmond Clark, "Two Chemical Groups of Dichroic Glass Beads from West Africa," *Man* 6, no. 4 (1971): 645–59, and Suzanne Gott, "Ghana's Glass Beadmaking Arts in Transcultural Dialogues," *African Arts* 47, no. 1 (2014): 10–29. See also Márcia de Castro and Guy Maurette, *Perles de troc: African Trade Beads: VII—Milieu XXe Siècle* (Paris: Édition La Traversée des Arts, 2018).

9 Araujo, *Public Memory of Slavery*, 158.

10 Richard Dyer, "Out of Africa," *Third Text* 7, no. 22 (1993): 112.

11 La bouche du roi: An artwork by Romuald Hazoumè, http://www.britishmuseum.org/about_us/news_and_press/press_releases/2007/la_bouche_du_roi.aspx.

12 Caroline Jacobs, Review of "Uncomfortable Truths: The Shadow of Slave Trading on Contemporary Art and Design," *African Arts* 41, no. 2 (2008): 92.

13 Christine Mullen Kreamer, "A Universe of Possibilities: Contemporary Artists' Perspectives on the Cosmos," in *African Cosmos: Stellar Arts*, ed. Christine Mullen Kreamer (Washington DC: National Museum of African Art, Smithsonian Institution, 2012), exhibition catalog, 304.

14 Victoria and Albert Museum, "Uncomfortable Truths: The Shadow of Slave Trading on Contemporary Art and Design," press release, 2007, 4.

15 Paul Gilroy, *The Black Atlantic: Modernity and Double-Consciousness* (Cambridge, MA: Harvard University Press, 1995).

16 Abigail E. Celis and Fried Ekotto, ed. *And Endlessly, I Create Myself, William-Adjété Wilson and the Black Ocean*, Ann Arbor: GalleryDAAS, Department of Afroamerican Studies University of Michigan Ann Arbor, September 18 to November 7, 2014, exhibition catalog, 51.

17 "Since the reign of Agoli-Agobo, a dust cover, initially made from a calabash then in silver, allowed to limit inhalation. The practice is visible only with Agoli-Agbo I and Dedjalagni Agoli-Agbo." See Beaujean, *L'art de la cour d'Abomey*, 79.

18 Kimberly L. Cleveland, *Black Art in Brazil: Expressions of Identity* (Gainesville: University Press of Florida, 2013), 128. On Paulino's work and how she describes it, see the artist's website, http://www.rosanapaulino.com.br/.

19 On visual representations of Afro-Brazilian wet nurses, see Isabel Löfgren and Patrícia Gouvêa, eds. *Mãe Preta* (São Paulo: Frida Projetos Culturais, 2018), exhibition catalog, and Kimberly Cleveland, *Black Women Slaves Who Nourished a Nation: Artistic Renderings of Wet Nurses in Brazil* (Amherst: Cambria Press, 2019).

20 On these visual records, see Maria Helena P. T. Machado and Sasha Huber, *(T)races of Louis Agassiz: Photography, Body, and Science, Yesterday and Today, Rastros e Raças de Louis Agassiz: Fotografia, Corpo e Ciência, Ontem e Hoje* (São Paulo: Capacete Entretenimentos, 2010), and Maria Helena P. T. Machado, "Race and Visual Representation," in *African Heritage and Memories of Slavery in Brazil and the South Atlantic World*, ed. Ana Lucia Araujo (Amherst: Cambria Press, 2015), 45–70.

21 Several works presented in the Lisbon's exhibition were also featured in the exhibition *Rosana Paulino: a costura da memória* at Pinacoteca de São Paulo, Brazil, December 8, 2018, to March 4, 2019, see *Rosana Paulino: a costura da memória, Rosana Paulino: The Sewing of Memory*, ed. Valéria Picoli and Pedro Nery (São Paulo: Pinacoteca de São Paulo, 2018), exhibition catalog.

22 Cleveland, *Black Art in Brazil*, 143.

23 This photograph is part of the Pure Race Series Africa Album's *Somatological tryptich, identified as Mina Aouni*, today housed at the Peabody Museum of Archaeology and Ethnology at Harvard University, and reproduced in Machado and Turner, *(T)races of Louis Agassiz*, 89.

24 Nona Faustine, "Conjuring Past Injustices through Contemporary Critique," interview by Jessica Holmes, *Degree Critical*, April 8, 2016, https://artwriting.sva.edu/journal/post/conjuring-past-injustices-through-contemporary-critique.

25 For an overview of these connections between slavery in the South and development of capitalism in the North, see Edward Baptist, *The Half Has Never Been Told: Slavery and the Making of American Capitalism* (New York: Basic Books 2016), and Sven Beckert and Seth Rockman, eds. *Slavery's Capitalism: A New History of American Economic Development* (Philadelphia: University of Pennsylvania Press, 2016). On the connections between slavery and US universities, see Wilder, *Ebony and Ivy*.

26 Faustine, "Conjuring Past Injustices through Contemporary Critique," https://artwriting.sva.edu/journal/post/conjuring-past-injustices-through-contemporary-critique.

27 On slavery in New York, see Ira Berlin and Leslie M. Harris, *Slavery in New York* (New York: The New Press, 2005).

28 See The Studio Museum in Harlem, Nona Faustine, *From Her Body Sprang Their Greatest Wealth*, White Shoes series, archival pigment print, 2013, https://www.artsy.net/artwork/nona-faustine-from-her-body-sprang-their-greatest-wealth-from-the-white-shoes-series.

29 "A Local Law in Relation to Requiring the Placement of an Informational Sign Near the Intersection of Wall Streets in Manhattan to Mark the Site of New York's First Slave Market," Int. 0036–2014, http://legislation.nyc/id/1655736.

30 The Official Website of the City of New York, "Transcript: Mayor de Blasio and First Lady Mccray Dedicate Marker Commemorating Wall Street Slave Market," June 27, 2015.

31 Evidence that enslaved individuals were buried in the cemetery appears in "Adriance Van Brunt diary (1828–1830)," Manuscript and Archives Division, The New York Public Library.

32 See Nona Faustine, White Shoes, http://nonafaustine.virb.com/home.

33 Matthieu Dussauge and François Piquet, *François Piquet: Réparations*, exhibition catalog, Saint-Claude, Habitation Beausoleil-Fonds d'art contemporain, March 12–June 25, 2016, Carte Blanche (Basse-Terre: Conseil départemental de la Guadeloupe, 2016), 9.
34 Dussauge and Piquet, *François Piquet: Réparations*, 25.
35 Dussauge and Piquet, *François Piquet: Réparations*, 33.
36 François Piquet, "François Piquet talks about Timalle," interview by Sarah Webster, http://www.reparations-art.org/Timalle-ENG.html.
37 Mbembe, *Critique of Black Reason*, 173.

REFERENCES

Museums, Memorials, and Heritage Sites

African Burial Ground, New York City, United States.
Colston's statue, Bristol, UK.
Faneuil Hall, Boston, MA, United States.
Institute of New Blacks (Instituto dos Pretos Novos), Rio de Janeiro, Brazil.
International Slavery Museum, Liverpool, UK.
Iziko Slave Lodge Museum, Cape Town, South Africa.
Le cri, L'écrit (The Cry, Writing) Jardin du Luxembourg, Paris, France.
Memorial to the Abolition of Slavery (Mémorial de l'abolition de l'esclavage), Nantes, France.
Monticello, Charlottesville, VA, United States.
Mount Vernon, VA, United States.
Museum of Aquitaine (Musée d'Aquitaine), Bordeaux, France.
Museum of London Docklands, London, UK.
Nantes History Museum (Musée d'histoire de Nantes), Nantes, France.
National Museum of African American History and Culture, Washington, DC, United States.
National Museum of American History, Washington DC, United States.
National 9/11 Pentagon Memorial, Arlington, VA, United States.
National September 11 Memorial and Museum, New York City, United States.
Shoah Memorial (Mémorial de la Shoah), Paris, France.
United States Holocaust Memorial Museum, Washington DC, United States.
Valongo Wharf (Cais do Valongo), Rio de Janeiro, Brazil.
Vietnam Veterans Memorial, Washington DC, United States.
Whitney Plantation Museum, Wallace, LA, United States.

Printed and Digital Primary Sources

"À Bordeaux, une sculpture pour rappeler le passé négrier de la ville." *Le Monde*, December 3, 2019.

"Adriance Van Brunt diary (1828-1830)." Manuscript and Archives Division. The New York Public Library.

"Advertisement for a Runaway Slave, 7 September 1769." Founders Online, National Archives, https://founders.archives.gov/documents/Jefferson/01-01-02-0021. [Original source: The Papers of Thomas Jefferson, vol. 1, 1760–1776, ed. Julian P. Boyd. Princeton: Princeton University Press, 1950, p. 33.]

Arrowsmith, James Williams. *How to See Bristol: A Complete, Up-To-Date, and Profusely Illustrated Guide*. Bristol: J. W. Arrowsmith, 1906.
Astor, Maggie. "Protester in Durham Topple a Confederate Monument." *New York Times*, August 14, 2017.
Amsdem, David. "Building the First Slavery Museum in America." *The New York Times Magazine*, March 1, 2015.
Baars, Samantha. "With a Tough Year for Tourism in Our Rearview, the Road Ahead Looks Bright." *C-ville*, June 15, 2018, http://www.c-ville.com/tough-year-tourism-rearview-road-ahead-looks-bright/.
Becker, Isaac Stanley. "Yale Keeps the Calhoun Name despite Racial Controversy but Ditches the 'Master Title.'" *Washington Post*, April 27, 2016.
Betancourt, Sarah. "Boycott Looms for Landmark Named after Slave Owner." *Philadelphia Tribune*, August 3, 2018.
Bordeaux, le commerce atlantique et l'esclavage: Nouvel espace permanent au Musée d'Aquitaine à Bordeaux, ouverture le 10 mai 2009. Bordeaux: Musée d'Aquitaine, 2009, press pack.
Brown, Abram English. *Faneuil Hall and Faneuil Hall Market or Peter Faneuil and His Gift*. Boston: Lee and Shepard, 1900.
Brown University. *Slavery and Justice: Report of the Brown University Steering Committee on Slavery and Justice*. Providence: Brown University, 2007.
Brown, William Wells. *Clotel; or the President's Daughter: A Narrative of Slave Life in the United States*. London: Partridge & Oakey, Paternoster Row, 1853.
Browning, Kellen. "Artist Pulls Out of Faneuil Hall Slave Memory Project After NAACP Announces Opposition." *Boston Globe*, July 12, 2019.
Buncombe, Andrew. "Yale University Keeps College Named after White Supremacist despite Protests." *Independent*, April 26, 2015.
Camus, Thibault. "Esclavage: une Fondation pour la mémoire à l'hôtel de la Marine." *Radio France Internationale*, April 28, 2018, http://www.rfi.fr/france/20180428-esclavage-traite-fondation-memoire-hotel-marine-macron-pantheon.
Catlin, Roger. "Smithsonian to Receive Artifacts from Sunken 18th-Century Slave Ship." *Smithsonian Magazine*, May 31, 2015, https://www.smithsonianmag.com/smithsonian-institution/sunken-18th-century-slave-ship-found-south-africa-180955458/.
Césaire, Aimé. "Discours prononcé par M. Aimé Césaire." In *Commémoration du centenaire de l'abolition de l'esclavage: Discours prononcés à la Sorbonne le 27 avril 1948*, edited by Gaston Monnerville, Léopold Sédar Senghor and Aimé Césaire, 21–33. Paris: Presses Universitaires de France, 1948.
Coates, Tim. *King Gezo of Dahomey, 1850–52: The Abolition of Slave Trade on the West Coast of Africa*. London: The Stationary Office, Uncovered Editions, 2001.
Colton, J. H. *Colton's Traveler and Tourist's Guide-Book through the United States of America and the Canadas: Containing the Routes and Distances on the Great Lines of Travel, by Railroads, Canals, Stage-Roads, and Steamboats; Together with Descriptions of the Several States, and of the Principal Cities, Towns, and Villages in Each*. New York: J.H. Colton, 1850.
Comité pour la mémoire de l'esclavage. "Mémoires de la traite négrière, de l'esclavage et de leurs abolitions." April 12, 2005.

Commission de réflexion sur la traite négrière et l'esclavage. "La mémoire de l'esclavage et de la traite négrière à Bordeaux: Visibilité, pédagogie, cohésion." Rapport final, May 3, 2018.

Cork, Tristan. "100 Human Figures Placed in Front of Colston Statue in City Centre." *BristoLive*, October 18, 2018, https://www.bristolpost.co.uk/news/bristol-news/100-human-figures-placed-front-2122990.

Cummings, Amos J. "A National Humiliation." *New York Sun*, August 24, 1902.

Duncan, John. *Travels in Western Africa in 1845 & 1846: Comprising a Journey from Whydah, through the Kingdom of Dahomey to Adfoodia in the Interior.* London: Cass, 1968, vol. 1.

The Englishman's Illustrated Guide Book to the United States and Canada. London: Longmans, Green Reader, and Dyer, 1880.

Faustine, Nona. "Conjuring Past Injustices through Contemporary Critique." Interview by Jessica Holmes, *Degree Critical*, April 8, 2016, https://artwriting.sva.edu/journal/post/conjuring-past-injustices-through-contemporary-critique.

Foner, Eric. "The South's Hidden Heritage." *New York Times*, February 22, 1997.

Forbes, Frederick Edwyn. *Dahomey and the Dahomans: Being the Journals of Two Missions to the King of Dahomey and Residence at His Capital in the Years 1849 and 1850.* London: Cass, 1966, vol. 1.

Gans, Felicia. "Protestors Reenact Slave Auction to Demand Change for Faneuil Hall." *Boston Globe*, November 10, 2018.

Gilliam, Dorothy. "Remembrance." *Washington Post*, February 6, 1982.

Gilliam, Dorothy. "Memorial." *Washington Post*, February 28, 1983.

Glendinning, Lee. "Renaming Row Darkens Penny Lanes's Blue Suburban Skies." *The Guardian*, July 10, 2006.

Hening, William Waller, ed. *The Statutes at Large; being a Collection of All the Laws of Virginia from the First Session of the Legislature, in the Year 1619.* Richmond: J. & G. Cochran, 1821, vol. 11.

Holloway, Kali. "Confederate Monuments: Where Are They Now?" *Salon*, August 18, 2019.

Holley, Peter and DeNeen L. Brown. "Woman Takes Down Confederate Flag in Front of South Carolina Statehouse." *Washington Post*, June 27, 2015.

Hurston, Zora Neale, Debora G. Plant and Alice Walker. *Barracoon: The Story of the Last "Black Cargo."* New York: Amistad, 2018.

Jacobs, Jack. "Former Historical Interpreters Reflect on Early Days of African American Programming at Colonial Williamsburg." *The Virginia Gazette*, May 14, 2019.

Jefferson Club of St. Louis, MO. *The Pilgrimage to Monticello: The Home and Tomb of Thomas Jefferson.* St. Louis: Con. P. Curran Printing Company, 1908.

Jefferson, Isaac. *Memoirs of a Monticello Slave: As Dictated to Charles Campbell in the 1840's by Isaac, One of Thomas Jefferson's Slaves.* Charlottesville: University of Virginia Press, 1951.

Jirran, Raymond J. "To the Editor." The Crisis 82, no. 9 (November 1975): 370.

"La bouche du roi: An artwork by Romuald Hazoumè," http://www.britishmuseum.org/about_us/news_and_press/press_releases/2007/la_bouche_du_roi.aspx.

Leflouria, Talitha. "When Slavery Is Erased from Plantations." *The Atlantic*, September 2, 2018.
"Le Musée d'Aquitaine affiche un cartel aux relents révisionnistes sur la traite négrière." *Le Monde*, May 21, 2009.
"Le Musée d'Aquitaine est un musée d'histoire, locale, régionale et mondiale." *Le Monde*, June 13, 2019.
Le Voyage à Nantes: Dossier de presse, Bilan de fréquentation du voyage à Nantes 2017. August 31, 2017.
Littleton, Mrs. and W. Martin. *One Wish*. Washington, 1912.
Lossing, Benson J. *Mount Vernon and Its Associations, Historical, Biographical, and Pictorial*. New York: W. A. Towsend & Company, 1859.
"Mayor Announces Acceleration of Construction Schedule of City's Third Water Tunnel." *New York Voice*, March 14, 1992.
Melton, Desiree H. "Monticello's Whitewashed Version of History." *Washington Post*, August 14, 2015.
Mills, Jane. *Equalities Profile: African Caribbeans Living in Bristol*. Bristol: Performance, Information, and Intelligence, Bristol City Council, October, 2014.
Mills, Jane. *Equality Profile: Black Africans Living in Bristol*. Bristol: Performance, Information, and Intelligence, Bristol City Council, October, 2014.
Morris, Steven. "Slave Trader's Portrait Removed from Bristol Lord Mayor's Office." *The Guardian*, June 19, 2018.
Mount Vernon's Ladies' Association. *George Washington's Mount Vernon: Official Guidebook*. Mount Vernon: Mount Vernon's Ladies' Association, 2017.
Mount Vernon Ladies' Association of the Union. *Historical Sketch of Ann Pamela Cunningham, "The Southern Matron," Founder of The Mount Vernon Ladies' Association."* Jamaica, NY: Printed for the Association at the Marion Press, 1988.
Mount Vernon Ladies' Association of the Union. *Illustrated Handbook of Mount Vernon, the Home of George Washington*. Washington DC: Lee Brothers, 1912.
"Monticello Passes 25 Million Plateau." *Monticello Newsletter* 15, no. 2 (2004).
"Mrs. Littleton vs. Mrs. Walke." *Times-Dispatch*, November 18, 1912.
National Museums Liverpool, Museum of Liverpool, *Liverpool Black Community Trail*, Liverpool, 2020, pamphlet.
Neild, Larry. "Slavery Streets May Be Wiped from the Map." *Daily Post*, July 7, 2006.
"Nineteenth Annual Report, 1914, of the American Scenic and Historic Preservation Society to the Legislature of the State of New York, Transmitted to the Legislature March 24, 1914." Albany: J. B. Lyon Company, Printers, 1914.
The Official Website of the City of New York. "Transcript: Mayor de Blasio and First Lady Mccray Dedicate Marker Commemorating Wall Street Slave Market." June 27, 2015.
Oliveira, Flávia. "História desenterrada." *O Globo*, June 29, 2017.
O'Hara, Mary. "Museums Show Up Past and Present." *The Guardian*, July 25, 2007.
Pattison-Gordon, Jule. "Bostonians Mark City's History with Slavery." *The Boston Banner*, August 27, 2015.
Philip, Marcelo. "Should Boston Rename Meeting Hall with Slave Ties?" *Philadelphia Tribune*, August 25, 2017.
Pratt, Mark. "Should Liberty Icon Faneuil Hall's Slave Ties Mean Renaming." *Philadelphia Tribune*, June 18, 2018.

Return of the Whole Number of Persons within Several Districts of the United States, According to "An Act Providing for the Enumeration of the Inhabitants of the United States," Passed March the First, One Thousand Seven Hundred and Ninety-One. Philadelphia: Childs And Swaine, 1793.

Roberts, Nigel. "New Confederate Monuments Going Up despite Uproar." *The Jacksonville Free Press* 30, no. 47 (2017): 2.

Rosemont Plantation National Register of Historic Places Registration Form, April 28, 1993, OMB No. 110024-0018.

Sebastian, Shelvin. "Sue Williamson and the Slave Trade Narrative." *The New Indian Express*, January 2, 2019, http://www.newindianexpress.com/cities/kochi/2019/jan/02/sue-williamson-and-the-slave-trade-narrative-1919335.html.

Sengstacke, Myiti. "Masses Honor Slave Remains." *Chicago Defender*, October 6, 2003.

Smith, Ruth Serven. "UVA Begins Project to Identify, Contact Descendants of Slaves." *Richmond Times-Dispatch*, July 19, 2019.

The Studio Museum in Harlem. Nona Faustine, from Her Body Sprang Their Greatest Wealth, White Shoes Series, archival pigment print, 2013, https://www. artsy.net/artwork/nona-faustine-from-her-body-sprang-their-greatest-wealthfrom-the-white-shoes-series.

Svrluga, Susan. "College of William & Mary to Explore the Legacies of Slavery and Racism." *Washington Post*, July 31, 2019.

Swarns, Rachel L. "Yale College Dean Torn by Racial Protests." *New York Times*, November 15, 2015.

"Thomas Jefferson: Will and Codicil, 16-17 Mar. 1826, 16 March 1826." Founders Online, National Archives, https://founders.archives.gov/documents/Jefferson/98-01-02-5963.

Thompson, Charles Manfred. *History of the United States: Political, Industrial, Social*. Chicago: Benj. H. Sanborn & Co, 1917.

Tourisme en Gironde: Les chiffres clés 2018. Bordeaux: Gironde Tourisme, 2018.

Tucker, Neely and Peter Holley. "Dylann Roof's Eerie Tour of American Slavery at Its Beginning, Middle, and End." *Washington Post*, July 1, 2015.

"U.S. President Had 5 Colored Children. He Acknowledged and Many More He Didn't because That Was the Custom of His Day." *The Afro-American*, April 20, 1940.

Vagrancy Act 1824, https://www.legislation.gov.uk/ukpga/Geo4/5/83/section/4.

Victoria and Albert Museum. "Uncomfortable Truths: The Shadow of Slave Trading on Contemporary Art and Design." press release, 2007.

Walker, Adrian. "The Nearly Erased Artist behind the Hidden Face of the Proposed Faneuil Hall Memorial." *Boston Globe*, August 21, 2018.

Welles, Albert. *The Pedigree and History of the Washington Family: Derived from Odin, the Founder of Scandinavia, B. C. 70, Involving a Period of Eighteen Centuries and Including Fifty-Five Generations, Down to General George Washington, First President of the United States*. New York: Society Library, 1879.

Yale University, Office of the President, Decision on the Name of Calhoun College, https://president.yale.edu/decision-name-calhoun-college.

Yong, Michael. "Ball and Chain Attached to Edward Colston's Statue in Bristol City Centre." *BristolLive*, May 6, 2018, https://www.bristolpost.co.uk/news/bristol-news/ball-chain-attached-edward-colstons-1539315.

Secondary Sources

Alderman, Derek H. Candace Forbes Bright, David Butler, Perry Labron Carter, Stephen P. Hanna, Arnold Modlin and Amy E. Potter. "Whitney Plantation Exit Survey Results, National Science Foundation [Grant Number 1359780]." unpublished report, 2015.

Amos, Alcione Meira. *Os que voltaram: A história dos retornados afro-brasileiros na África Ocidental no século XIX*. Belo Horizonte: Tradição Planalto, 2007.

Anderson, Benedict. *Imagined Communities: Reflections on the Origin and Spread of Nationalism*. London, New York: Verso, 2006.

Araujo, Ana Lucia. "Dahomey, Portugal, and Bahia: King Adandozan and the Atlantic Slave Trade." *Slavery and Abolition* 3, no. 1 (2012): 1–19.

Araujo, Ana Lucia. "History, Memory and Imagination: Na Agontimé, a Dahomean Queen in Brazil." In *Beyond Tradition: African Women and Their Cultural Spaces*, edited by Toyin Falola and Sati U. Fwatshak, 45–68. Trenton, NJ: Africa World Press, 2011.

Araujo, Ana Lucia. *Public Memory of Slavery: Victims and Perpetrators in the South Atlantic*. Amherst: Cambria Press, 2010.

Araujo, Ana Lucia. *Reparations for Slavery and the Slave Trade: A Transnational and Comparative History*. London, New York: Bloomsbury, 2017.

Araujo, Ana Lucia. *Shadows of the Slave Past: Memory, Heritage, and Slavery*. New York: Routledge, 2014.

Assmann, Jan. *Cultural Memory and Early Civilization: Writing, Remembrance, and Political Imagination*. Cambridge: Cambridge University Press, 2011.

Augé, Marc. *Oblivion*. Minneapolis: University of Minnesota Press, 2004.

Auslander, Mark. "Slavery's Traces: In Search of Ashley's Sack." *Southern Spaces*, November 29, 2016, https://southernspaces.org/2016/slaverys-traces-search-ashleys-sack.

Autry, Robyn. *Desegregating the Past: The Public Life of Memory in the United States and South Africa*. New York: Columbia University Press, 2017.

Bako-Arifari, Nassirou. "La mémoire de la traite négrière dans le débat politique au Bénin dans les années 1990." *Journal des Africanistes* 70, no. 1–2 (2000): 221–31.

Balme, Christopher. "Public Sphere." In *Performance Studies: Key Words, Concepts and Theories*, edited by Bryan Reynolds. New York: Palgrave Macmillan, 2015.

Baptist, Edward. *The Half Has Never Been Told: Slavery and the Making of American Capitalism*. New York: Basic Books, 2016.

Barasah, Jeffrey Andrew. *Collective Memory and Historical Past*. Chicago: University of Chicago Press, 2016.

Barker, Cyril Josh. "Respect Due: African Burial Ground Memorial Opened." *New York Amsterdam News*, October 11, 2007.

Bay, Edna G. "Cyprien Tokoudagba of Abomey." *African Arts* 8, no. 4 (1975): 24–9, 84.

Beaujean, Gaëlle. *L'art de la cour d'Abomey: Le sens des objets*. Paris: Presses du réel, 2019.

Beckert, Sven. *Empire of Cotton: A Global History*. New York: Alfred A. Knopf, 2014.

Beckert, Sven and Seth Rockman, eds. *Slavery's Capitalism: A New History of American Economic Development*. Philadelphia: University of Pennsylvania Press, 2016.

Benjamin, Richard. "Museums and Sensitive Histories: The International Slavery Museum." In *Politics of Memory: Making Slavery Visible in the Public Space*, edited by Ana Lucia Araujo, 178–96. New York: Routledge, 2012.

Berlin, Ira. "From Creole to African: Atlantic Creoles and the Origins of African-American Society in Mainland North America." *The William and Mary Quarterly* 53, no. 2 (1996): 251–88.

Berlin, Ira. *Many Thousands Gone: The First Two Centuries of Slavery in North America*. Cambridge: Harvard University Press, 1998.

Berlin, Ira and Leslie M. Harris. *Slavery in New York*. New York: The New Press, 2005.

Berlin, Ira, Marc Favreau and Steven F. Miller. *Remembering Slavery: African Americans Talk About Their Personal Experiences of Slavery and Emancipation*. New York: New Press, 1998.

Bernier, Celeste-Marie. "'Transatlantic Slavery: Against Human Dignity;' 'A Respectable Trade?: Bristol and Transatlantic Slavery;' 'Pero and Pinney Exhibit.'" *The Journal of American History* 88, no. 3 (2001): 1006–12.

Berry, Daina R. *The Price for Their Pound of Flesh: The Value of the Enslaved, from Womb to Grave, in the Building of a Nation*. New York: Beacon Press, 2017.

Blakey, Michael L. and Lesley M. Rankin-Hill. *The Skeletal Biology of the New York African Burial Ground*. Washington DC: Howard University Press, 2009.

Blier, Suzanne Preston. *African Vodun: Art, Psychology, and Power*. Chicago: University of Chicago Press, 1995.

Bloch, Marc. *Apologie pour l'histoire ou Métier d'historien*. Paris: Armand Colin, 2013.

Bonilla-Silva, Eduardo. *White Supremacy and Racism in the Post-Civil Rights Era*. Boulder: Lynne Rienner Publishers, 2001.

Boule, John B. *Jefferson: Architect of American Liberty*. New York: Basic Books, 2017.

Brandt, Lydia Mattice. *First in the Homes of His Countrymen: George Washington's Mount Vernon in the American Imagination*. Charlottesville: University of Virginia Press, 2016.

Brito, Luciana da Cruz. *Temores da África: Segurança, legislação e população africana na Bahia oitocentista*. Salvador: Editora da Universidade Federal da Bahia, 2016.

Brodie, Fawn M. *Thomas Jefferson: An Intimate History*. New York: W. W. Norton, 1974.

Brown, Jacqueline Nassy. *Dropping Anchor, Setting Sail: Geographies of Race in Black Liverpool*. Princeton: Princeton University Press, 2005.

Brundage, W. Fitzhugh. *The Southern Past: A Clash of Race and Memory*. Cambridge: Belknap, 2005.

Butler, David L. "Whitewashing Plantations: The Commodification of a Slave-Free Antebellum South." *International Journal of Hospitality and Tourism Administration* 2, no. 3–4 (2001): 163–75.

Carson, Cary. "Colonial Williamsburg and the Practice of Interpretive Planning in American History Museums." *The Public Historian* 20, no. 3 (1998): 11–51.

Casbeard, Rebecca. "Slavery Heritage in Bristol: History, Memory, and Forgetting." *Annals of Leisure Research* 13, no. 1–2 (2010): 143–66.
Casper, Scott E. *Sarah Johnson's Mount Vernon: The Forgotten History of an American Shrine*. New York: Hill and Wang, 2008.
Castillo, Lisa Earl. "Mapping the Nineteenth-Century Brazilian Returnee Movement: Demographics, Life Stories, and the Question of Slavery." *Atlantic Studies: Global Currents* 13, no. 1 (2016): 25–52.
Castro, Márcia de and Guy Maurette. *Perles de troc: African Trade Beads: VII - milieu XXe siècle*. Paris: Édition La Traversée des Arts, 2018.
Celis, Abigail E. and Fried Ekotto, eds. *And Endlessly, I Create Myself, William-Adjété Wilson and the Black Ocean*. Ann Arbor: GalleryDAAS, Department of Afroamerican Studies University of Michigan Ann Arbor, September 18 to November 7, 2014, exhibition catalog.
Chatwin, Bruce. *The Viceroy of Ouidah*. London: Jonathan Cape, 1980.
Chérel, Emmanuelle. *Le memorial de l'abolition de l'esclavage de Nantes: enjeux et controversies*. Rennes: Presses universitaires de Rennes, 2012.
Chivallon, Christine. "Bristol and Eruption of Memory: Making the Slave-Trading Past Visible." *Social and Cultural Geography* 2, no. 3 (2001): 347–63.
Chivallon, Christine. "L'émergence récente de la mémoire de l'esclavage dans l'espace public: Enjeux et significations." *Revue d'histoire moderne et contemporaine* no. 52–4 (2005): 64–81.
Chivallon, Christine. "Resurgence of the Memory of Slavery in France: Issues and Significations of a Public and Academic Debate." In *Living History: Encountering the Memory of the Heirs of Slavery*, edited by Ana Lucia Araujo, 83–97. Newcastle: Cambridge Scholars Publishing, 2009.
Christian, Mark. "An African-Centered Approach to the Black British Experience: With Special Reference to Liverpool." *Journal of Black Studies* 28, no. 3 (1998): 291–308.
Ciarcia, Gaetano. *Le revers de l'oubli. Mémoires et commémorations de l'esclavage au Bénin*. Paris: Karthala, 2016.
Cicalo, André. "From Public Amnesia to Public Memory: Rediscovering Slavery Heritage in Rio de Janeiro." In *African Heritage and Memories of Slavery in Brazil and the South Atlantic*, edited by Ana Lucia Araujo, 179–211. Amherst: Cambria Press, 2015.
Clark-Pujara, Christy. *Dark Work: The Business of Slavery in Rhode Island*. New York: New York University Press, 2016.
Cleveland, Kimberly. *Black Women Slaves Who Nourished a Nation: Artistic Renderings of Wet Nurses in Brazil*. Amherst: Cambria Press, 2019.
Cleveland, Kimberly L. *Black Art in Brazil: Expressions of Identity*. Gainesville: University Press of Florida, 2013.
Clinton, Catherine, ed. *Confederate Statues and Memorialization*. Athens: University of Georgia Press, 2019.
Coates, Ta-Nehisi. "Killing Dylann Roof." *The Atlantic*, May 26, 2016.
Cogliano, Francis D. *Thomas Jefferson: Reputation and Legacy*. Edinburgh: Edinburgh University Press, 2006.
Commander, Michelle D. "Plantation Counternarratives: Disrupting Master Accounts in Contemporary Cultural Production." *The Journal of American Culture* 41, no. 1 (2018): 28–44.

Cook, Matthew and Micheline van Riemsdijk. “Agents of Memorialization: Gunter Demnig’s Stolpersteine and the Individual (Re-)creation of a Holocaust Landscape in Berlin.” *Journal of Historical Geography* 43 (2014): 138–47.

Cook, Matthew R. “Counter-Narratives of Slavery in the Deep South: The Politics of Empathy along and beyond River Road.” *Journal of Heritage Tourism* 11, no. 3 (2015): 290–308.

Coombes, Annie E. *History after Apartheid Visual Culture and Public Memory in a Democratic South Africa*. Durham, NC: Duke University Press, 2005.

Costa E. Silva, Alberto da. *Francisco Félix de Souza: mercador de escravos*. Rio de Janeiro: Nova Fronteira, 2004.

Coughtry, Jay. *The Notorious Triangle: Rhode Island and the African Slave Trade, 1700–1807*. Philadelphia: Temple University Press, 1981.

Cox, Karen L. *Dixie’s Daughters: The United Daughters of the Confederacy and the Preservation of Confederate Culture*. Gainesville: University Press of Florida, 2003.

Cubitt, George. *History and Memory*. Manchester: University of Manchester Press, 2007.

d’Aquitaine, Musée. *Bordeaux au XVIIIe siècle: Le commerce atlantique et l’esclavage*. Bordeaux: Le Festin and Musée d’Aquitaine, 2018, exhibition catalog.

d’Aquitaine, Musée. *Regards sur les Antilles: collection Marcel Châtillon*. Bordeaux and Paris: Musée d’Aquitaine and Réunion des musées nationaux, 1999, exhibition catalog.

Davis, Charles T. and Henry Louis Gates, Jr. *The Slave’s Narratives*. New York: Oxford University Press, 1985.

Davison, Claire C., Robert D. Giauque and J. Desmond Clark. “Two Chemical Groups of Dichroic Glass Beads from West Africa.” *Man* 6, no. 4 (1971): 645–59.

Dean, David. “Introduction.” *A Companion to Public History*, edited by David Dean, 1–11. Malden, MA: Wiley Blackwell, 2018.

DeWolf, Thomas Norman. *Inheriting the Trade: A Northern Family Confronts Its Legacy as the Largest Slave-Trading Dinasty in U.S. History*. Boston: Beacon Press, 2008.

Donington, Katie, Ryan Hanley and Jessica Moody, eds. *Britain’s History and Memory of Transatlantic Slavery: Local Nuances of a “National Sin.”* Liverpool: Liverpool University Press, 2016.

Doss, Erica. *Memorial Mania: Public Feeling in America*. Chicago: Chicago University Press, 2010.

Drayton, Richard. “Rhodes Must Not Fall? Statues, Postcolonial ‘Heritage’ and Temporality.” *Third Text* 33 (2019): 1–16.

Dresser, Madge. “Remembering Slavery and Abolition in Bristol.” *Slavery and Abolition* 30, no. 3 (2009): 223–46.

Dresser, Madge. “Set in Stone? Statues and Slavery in London.” *History Workshop Journal* 64 (2007): 163–99.

Dresser, Madge. *Slavery Obscured: The Social History of the Slave Trade in an English Provincial Port*. London: Continuum, 2001.

Dresser, Madge. Slavery Obscured: The Social History of the Slave Trade in an English Provincial Port. London: Bloomsbury, 2018.

Dresser, Madge, Caletta, Jordan and Doreen Taylor. *Slave Trade Trail around Central Bristol*. Bristol: Bristol Museums and Art Gallery, 1998.
Dunbar, Erica. *Never Caught: The Washingtons' Relentless Pursuit of Their Runaway Slave, Ona Judge*. New York: Atria/37 INK, 2017.
Dussauge, Matthieu and François Piquet. *François Piquet, Réparations*, Saint-Claude, Habitation Beausoleil-Fonds d'art contemporain, March 12–June 25, 2016, Carte Blanche. Basse-Terre: Conseil départemental de la Guadeloupe, 2016, exhibition catalog.
Dyer, Richard. "Out of Africa." *Third Text* 7, no. 22 (1993): 111–12.
Eichstedt, Jennifer L. and Stephen Small. *Representations of Slavery: Race and Ideology in Southern Plantation Museums*. Washington DC: Smithsonian Books, 2002.
Erll, Astrid. *Memory in Culture*. New York: Palgrave McMillian, 2011.
Faulkner, William. *Requiem for a Nun*. New York: Vintage Books, 2011.
Fleming, Crystal. *Resurrecting Slavery: Racial Legacies and White Supremacy in France*. Philadelphia: Temple University Press, 2017.
Forest, Benjamin and Juliet Johnson. "Unraveling the Threads of History: Soviet-Era Monuments and Post-Soviet National Identity in Moscow." *Annals of the Association of American Geographers* 92, no. 3 (2002): 524–47.
Forsdick, Charles. "Monuments, Memorials, Museums: Slavery Commemoration and the Search for Alternative Spaces." *Francosphères* 3, no. 1 (2014): 81–98.
Forsdick, Charles. "The Panthéon's Empty Plinth: Commemorating Slavery in Contemporary France." *Atlantic Studies* 9, no. 3 (2012): 279–97.
Foster, Thomas A. *Sex and the Founding Fathers: The American Quest for a Relatable Past*. Philadelphia: Temple University Press, 2016.
Fraser, Nancy. "Rethinking the Public Sphere: A Contribution to the Critique of Actually Existing Democracy." *Social Text*, no. 25/26 (1990): 56–80.
French, Scot A. and Edward L. Ayers. "The Strange Career of Thomas Jefferson: Race and Slavery in American Memory, 1943–1993." In *Jeffersonian Legacies*, edited by Peter S. Onuf, 418–56. Charlottesville, VA: University of Virginia Press, 1993.
Frith, Nicola. "The Art of Reconciliation: The Memorial to the Abolition of Slavery in Nantes." In *At the Limits of Memory: Legacies of Slavery in the Francophone World*, edited by Nicola Frith and Kate Hodgson, 68–89. Liverpool: Liverpool University Press, 2015.
Frohne, Andrea E. *The African Burial Ground in New York City: Memory, Spirituality, and Space*. Syracuse: Syracuse University Press, 2015.
Fryer, Peter. *Staying Power: The History of Black People in Britain*. London: Pluto Press, 2010.
Gardullo, Paul. "Meditation." In *From No Return: The 221-Year Journey of the Slave Ship São José, 1794*, edited by Jaco Jacques Boshoff, Lonnie G. Bunch III, Paul Gardullo and Stephen Lubkemann, 1–17. Washington DC: Smithsonian National Museum of African American History and Culture, 2016.
Gifford, Tony, Wally Brown and Ruth Bundey. *Loosen the Shackles: First Report of the Liverpool 8 into Race Relations in Liverpool*. London: Karia Press, 1989.
Gikandi, Simon. *Slavery and the Culture of Taste*. Princeton, NJ: Princeton University Press, 2014.

Giles, Sue. "The Great Circuit: Making the Connection between Bristol's Slaving History and the African-Caribbean Community." *Journal of Museum Ethnography*, no. 13 (2001): 15–21.

Gilroy, Paul. *The Black Atlantic: Modernity and Double-Consciousness*. Cambridge, MA: Harvard University Press, 1995.

Gilroy, Paul. *There Ain't No Black in the Union Jack: The Cultural Politics of Race and Nation*. New York: Routledge, 1992.

Glissant, Édouard. *Mémoires des esclavages*. Paris: Gallimard, 2007.

Glymph, Thavolia. *Out of the House of Bondage: The Transformation of the Plantation Household*. New York: Cambridge University Press, 2003.

Gordon-Reed, Annette. *The Hemingses of Monticello: An American Family*. New York: W. W. Norton, 2009.

Gordon-Reed, Annette and Peter S. Onuf. "*Most Blessed of the Patriarchs*": *Thomas Jefferson and the Empire of Imagination*. New York: Liveright, 2016.

Gordon-Reed, Annette. *Thomas Jefferson and Sally Hemings: An American Controversy*. Charlottesville: University of Virginia Press, 1997.

Gott, Suzanne. "Ghana's Glass Beadmaking Arts in Transcultural Dialogues." *African Arts* 47, no. 1 (2014): 10–29.

Graham, Pearl M. "Thomas Jefferson and Sally Hemings." *The Journal of Negro History* 46, no. 2 (1961): 89–103.

Greenfield, Thomas A. "Race and Passive Voice at Monticello." *The Crisis*, April 1975, 146–7.

Gregory, Philippa. *A Respectable Trade*. Toronto: HarperCollins, 1995.

Grieve, Averil M. *The Last Years of the English Slave Trade: Liverpool 1750–1807*. London: Frank Cass, 1968.

Gueye, Abdoulaye. "The Past Is a Contentious Field: The Memory of the Atlantic Slave Trade in the Black Organizational Debate." In *A Stain on Our Past: Slavery and Memory*, edited by Abdoulaye Gueye and Johann Michel, 91–114. Trenton: Africa World Press, 2018.

Habermas, Jurgen. *The Structural Transformation of the Public Sphere: An Inquiry into a Category of Bourgeois Society*. Cambridge, MA: Massachusetts Institute of Technology Press, 1989.

Halbwachs, Maurice. *On Collective Memory*. Chicago: University of Chicago Press, 1992.

Halbwachs, Maurice. *Les cadres sociaux de la mémoire*. Paris: Albin Michel, 1994.

Haley, Alex. *Roots: The Saga of an American Family*. New York: Doubleday, 1976.

Hardesty, Jared Ross. "'The Negro at the Gate': Enslaved Labor in Eighteenth-Century Boston." *The New England Quarterly* 87, no. 1 (2014): 72–98.

Harjes, Kirsten. "Stumbling Stones: Holocaust Memorials, National Identity, and Democratic Inclusion in Berlin." *German Politics and Society* 23, no. 74 (2005): 138–51.

Harris, Leslie M., James T. Campbell and Alfred L. Brophy, eds. *Slavery and the University: Histories and Legacies*. Athens: University of Georgia Press, 2019.

Hemings, Madison. "Life among the Lowly, no. 1." *Pike County Republican*, March 13, 1873.

Hirschfeld, Fritz. *George Washington and Slavery: A Documentary Portrayal*. Columbia: University of Missouri Press, 1998.

Hopkins, Caitlin Galante-DeAngelis. "The Beautiful, Forgotten, and Moving Graves of New England's Slaves." *Atlas Obscura*, October 26, 2016, https://www.atlasobscura.com/articles/the-beautiful-and-forgotten-gravesites-of-new-englands-slaves.

Hopkins, Caitlin Galante-DeAngelis. "Pompe Setevens, Enslaved Artisan." *Common-Place*, 13, no. 3 (2013), http://www.common-place-archives.org/vol-13/no-03/lessons/index2.shtml.

Horton, Lois E. "Avoiding History: Thomas Jefferson, Sally Hemings, and the Uncomfortable Public Conversation on Slavery." In *Slavery and Public History: The Tough Stuff of American Memory*, edited by James Oliver Horton and Lois E. Horton, 135–49. Chapel Hill: University of North Carolina Press, 2006.

Hosmer, Charles B. Jr. "The Levys and the Restoration of Monticello." *American Jewish Historical Quarterly* 53, no. 3 (1964): 219–52.

Hourcade, Renaud. "Commemorating a Guilty Past: The Politics of Memory in the French Former Slave Trade Cities." In *Politics of Memory: Making Slavery Visible in the Public Space*, edited by Ana Lucia Araujo, 124–40. New York: Routledge, 2012.

Hourcade, Renaud. *Les ports négriers face à leur histoire: politiques de la mémoire à Nantes, Bordeaux et Liverpool.* Paris: Dalloz, 2014.

Howe, Barbara J. "Women in Historic Preservation: The Legacy of Ann Pamela Cunningham." *The Public Historian* 12, no. 1 (1990): 31–61.

Howe, Geo. *Mount Hope: A New England Chronicle.* New York: Viking, 1959.

Hulser, Kathleen. "Exhibiting Slavery at the New York Historical Society." In *Politics of Memory: Making Slavery Visible in the Public Space*, edited by Ana Lucia Araujo, 232–51. New York: Routledge, 2012.

Jacobs, Caroline. "Uncomfortable Truths: The Shadow of Slave Trading on Contemporary Art and Design." *African Arts* 41, no. 2 (2008): 92–3.

Jindra, Michael and Joël Noret. "African Funerals and Sociocultural Change: A Review of Momentous Transformations across a Continent." In *Funerals in Africa: Explorations of a Social Phenomenon*, edited by Michael Jindra and Joël Noret, 16–40. New York: Berghahn, 2013.

Jong, Steffi de. *The Witness as Object: Video Testimonies in Memorial Museums.* New York: Berghahn, 2018.

Jones-Rogers, Stephanie E. *They Were Her Property: White Women as Slave Owners in the American South.* New Haven: Yale University Press, 2019.

Jump Ship Rat. "Getting Away with It." In *Cultural Hijack: Rethinking Intervention*, edited by Ben Perry, Myriam Tahir and Sally Medlyn, 276–305. Liverpool: Liverpool University Press, 2011.

Kardux, Johanna C. "Slavery, Memory, and Citizenship in Transatlantic Perspective." In *American Multiculturalism after 9/11: Transatlantic Perspectives*, edited by Derek Rubin and Jaap Verheul, 165–80. Amsterdam: Amsterdam University Press, 2009.

Kaufmann, Miranda. *Black Tudors: The Untold Story.* London: One World, 2017.

Kern, Susan. "The Material World of the Jeffersons at Shadwell." *The William and Mary Quarterly* 62, no. 2 (2005): 213–42.

Kerr-Ritchie, Jeffrey R. *Rites of August First: Emancipation Day in the Black Atlantic World.* Baton Rouge: Louisiana State University Press, 2007.

Kerrison, Catherine. *Jefferson's Daughters: Three Sisters, White and Black, in a Young America.* New York: Ballantine Books, 2019.

Khadraoui-Fortune, Sophia. "The Abolition of Slavery." In *Postcolonial Realms of Memory: Sites and Symbols in Modern France*, edited by Etienne Achille, Charles Forsdick and Lydie Moudileno, 195–203. Liverpool: Liverpool University Press, 2020.

Kiddy, Elizabeth W. "Who Is the King of Congo? A New Look at African and Afro-Brazilian Kings in Brazil." In *Central Africans and Cultural Transformations in the American Diaspora*, edited by Linda M. Heywood, 153–82. New York: Cambridge University Press, 2002.

Knoblock, Glenn A. *African American Historic Burial Grounds and Gravesites of New England*. Jefferson: McFarland & Company, 2016.

Kreamer, Christine Mullen. "A Universe of Possibilities: Contemporary Artists' Perspectives on the Cosmos." In *African Cosmos: Stellar Arts*, edited by Christine Mullen Kreamer, 307–28. Washington DC: National Museum of African Art, Smithsonian Institution, 2012, exhibition catalog.

Krutko, Erin. "Colonial Williamsburg's Slave Auction Re-enactment: Controversy, African American History and Public Memory." MA thesis, College of William and Mary, 2003.

Kytle, Ethan J. and Blain Roberts. *Denmark Vesey's Garden: Slavery and Memory in the Cradle of the Confederacy*. New York: The New Press, 2018.

Lacqueur, Thomas A. *The Work of the Dead: A Cultural History of Human Remains*. Princeton: Princeton University Press, 2015.

Law, Robin. "A carreira de Francisco Félix de Souza na África Ocidental (1800–1849)." *Topoi*, 2 (2001): 9–39.

Law, Robin. "Commemoration of the Atlantic Slave Trade in Ouidah." *Gradhiva*, no. 8 (2008): 11–27.

Law, Robin. *Ouidah: The Social History of a West African Slaving "Port," 1727–1892*. Athens: Ohio University Press, 2004.

Law, Robin. *The Slave Coast of West Africa, 1550–1750: The Impact of the Atlantic Slave Trade on an African Society*. Oxford: Clarendon Press, 1991.

Lawers, Michel and Aurélie Zemour. "Introduction: des morts, de la sépulture et des sciences sociales." In *Qu'est-ce qu'une sépulture?: Humanités et systèmes funéraires de la Pré-histoire à nos jours. XXXVIe Rencontres internationales d'archéologie et d'histoire d'Antibes*, edited by Michael Lawers et Aurélie Zemour, 11–21. Antibes: Éditions de l'Association pour la diffusion et la connaissance de l'archéologie, 2016.

Le Goff, Jacques. *Histoire et mémoire*. Paris: Gallimard, 1988.

Leepson, Marc. *Saving Monticello: The Levy Family's Epic Quest to Rescue the House That Jefferson Built*. New York: Free Press, 2001.

Leepson, Marc. *Saving Monticello: The Levy Family's Epic Quest to Rescue the House That Jefferson Built*. Charlottesville: University of Virginia Press, 2003.

Lepore, Jill. *The Story of America: Essays on Origins*. Princeton: Princeton University Press, 2012.

Levin, Kevin M. *Searching for Black Confederates: The Civil War's Most Persistent Myth*. Chapel Hill: University of North Carolina Press, 2019.

Lewis, Jan Ellen. "The White Jeffersons." In *Sally Hemings and Thomas Jefferson: History, Memory, and Civic Culture*, edited by Jan Ellen Lewis and Peter S. Onuf, 127–60. Charlottesville: University of Virginia, 1999.

Lima, Tania, Andrade, Marcos André Torres de Souza and Glaucia Malerba Sene. "Weaving the Second Skin: Protection against Evil among the Valongo Slaves in

Nineteenth-Century Rio de Janeiro." *Journal of African Diaspora Archaoelogy and Heritage* 3, no. 2 (2014): 103–36.
Lima, Tania Andrade, Glaucia Malerba Sene and Marcos André Torres de Souza. "Em busca do Cais do Valongo, Rio de Janeiro, século XIX." *Anais do Museu Paulista* 24, no. 1 (2016): 299–391.
Lisanti, Linda M. Thomas Jefferson Memorial Foundation, *Finding Isaac Jefferson: A Monticello Slave*. Charlottesville: Monticello Education Department, 1991.
Locke, Steven. "Why I Withdrew My Proposed Slave Memorial at Faneuil Hall." *Boston Globe*, August 4, 2019.
Löfgren, Isabel and Patrícia Gouvêa, eds. *Mãe Preta*. São Paulo: Frida Projetos Culturais. 2018, exhibition catalog.
Lowenthal, David. *The Heritage Crusade and the Spoils of History*. London: Cambridge University Press, 1998.
Lowenthal, David. *The Past Is a Foreign Country: Revisited*. London: Cambridge University Press, 2015.
Machado, Maria Helena P. T. "Race and Visual Representation." In *African Heritage and Memories of Slavery in Brazil and the South Atlantic World*, edited by Ana Lucia Araujo, 45–70. Amherst: Cambria Press, 2015.
Machado, Maria Helena P. T. and Sasha Huber. *(T)races of Louis Agassiz: Photography, Body, and Science, Yesterday and Today, Rastros e Raças de Louis Agassiz: Fotografia, Corpo e Ciência, Ontem e Hoje*. São Paulo: Capacete Entretenimentos, 2010.
Mbembe, Achille and Laurent Dubois. *Critique of Black Reason*. Durham: Duke University Press, 2017.
Medford, Edna G. "Beyond Mount Vernon: George Washington's Emancipated Laborers and Their Descendants." In *Slavery at the Home of George Washington*, edited by Philip J. Schwarz, 137–58. Mount Vernon: Mount Vernon's Ladies' Association, 2001.
Medford, Edna G. *Historical Perspectives of the African Burial Ground: New York Blacks and the Diaspora*. Washington DC: Howard University Press, 2009, vol. 3.
Merritt, Keri Leigh. *Masterless Men: Poor Whites and Slavery in the Antebellum South*. New York: Cambridge University Press, 2017.
Michel, Johann. *Devenir descendant d'esclave: Enquête sur les régimes mémorielles*. Rennes: Presses Universitaires de Rennes, 2015.
Miller, Charles and Peter Miller. *Monticello: The Official Guide to Thomas Jefferson's World*. Washington DC: National Geographic, 2016.
Mills, Charles. *The Racial Contract*. Ithaca: Cornell University Press, 1997.
Mitchell, Margaret. *Gone with the Wind*. New York: Macmillan, 1936.
Modlin, E. Arnold, Stephen P. Hanna, Perry L. Carter, Amy E. Potter, Candace Forbes Bright and Derek H. Alderman. "Can Plantation Museums Do Full Justice to the Story of the Enslaved? A Discussion of Problems, Possibilities, and the Place of Memory." *GeoHumanities* (2018): 335–59.
Moody, Jessica. "Liverpool's Local Tints: Drowning Memory and 'Maritimising' Slavery in a Seaport City." In *Britain's History and Memory of Transatlantic Slavery: Local Nuances of a "National Sin,"* edited by Katie Donington, Ryan Hanley and Jessica Moody, 150–71. Liverpool: Liverpool University Press, 2016.

Moody, Jessica. "The Memory of Slavery in Liverpool in Public Discourse from the Nineteenth Century to the Present Day." PhD dissertation, University of York, 2014.

Moody, Jessica. "Remembering the Imperial Context of Emancipation Commemoration in the Former British Slave-Port Cities of Bristol and Liverpool, 1933–1934." *Slavery and Abolition* 3.9, no. 1 (2018): 168–89.

Moody, Jessica and Stephen Small. "Slavery and Public History at the Big House: Remembering and Forgetting at American Plantation Museums and British Country Houses." *Journal of Global Slavery* 4, no. 1 (2019): 34–68.

Morgan, Kenneth. *Bristol and the Atlantic Trade in the Eighteenth Century*. Cambridge: Cambridge University Press, 1993.

Morgan, Kenneth. *Edward Colston and Bristol*. Bristol: Bristol Branch of the Historical Association, 1999.

Morgan, Kenneth. "Liverpool's Dominance in the British Slave Trade, 1740–1807." In *Liverpool and Transatlantic Slavery*, edited by David Richardson, Suzanne Schwarz and Anthony Tibbles, 14–42. Liverpool: Liverpool University Press, 2007.

Nora, Pierre. "Between Memory and History: Les Lieux de Mémoire." *Representations*, no. 26 (1989): 7–29.

Noret, Joel. *Deuil et funérailles dans le Bénin méridional: Enterrer à tout prix*. Brussels: Éditions de l'Université de Bruxelles, 2010.

North, Samuel. "Museums as Tools for Understanding Slavery and Its Legacies in South Africa." *South African Historical Journal* 69, no. 1 (2017): 82–100.

Obama, Michelle. *Becoming*. New York: Crown, 2018.

Ofer, Dalia. "The Strength of Remembrance: Commemorating the Holocaust during the First Decade of Israel." *Jewish Social Studies* 6, no. 2 (2000): 24–55.

Oldfield, John R. *Chords of Freedom: Commemoration, Ritual and British Transatlantic Slavery*. Manchester: Manchester University Press, 2007.

Ologoudou, Émile-Désiré. "Tours et détours des mémoires familiales à Ouidah: La place de l'esclavage en question." *Gradhiva* 8 (2008): 80–6.

Olusoga, David. *Black and British: A Forgotten History*. London: Pan Books, 2017.

Oostindie, Gert. "Public Memories of the Atlantic Slave Trade and Slavery in Contemporary Europe." *European Review* 17, no. 3 and 4 (2009): 611–26.

Otele, Olivette. "Bristol, Slavery, and the Politics of Representation: The Slave Trade Gallery in the Bristol Museum." *Social Semiotics* 22, no. 2 (2012): 155–72.

Otele, Olivette. "Colston: What Can Britain Learn from France." *Rhodes Must Fall: The Struggle to Decolonise the Racist Heart of Empire*, edited by Roseanne Chantiluke, Brian Kwoba and Athniangamso, 174–8. London: Zed Books, 2018.

Otele, Olivette. "History of Slavery, Sites of Memory, and Identity Politics in Contemporary Britain." In *A Stain on Our Past: Slavery and Memory*, edited by Abdoulaye Gueye and Johann Michel, 189–210. Trenton: Africa World Press, 2017.

Perry, Warren R., Jean Howson and Barbara A. Bianco. *The Archaeology of the New York African Burial Ground*. Washington DC: Howard University Press, 2009, vol. 2.

Philips, Caryl. *The Atlantic Sound*. London: Faber and Faber, 2000.

Picoli, Valéria and Pedro Nery, ed. *Rosana Paulino: a costura da memória, Rosana Paulino: The Sewing of Memory*. São Paulo: Pinacoteca de São Paulo, 2018, exhibition catalog.

Pierre, Jemima. *The Predicament of Blackness: Postcolonial Ghana and the Politics of Race*. Chicago: University of Chicago Press, 2012.

Piqué, Francesca and Leslie H. Rainer. *Palace Sculptures of Abomey: History Told in Walls*. Los Angeles: The Getty Conservation Institute and the J. Paul Getty Museum, 1999.

Pogue, Dennis J. "The Domestic Architecture of Slavery at George Washington's Mount Vernon." *Winterthur Portfolio: A Journal of American Material Culture* 37, no. 1 (2002): 3–22.

Rees, James C. "Looking Back, Moving Forward: The Changing Interpretations of Slave Life on the Mount Vernon Estate." In *Slavery at the Home of George Washington*, ed. Philip J. Schwarz. Mount Vernon: Mount Vernon's Ladies' Association, 2001.

Reinhardt, Catherine. *Claims to Memory: Beyond Slavery and Emancipation in the French Caribbean*. New York: Berghahn, 2008.

Reis, João José. "De Escravo a Rico Liberto: A Trajetória do Africano Manoel Joaquim Ricardo na Bahia Oitocentista." *Revista de História*, no. 174 (2016): 15–68.

Reis, João José. *Slave Rebellion in Brazil: The Muslim Uprising of 1835 in Bahia*. Baltimore: Johns Hopkins University Press, 1997.

Reis, João José. "From Slave to Wealthy African Freedman: The Story of Manoel Joaquim Ricardo." In *Black Atlantic Biography*, edited by Lisa Lindsay and John Wood Sweet, 131–45. Philadelphia: University of Pennsylvania Press, 2013.

Rice, Alan. *Creating Memorials, Building Identities: The Politics of Memory in the Black Atlantic*. Liverpool: Liverpool University Press, 2012.

Rice, Alan. "The History of the Transatlantic Slave Trade and Heritage from below in Action: Guerrilla Memorialisation in the Era of Bicentennial Commemoration." In *Heritage from Below*, edited by Iain J. M. Robertson, 209–36. New York, London: Routledge, 2016.

Richardson, David. *Bristol, Africa and the Eighteenth-Century Slave Trade to America: The Years of Expansion 1698–1729*. Bristol: The Bristol Record Society, 1986.

Richardson, David. *Bristol, Africa and the Eighteenth-Century Slave Trade to America: The Years of Ascendancy 1730–1745*. Bristol: The Bristol Record Society, 1987.

Richardson, David. *Bristol, Africa and the Eighteenth-Century Slave Trade to America: The Years of Decline 1746–1769*. Bristol: The Bristol Record Society, 1991.

Richardson, David. *Bristol, Africa and the Eighteenth-Century Slave Trade to America: The Final Years 1770–1807*. Bristol: The Bristol Record Society, 1996.

Richardson, David, Suzanne Schwarz and Anthony Tibbles, eds. *Liverpool and Transatlantic Slavery*. Liverpool: Liverpool University Press, 2010.

Ricoeur, Paul. *La mémoire, l'histoire, l'oubli*. Paris: Seuil, 2000.

Ricoeur, Paul. *Memory, History, Forgetting*. Chicago: Chicago University Press, 2006.

Robben, Antonius C. G. M. *Argentina Betrayed: Memory, Mourning, and Accountability*. Philadelphia: Pennsylvania University Press, 2018.

Roger Anstey and P. E. H. Hair. *Liverpool, the African Slave Trade, and Abolition: Essays to Illustrate Current Knowledge and Research*. Liverpool: Historic Society of Lancashire and Cheshire, 1989.

Rothberg, Michael. *Multidirectional Memory: Remembering the Holocaust in the Age of Decolonization*. Palo Alto: Stanford University Press, 2009.

Rush, Dana. *Vodun in Coastal Benin: Unfinished, Open-Ended, Global*. Nashville: Vanderbilt University Press, 2013.

Saillant, Francine and Pedro Simonard. "Afro-Brazilian Heritage and Slavery in Rio de Janeiro Community Museums." In *Politics of Memory: Making Slavery Visible in the Public Space*, edited by Ana Lucia Araujo, 213–31. New York: Routledge, 2012.

Saugera, Éric. *Bordeaux port négrier: Chronologie, économie, idéologie, XVIIe–XIXe siècles*. Biarritz: J & D, 1995.

Savage, Kirk. *Monument Wars: Washington, D.C., the National Mall, and the Transformation of the Memorial Landscape*. Los Angeles: University of California, 2011.

Schmidt, Nelly. "Teaching and Commemorating Slavery and Abolition in France: From Organized Forgetfulness to Historical Debates." In *Politics of Memory: Making Slavery Visible in the Public Space*, edited by Ana Lucia Araujo, 106–23. New York: Routledge, 2012.

Schoelwer, Susan P. ed. *Lives Bound Together: Slavery at George Washington Mount Vernon*. Mount Vernon: Mount Vernon Ladies' Association, 2016, exhibition catalog.

Scholnick, Jonathan, Derek Wheeler and Fraser Neiman. "Mulberry Row Reassessment: The Building l Site." Charlottesville: Monticello Department of Archaeology Technical Report Series, no. 3, 2001.

Schwarz, Philip J. "Introduction." In *Slavery at the Home of George Washington*, edited by Philip J. Schwarz, 1–12. Mount Vernon: Mount Vernon's Ladies' Association, 2001.

Schwarz, Suzanne. *Slave Captain: The Career of James Irving in the Liverpool Slave Trade*. Liverpool: Liverpool University Press, 2008.

Sean, Margaret. *The Sun Is My Undoing*. London: Collins, 1941.

Seck, Ibrahima. *Bouki Fait Gombo: A History of the Slave Community of Habitation Haydel (Whitney Plantation) Louisiana, 1750–1860*. New Orleans: University of New Orleans Press, 2014.

Seeman, Erik S. "Sources and Interpretations: Reassessing the '*Sankofa* Symbol' in New York's African Burial Ground." *William and Mary Quarterly* 67, no. 1 (2010): 101–22.

Shaw, Rosalind. *Memories of the Slave Trade: Ritual and the Historical Imagination in Sierra Leone*. Chicago: University of Chicago, 2002.

Silva, Júlio César Medeiros da. *À flor da terra: O cemitério dos pretos novos no Rio de Janeiro*. Rio de Janeiro: Garamond, 2007.

Small, Stephen. "Racialised Relations in Liverpool: A Contemporary Anomaly." *New Community* 17, no. 4 (1991): 511–37.

Small, Stephen. "Slavery, Colonialism and Museums Representations in Great Britain: Old and New Circuits of Migration." *Human Architecture: Journal of the Sociology of Self-Knowledge* 9, no. 4 (2011): 117–28.

Small, Stephen. "Still Back of the Big House: Slave Cabins and Slavery in Southern Heritage Tourism." *Tourism Geographies: An International Journal of Tourism Space, Place and Environment* 15, no. 3 (2013): 405–23.

Snow, Caleb Hopkins. *A History of Boston: The Metropolis of Massachusetts from Its Origin to the Present Period with Some Account of the Environs*. Boston: Abel Bowen, 1825.

Soares, Carlos Eugênio Líbano. "Valongo, Cais dos Escravos: Memória da diáspora e modernização portuária na cidade do Rio de Janeiro, 1668–1911." Postdoctoral report, Universidade Federal do Rio de Janeiro, 2013.

Soares, Mariza de Carvalho. *Devotos da cor: Identidade étnica, religiosidade e escravidão no Rio de Janeiro, século XVIII*. Rio de Janeiro: Civilização Brasileira, 2000.

Spence, David. "Making the London, Sugar and Slavery Gallery at the Museum of London Docklands." In *Representing Enslavement and Abolition in Museums: Ambiguous Engagements*, edited by Laurajane Smith, Geoffrey Cubitt, Ross Wilson and Kalliopi Fouseki, 149–63. New York: Routledge, 2011.

Stanton, Lucia. "The Other End of the Telescope: Jefferson through the Eyes of His Slaves," *The William and Mary Quarterly* 57, no. 1 (2000): 139–52.

Stanton, Lucia and Dianne Swann-Wright. "Bonds of Memory: Identity and the Hemings Family." In *Sally Hemings and Thomas Jefferson: History, Memory, and Civic Culture*, edited by Jan Ellen Lewis and Peter S. Onuf, 161–83. Charlottesville: University of Virginia, 1999.

Stewart, Catherine A. *Long Past Slavery: Representing Race in the Federal Writers' Project*. Chapel Hill: University of North Carolina Press, 2016.

Stockman, Farah. "Monticello Is Done Avoiding Jefferson's Relationship with Sally Hemings." *New York Times*, June 16, 2018.

Sturken, Marita. "The Wall, the Screen, and the Image: The Vietnam Veterans Memorial." *Representations* 35 (1991): 118–42.

Tall, Emmanuelle Kadya. "De la démocratie et des cultes voduns au Bénin." *Cahiers d'études africaines* 137 (1995): 195–208.

Telles, Edward. "The Project on Ethnicity and Race in Latin America (PERLA): Hard Data and What Is at Stake." In *Pigmentocracies: Ethnicity, Race, and Color in Latin America*, edited by Edward Telles, 1–35. Chapel Hill: University of North Carolina Press, 2014.

Thompson, Mary V. "*The Only Unavoidable Subject of Regret: George Washington, Slavery, and the Enslaved Community of Mount Vernon*." Charlottesville: University of Virginia Press, 2019.

Thompson, Mary V. "'They Appear to Live Comfortable Together': Private Lives of the Mount Vernon Slaves." In *Slavery at the Home of George Washington*, edited by Philip J. Schwarz, 79–110. Mount Vernon: Mount Vernon's Ladies' Association, 2001.

Tibbles, Anthony. *Liverpool and the Slave Trade*. Liverpool: Liverpool University Press, 2018.

Todorov, Tzvetan. *Les abus de la mémoire*. Paris: Arléas, 1995.

Trouillot, Michel-Rolph. *Silencing the Past: Power and the Production of History*. Boston: Beacon Press, 2015.

Urofsky, Melvin I. *The Levy Family and Monticello, 1834–1923: Saving Thomas Jefferson's House*. Charlottesville: Thomas Jefferson Foundation, 2001.

Videau, André. "Les Anneaux de la Mémoire à Nantes jusqu'au 4 février 1994 au château des ducs de Bretagne." *Hommes et migrations*, no. 1170 (1993): 63–4.

Wallace, Elizabeth Kowaleski. *The British Slave Trade and Public Memory*. New York: Columbia University Press, 2006.

Walsh, Lorena S. "Slavery and Agriculture at Mount Vernon." In *Slavery at the Home of George Washington*, edited by Philip J. Schwarz, 47–78. Mount Vernon: Mount Vernon's Ladies' Association, 2001.
Walvin, James. *The Zong: A Massacre, the Law and the End of Slavery*. New Haven: Yale University Press, 2011.
Webb, Peter. *Exploring the Networked Worlds of Popular Music: Milieux Cultures*. New York, London: Routledge, 2007.
Westgaph, Laurence. *Read the Signs: Street Names with a Connection to the Transatlantic Slave Trade and Abolition in Liverpool*. Liverpool: Liverpool City Council, 2007.
White, Gwendolyn K. "Commerce and Community: Plantation Life at George Washington's Mount Vernon, 1754 to 1799." PhD dissertation, George Mason University, 2016.
Wiencek, Henry. *Master of the Mountain: Thomas Jefferson and His Slaves*. New York: Farrar, Straus and Giroux, 2012.
Wilder, Craig Steven. *Ebony and Ivy: Race, Slavery, and the Troubled History of America's Universities*. New York: Bloomsbury, 2013.
Wilkins, H. J. *Edward Colston: A Chronological Account of His Life and Work*. Bristol: J. W. Arrowsmith, 1920.
Williams, Gomer and David Eltis. *History of the Liverpool Privateers and Letters of Marque with an Account of the Liverpool Slave Trade, 1744–1812*. Montreal: McGill-Queen's University Press, 2004.
Worden, Nigel. *Trials of Slavery: Selected Documents Concerning Slaves from the Criminal Records of the Council of Justice at the Cape of Good Hope, 1704–1794*. Cape Town: Van Riebeeck Society for the Publication of South African Historical Documents, 2005.
Worden, Nigel, Ruth Versfeld, Dorothy Dyer and Claudia Bickford-Smith. *The Chains That Bind Us: A History of Slavery at the Cape*. Kenwyn, South Africa: Juta, 1996.
Young, James Edward. *The Stages of Memory: Reflections on Memorial Art, Loss, and the Spaces Between*. Amherst: University of Massachusetts Press, 2018.

Archival Collections, Online Repositories, and Websites

"A Local Law in Relation to Requiring the Placement of an Informational Sign near the Intersection of Wall Streets in Manhattan to Mark the Site of New York's First Slave Market," Int. 0036-2014, http://legislation.nyc/id/1655736.
"Establishment of the African Burial Ground National Monument: A Proclamation by the President of the United States of America," February 27, 2006, http://georgewbush-whitehouse.archives.gov/news/releases/2006/02/20060227-6.html.
African Burial Ground, National Monument, New York City, http://www.nps.gov/afbg/index.htm.
American Jewish Historical Society, Center for Jewish History, New York City, United States.
Ask a Slave: A Web Series, http://www.askaslave.com/home.html.

Association of Leading Visitors Attractions, 2018 visitor figures, http://www.alva.org.uk/details.cfm?p=609.
Berlin's Memorial to the Murdered Jews of Europe, https://www.holocaust-denkmal-berlin.de/.
Countering Colston: Campaign to Decolonise Bristol, https://counteringcolston.wordpress.com/colston-statue/.
Faustine, Nona. *Of My Body I Will Make Monuments in Your Honor*, 2014, *White Shoes* series, http://nonafaustine.virb.com/home.
Getting Word, https://www.monticello.org/getting-word.
Institut National de l'Audiovisuel, "Les Anneaux de la mémoire," France 3, December 5, 1992, https://fresques.ina.fr/auran/fiche-media/Auran000105/les-anneaux-de-la-memoire.html.
Layers of the Old Dock, https://layers-of.net/olddock/about.html.
Legacies of British Slave-Ownership, https://www.ucl.ac.uk/lbs/.
The Lemon Project: A Journey of Reconciliation, https://www.wm.edu/sites/lemonproject/.
Les noms de familes guadeloupéennes et martiniquaises, http://www.anchoukaj.org/.
The Life of Sally Hemings, https://www.monticello.org/sallyhemings/.
Liverpool's Abercromby Square and the Confederacy during the U.S. Civil War, curated by Christopher Williams, Jim Powell and Joseph Kelly, University of Liverpool, 2005, http://ldhi.library.cofc.edu/exhibits/show/liverpools-abercromby-square.
Manuscript and Archives Division, New York City, United States.
Mémoire de l'esclavage et de la traite négrière, https://www.memoire-esclavage-bordeaux.fr/histoire.
Memorial to Enslaved Laborers at the University of Virginia, https://www2.virginia.edu/slaverymemorial/.
Moorland Spingarn Research Center, Manuscript Division, Howard University, Washington DC.
National Archives, Founders Online, http://founders.archives.gov/documents/Jefferson/98-01-02-5963.
National Archives, Founders Online, https://founders.archives.gov/documents/Jefferson/01-01-02-0021.
Portal Arqueológico dos Pretos Novos, http://www.pretosnovos.com.br/.
Piquet, François. "François Piquet Talks about Timalle." Interview with Sarah Webster, http://www.reparations-art.org/Timalle-ENG.html.
Rosana Paulino, http://www.rosanapaulino.com.br/.
Smithsonian National Museum of African American History and Culture, the Collection, https://nmaahc.si.edu/explore/collection.
Stolpersteine, http://www.stolpersteine.eu.
Tours of Liverpool's Old Dock, http://www.liverpoolmuseums.org.uk/maritime/visit/old_dock_tours.aspx.
UNESCO, World Heritage Convention, Liverpool Maritime Mercantile City, https://whc.unesco.org/en/list/1150/.
UNESCO, World Heritage List, Valongo Wharf Archaeological Site, https://whc.unesco.org/en/list/1548/.

United States Census Bureau, Boston, Massachusetts, https://www.census.gov/quickfacts/bostoncitymassachusetts.
United States Holocaust Memorial Museum, behind Every Name a Story, https://www.ushmm.org/remember/holocaust-reflections-testimonies/behind-every-name-a-story.
University of Massachusetts Special Collections and University Archives.
Voyages: The Transatlantic Slave Trade Database: Voyages, www.slavevoyages.org.
West of England Partnership, Office for National Statistics, 1991 Census of population, Ethnic Groups by Unitary Authority, http://www.westofengland.org/research–statistics/census-/1991-census.
Witness Stones, "What Is the Witness Stones Project," https://witnessstones.org/.
Yad Vashem, The World Holocaust Remembrance Center, https://www.yadvashem.org/.

Motion Pictures and Documentary Films

Browne, Katrina. *Traces of the Trade: A Story from the Deep North*. San Francisco, CA: California Newsreel, 2008, DVD video.
Herzog, Werner. *Cobra Verde*. West Germany: Werner Herzog Filmproduktion, ZDF, and the Ghana Film Industry Corporation, 2002 [1987], DVD video.
Selznick, David O. *Gone with the Wind*. Burbank, CA: Warner Home Video, 2004 [1939], DVD video.

INDEX